D1561975

The Dutch and English East India Companies

Asian History

The aim of the Asian History series is to offer a forum for writers of monographs and occasionally anthologies on Asian history. The series focuses on cultural and historical studies of politics and intellectual ideas and crosscuts the disciplines of history, political science, sociology and cultural studies.

The Dutch and English East India Companies

Diplomacy, Trade and Violence in Early Modern Asia

Edited by
Adam Clulow and Tristan Mostert

Amsterdam University Press

Cover illustration: Detail from Japanese lacquer screen showing Dutch ship and Chinese junk. Nagasaki, Japan, c. 1759. Rijksmuseum

Cover design: Coördesign, Leiden
Lay-out: Crius Group, Hulshout

ISBN	978 94 6298 329 8 (Hardback)
ISBN	978 94 6298 527 8 (Paperback)
e-ISBN	978 90 4853 338 1
DOI	10.5117/9789462983298
NUR	691 | 692

© Adam Clulow and Tristan Mostert / Amsterdam University Press B.V., Amsterdam 2018

For Leonard Blussé, whose work has shown the way

Map 1   Southeast Asia

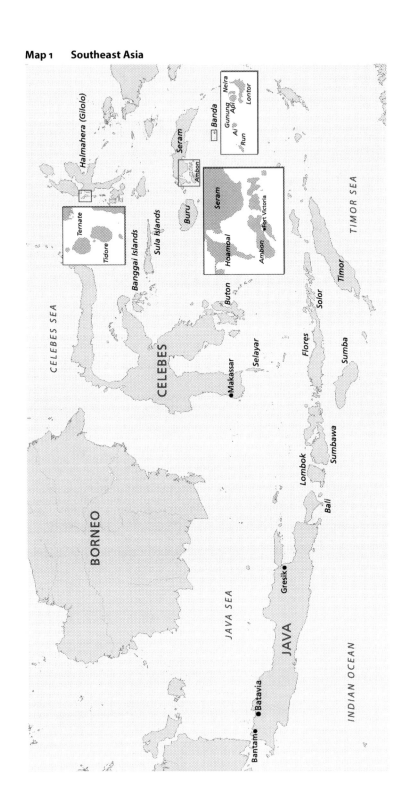

Map 2 East Asia

Map 3 South Asia and the Arabian Sea

Table of Contents

Part 3   Violence

Epilogue

List of Illustrations

Illustrations

Acknowledgements

This volume grew out of a 2015 conference held at the Internationales Wissenschaftsforum Heidelberg at the University of Heidelberg. The conference was sponsored by the International Research Award in Global History, which was offered jointly by the Department of History and the Cluster of Excellence 'Asia and Europe in a Global Context' at Heidelberg University, the Institute for European Global Studies at the University of Basel, and the Laureate Research Program in International History at the University of Sydney. The editors would like to thank Roland Wenzlhuemer, Glenda Sluga and Madeleine Herren-Oesch for their generous support which made this volume possible. 24 scholars participated in the original conference and we would like to thank them all for their many contributions, only some of which could be included here. Finally, we owe a great debt of gratitude to Susanne Hohler, the indefatigable organiser of the conference who did so much to make it possible.

Introduction

The Companies in Asia

Adam Clulow and Tristan Mostert

Although they were dissolved centuries ago, we do not have to look far to find signs of the East India Companies today. In recent years, both organisations have featured prominently in popular culture, in the commercial world and in public debate. In 2009, a Finnish games developer, Nitro Games, released the popular *East India Company* video game which places players in the role of Governor Director in charge of a process of economic and commercial expansion designed to parallel the real development of these organisations. In the Netherlands, the corporate logo of the Dutch East India Company (*Vereenigde Oostindische Compagnie* or VOC), widely considered to be the oldest in the world, has been used to market a range of products from souvenirs to gin even as the organisation's legacy has become the object of increasingly intense public debate.[1] When in 2006 the then Prime Minister Jan Peter Balkenende, while addressing the Dutch House of Representatives, called for more optimism and a revival of the 'VOC mentality', he voiced a strikingly resilient view of the Company, which is still regularly praised as a dynamic force in global trade and the world's first multinational. His comments, however, were met with immediate resistance from a range of groups that pointed to the violence and repression also associated with the organisation's long and frequently brutal history.

Across the North Sea, the VOC's great rival, the English East India Company (EIC) has famously been reborn as a high-end purveyor of luxury goods. Over a century after it exited from the global stage, it is once again possible to see EIC branded goods for sale in London and stores scattered across the globe. The agent of this rebirth is Sanjiv Mehta, a wealthy Mumbai businessman with a family history in the diamond trade in Surat. It makes for a compelling story – an Indian businessman buying the company that once colonised large swathes of his country – and it has, not surprisingly, generated a powerful response on social media.[2] The reality, however, is

---

1   For one example, see www.v2cgin.com/, which uses a modified version of the famous VOC logo.

2   See the comments for: http://economictimes.indiatimes.com/news/company/corporate-trends/the-indian-owners-of-the-east-india-company-are-betting-on-its-future-by-leaning-on-its-past/articleshow/54535557.cms, accessed 2 February 2017.

considerably less clear-cut. The Company itself ceased to exist entirely in the nineteenth century, surrendering both its assets and legal identity. What Mehta seems to have purchased, then, although this is glossed over in the company's publicity materials which speak of its pioneering early modern heritage, was not the original organisation but a number of short-lived enterprises created during the closing decades of the twentieth century with similar names but no actual connection to the EIC itself.

If it is in fact not directly linked with the original, this latest iteration of the East India Company does at least share one feature both of its famous predecessor and its Dutch rival, the VOC, which was established two years later in 1602. These were elusive organisations that were notoriously difficult to pin down and affix singular identities to. From the beginning, observers struggled to explain exactly what the VOC and the EIC were and the place they occupied in diplomatic, commercial and military circuits. The problem was readily apparent when the first generation of Company ambassadors arrived in Asia charged to negotiate with local rulers. Not surprisingly, many early representatives opted to speak in the most general of terms or to actively conceal the true nature of their employers. The English Company famously dispatched Sir Thomas Roe, a courtier with a close connection to the monarch, to India in an effort to boost its prestige while effectively muddying the water as to whether he represented a company, a king or both at the same time.[3] Early VOC ambassadors opted for a more direct subterfuge, regularly passing themselves off as proxies of the 'King of Holland' without making any mention of the complicated organisational structure of the company or the fact that it was based in a Republic.[4]

For centuries now, writers and scholars have wrestled with the seemingly contradictory nature of these organisations and how to fit them into a wider schema. This struggle has continued even as the last decade in particular has witnessed an unexpected boom in studies of the two companies. A field that was once the preserve of a handful of pioneering specialists has now experienced a significant expansion, with a string of new books coming out every year.[5] And yet it sometimes seems as if we are no closer to explaining exactly what these organisations actually were. One solution is to locate the two companies in an uneasy space stuck somewhere between state and company by affixing labels like 'quasi-sovereign' or calling attention to

---

3   Mishra, 'Diplomacy at the Edge'.
4   Clulow, *The Company and the Shogun*, chapter 1.
5   See Stern's recent overview of EIC historiography. Stern, 'The History and Historiography of the English East India Company'.

their duelling characteristics.[6] While useful, the result can be to trap these organisations in a permanently liminal state, neither one thing nor the other. In his groundbreaking study of the English East India Company, Philip Stern argues against this view, asking us to assess the EIC as a 'body-politic on its own terms' rather than as a purely commercial organisation that strayed off its commercial path to embrace empire.[7]

Works by Stern and others provide a template for how we should think about these organisations both in Europe, where they had to negotiate a precarious and often awkward alliance with the state, but also in Asia, where there has been a fresh understanding of their impact on the region.[8] Even as scholars have become more and more interested in the companies, they have become less and less convinced of the uniqueness of these organisations or of their transformational impact on the Asian environment. The best new scholarship aims to walk a fine line, recognising that the Dutch and English East India Companies were formidable organisations but looking closely at the actual environment in which they operated. Founded in the first decade of the seventeenth century, they were, over time, gifted with expansive powers that allowed them to conduct diplomacy, raise armies and seize territorial possessions. But they did not move into an empty arena in which they were free to deploy these powers without resistance. Early modern Asia stood at the centre of the global economy and was crowded with powerful states that wielded economic, military and cultural resources that outstripped the most influential polities in Europe. The challenge for scholars working on these organisations has been to understand the peculiar strengths of the companies while at the same time placing them firmly into early modern Asia. Both organisations did bring powerful tools to the region, but they often found their sharpest weapons unexpectedly blunted; and for every military, diplomatic or economic success, there were other moments in which their efforts either faltered or failed.

This volume brings together new work from scholars of both companies focusing on their operations across Southeast, East and South Asia. It grew out of a conference, convened in Heidelberg in December 2015 and sponsored by Heidelberg University, the University of Basel, the University of Sydney, and Monash University. While it focuses on the Dutch and English East India Companies, these were not, it should be acknowledged, the only such

6   For one example of a much wider trend, see Ricklefs, *A History of Modern Indonesia since c. 1200*, p. 31.

7   Stern, *The Company-State*, p. 6.

8   See e.g. Mishra, *A Business of State*.

organisations operating in Asia and a strong case could be made for including, for example, the Danish East India Company, which has generated innovative new scholarship.[9] This said, the histories of the Dutch and English Companies are intertwined in ways that make it logical to study them as a pair. Looking at the EIC and the VOC together is by no means a new idea. For an earlier generation of Company scholars, it was standard to approach these organisations in this way. Works like George Masselman's *The Cradle of Colonialism* or Holden Furber's *Rival Empires of Trade* took it for granted that the two companies must be examined as a pair.[10] In recent years, this habit has largely lapsed and it is far more common now for monographs to focus on one of the companies usually in one part of the world.[11] There is, however, much to be gained from considering these organisations together. Most obviously, they were, despite moments of precarious alliance, in constant competition. Given their sweeping operations, the two companies fought across multiple arenas: on Asian seas for maritime dominance, in courts spread across the region for diplomatic advantage, and on land as both organisations claimed territorial footholds that morphed over time into expansive empires.

But even as they fought, the companies remained locked together in an intimate embrace. Across Asia, the Dutch and English companies operated in strikingly close proximity, with VOC and EIC officials living essentially on top of each other. On the island of Ambon, the site of perhaps the most famous flashpoint between the two companies, their representatives lived together for years, shared the same food and attended the baptism ceremonies of each other's children; while in Hirado in western Japan both companies opted to set up outposts in the same remote port city hundreds of kilometres from Japan's commercial centres. So close was this embrace that Company officials sometimes went to great lengths in an effort to distinguish themselves from their rivals. In Banten, for example, EIC officials made a great show of celebrating their monarch's coronation day by dressing up with 'Scarfes of white and red Taffata,' and decorating their lodge with 'a Flagge with the red Crosse through the middle' in order to made it clear that they were not Dutch.[12]

More important for this volume, the two organisations confronted similar problems as they pushed into Asia. Both companies were interlopers

9   See e.g. Wellen, 'The Danish East India Company's War'.

10   Masselman, *The Cradle of Colonialism*; Furber, *Rival Empires of Trade*.

11   There are a number of notable exceptions, such as Nierstrasz, *Rivalry for Trade in Tea and Textiles*.

12   Purchas, *Hakluytus posthumus*, 2:457.

in a crowded diplomatic world in which they did not fully understand the rules governing interaction; both sought the same markets and suffered the same lack of demand for Europeans goods; and both watched each other closely while attempting to learn, sometimes with success, from the other's experience. While not every chapter in this volume considers both companies together, those that do show the clear advantages of this approach. As Ghulam Nadri reveals, for example, in his contribution, both organisations were heavily (and similarly) dependent on brokers not simply to establish themselves in Asia but across the course of their long existence.

One of the difficulties in doing Company history is the vast differences between their trajectories in different parts of Asia and the way these organisations are remembered. In East Asia, for example, the companies were confined to the margins for long periods. In Japan, the EIC trading outpost lasted for just a decade, while the VOC presence was restricted to the tiny man-made island of Deshima which was placed under constant surveillance. In its attempts to gain access to Chinese markets, the VOC did succeed in establishing a colonial presence on Taiwan, but was ejected in 1662 after suffering a devastating military defeat at the hands of Zheng Chenggong (Koxinga). By contrast, in other parts of Asia, India for the English, Indonesia for the Dutch, the companies dug in deep roots that were not easily dislodged. Connecting these regions presents a challenge – how to take a place like Japan, where the VOC was utterly subservient to Tokugawa authorities, and compare it to the Banda islands, where the Company wiped out the local population and replaced them with imported slaves? But, even in the face of vast differences, there could be striking points of convergence. As Peter Good shows, for example, the companies' capacity to offer their services as naval mercenaries unifies Persia, Siam and Japan where different rulers attempted to press European vessels into service.

Our broad goal in the conference and now this volume was to collect new work on the companies with a focus on the contributions of more junior scholars. As a result, we have not aimed for or achieved a perfect split between EIC and VOC chapters, nor are all or even the majority of chapters comparative. But we believe that the contributions collected here shed light on some of the challenges that these organisations faced as they pushed into Asia. The volume is divided into three sections: diplomacy, trade and violence. These were, it must be said, never cordoned off: trade overlapped with diplomacy, which in turn spilled over into war, but Company officials returned again and again to this triumvirate.

Arriving in the region, the companies struggled to gain access to well-established diplomatic circuits. In recent years, scholars have followed the path blazed by John E. (Jack) Wills Jr., Leonard Blussé and others to map out the full extent of this diplomatic activity.[13] One of the most exciting recent developments has been the construction of a vast database of diplomatic engagement, *Diplomatic Letters 1625-1812*, for the Dutch East India Company.[14] Researchers attached to this database have catalogued more than 4,000 letters, exchanged across close to two centuries, that show the remarkable degree to which the Dutch Company became integrated into Asian diplomatic circuits.

The chapters gathered in this section reveal the complex task faced by the companies when they attempted to push into Asia. They show, first, that there were multiple centres, each with their own rules and regulations. East Asian diplomatic circuits could look very different from Southeast Asian ones and, as Fuyuko Matsukata reminds us, each centre had its own rules and conventions. Second, Asian structures were not static. If Europeans were pushing into diplomatic systems, Asian polities were, as Matsukata's chapter shows, improvising at the same time. She reveals how the Tokugawa *bakufu* was in the process of inventing a new category of 'Tokugawa subjects' just as the VOC was attempting to stabilise its diplomatic presence in Asia. Third, diplomacy took place at multiple levels. As Guido van Meersbergen demonstrates, the Company was compelled to interact with a range of officials, from powerful rulers down to local administrators. Given this, he cautions against the overwhelming focus on formal embassies. These could be grand affairs that came complete with detailed diaries and piles of documents but they frequently achieved very little. It was often the case that the real action took place in far less glamorous settings in the provinces where diplomacy was often improvised with local officials. Put together, these chapters show the need to develop a flexible understanding for diplomatic encounters that is able to accommodate a wide range of interactions.

Shifting the focus to alliances, Mostert's chapter reminds us that straightforward binaries do not translate well when applied to intricate regional networks. Mostert takes us to the eastern Indonesian archipelago where the VOC, in the process of expanding its power in the region, became increasingly enmeshed in local networks and rivalries. In the process, it

13   There are far too many works to cite here but two representative chapters are: Wills, 'Ch'ing Relations with the Dutch, 1662–1690'; and Blussé, 'Queen among Kings'.
14   https://sejarah-nusantara.anri.go.id/diplomatic-letters/), accessed 2 February 2017.

entered into a game in which it could not always set the rules or predict the dynamics. Mostert shows how the alliances constructed by VOC officials made the organisation a party to existing rivalries between expanding states in the Moluccas and their European allies.

Part 2 moves the focus to trade. Looking across an extended timeline, Ghulam Nadri shows how both companies' relationship with Indian merchants was characterised by a pronounced dependence on brokers and local intermediaries that waned but never disappeared. But if the companies required the services of brokers to prosper, these brokers also needed the companies to provide protection in a dangerous world, and Nadri's study reveals the development of a broadly reciprocal relationship. Martha Chaiklin continues the same focus on the two companies in Surat. Sanjay Subrahmanyam, another groundbreaking scholar of the companies, once wrote of the 'congealed power' of the Company archive that acts to draw in the researcher and blind them to the world outside European records.[15] The same theme is picked up in Chaiklin's reassessment of the traditional timeline that sees the fall of Surat following inevitably on from the rise of Bombay. Focusing on ivory, a vital trade but one that was not well captured by European records, her contribution gathers together clues from a wide range of sources to show how local demand and the presence of large numbers of craftsmen underpinned Surat's remarkable resilience into the eighteenth century.

The final section of the volume turns our attention to violence. While recent scholarship by Tonio Andrade and others has effectively blunted outdated notions of an overwhelming European military advantage, there can be no question that Europeans brought with them to Asia a formidable capacity for violence.[16] In her chapter, Martine van Ittersum cautions us not to go too far in our search for indigenous agency or resistance and thereby to lose sight of the devastating combination of treaties and violence deployed by these organisations. Treaties could be vehicles of indigenous agency but they could also be nothing more than a milestone along the route to dispossession, and we should be careful of freighting these documents with meanings that may not have existed when they were signed.

The history of the companies was underpinned by a consistent tension brought about by the fact that they were powerful on the waves but weak on land. The final chapters by Adam Clulow and Peter Good address this

15   Subrahmanyam, 'Frank Submissions', p. 70.
16   For one example of Andrade's numerous books, see Andrade, *Lost Colony*.

central problem in different ways. For Clulow, Japanese soldiers pressed into VOC service presented a way for the Dutch to compensate for their perennial lack of military manpower. In this case, Asian mercenaries became a vehicle, albeit one that never delivered on its promise, to expand European power on land by recruiting long columns of Japanese troops to march outwards under VOC banners. Peter Good describes the reverse case, in which the English Company was pressed into service by an Asian ruler as a 'navy for hire'. This pattern was duplicated in other parts of Asia, where local rulers attempted to turn the power of European vessels to their advantage. In such cases, naval resources represented a vital bargaining chip for these organisations that were deployed in order to carve out a position in Asia.

Put together, the chapters collected in this volume show the ways in which the companies were forced to accommodate themselves – economically, diplomatically and militarily – to existing structures in Asia. Even in situations where they had genuine advantages, in for example naval power, this did not necessarily translate to success, as these advantages were often offset by local circumstances. It was the resultant process of adaptation which underpinned the companies' longevity. The companies may have been established in Europe but they owed their development to a continual process of interaction and accommodation with Asian structures.

The field of Company history has been dominated by a string of extraordinary scholars who have shaped the way we understand these organisations today. This volume is dedicated to one of these giants, Leonard Blussé, who, by virtue of his remarkable scholarship, organisational capacities and sheer energy, shifted the focus of the field by placing the Dutch East India Company where it belongs, in Asian networks of goods and people, while opening up a vast array of new sources to consider these organisations. Across his long career and in addition to a steady stream of field-defining publications, Professor Blussé has been an indefatigable mentor to dozens of scholars across the world, including both of us and many of the contributors to this volume. The concluding chapter, written by Tonio Andrade, a hugely influential scholar of the VOC in his own right, charts the long trajectory of Dutch East India Company history from Marx until today while recognising the enormous contribution made by Professor Blussé in shaping the ways in which we now understand this organisation. While we cannot adequately repay Professor Blussé's generosity to so many of us, we hope this volume goes some small way to further acknowledging his vital role in the ongoing evolution of the field.

Works cited

Andrade, Tonio. *Lost Colony: The Untold Story of China's First Great Victory Over the West* (Princeton: Princeton University Press, 2011).

Blussé, Leonard. 'Queen among Kings: Diplomatic Ritual at Batavia'. In *Jakarta-Batavia*, ed. Kees Grijns and Peter Nas (Leiden: KITLV Press, 2000).

Clulow, Adam. *The Company and the Shogun: The Dutch Encounter with Tokugawa Japan* (New York: Columbia University Press, 2014).

Furber, Holden. *Rival Empires of Trade in the Orient, 1600-1800* (Minneapolis: University of Minnesota Press, 1976).

Masselman, George. *The Cradle of Colonialism* (New Haven: Yale University Press, 1963).

Mishra, Rupali. *A Business of State: Commerce, Politics, and the Birth of the East India Company* (Cambridge MA: Harvard University Press, 2018).

Mishra, Rupali. 'Diplomacy at the Edge: Split interests in the Roe Embassy to the Mughal court', *Journal of British Studies* 53 (January 2014): 1–24.

Nierstrasz, Chris. *Rivalry for Trade in Tea and Textiles: The English and Dutch East Indian Companies (1700–1800)* (Basingstoke: Palgrave Macmillan, 2015).

Purchas, Samuel. *Hakluytus posthumus, or, Purchas his Pilgrimes: contayning a history of the world in sea voyages and lande travells by Englishmen and others.* 20 vols. (Glasgow: J. MacLehose, 1905–1907).

Ricklefs, M.C. *A History of Modern Indonesia since c. 1200* (Stanford: Stanford University Press, 2001).

Stern, Philip J. 'The History and Historiography of the English East India Company: Past, Present and Future!', *History Compass* 7, no. 4 (2009): 474–83.

Subrahmanyam, Sanjay. 'Frank Submissions: The Company and the Mughals Between Sir Thomas Roe and Sir William Norris', in *The Worlds of the East India Company*, ed. H.V. Bowen, Margarette Lincoln and Nigel Rigby (Woodbridge, Suffolk: Boydell, 2002), pp. 69–96.

Wellen, Kathryn. 'The Danish East India Company's War against the Mughal Empire, 1642-1698', *Journal of Early Modern History* 19 (2015): 439–46.

Wills, John E., Jr., 'Ch'ing Relations with the Dutch, 1662–1690', in *The Chinese World Order*, ed. John. K. Fairbank (Cambridge MA: Harvard University Press, 1968).

Part 1

Diplomacy

1 Scramble for the spices

Makassar's role in European and Asian Competition in the Eastern Archipelago up to 1616

Tristan Mostert

Abstract

In the course of the 17th century the trade entrepôt of Makassar, and the state of Gowa-Tallo of which it was the capital, repeatedly clashed with the VOC over access to the Moluccan spices. This chapter investigates the early evolution of this conflict, highlighting the consequential role that the VOC's alliance with Ternate had for this relationship. Makassar has often been presented as merely an open trading port, or *bandar*, juxtaposed against the VOC's aggressive attempts to control the spice trade. This chapter tries to nuance this view by highlighting the active political and military role Gowa-Tallo played in the Moluccas.

After introducing the rise of both Ternate and Gowa-Tallo in the 16th century, the chapter follows the involvement of the various European colonial powers in the Moluccas just as Gowa-Tallo and Ternate were increasingly becoming rivals around the turn of the 17th century. It then argues that the VOC's alliance with Ternate against Spain and its allies was an important negative factor in its relationship with Gowa-Tallo, up to the years 1615 and 1616, when open hostilities between the two first broke out.

Keywords: Spice trade, Moluccas, Ternate, Makassar, East India Companies

In the course of the seventeenth century, the trade entrepôt of Makassar on South Sulawesi became a key site for European and Asian traders seeking to purchase spices and to trade in other high-value goods. They did so in defiance of Dutch East India Company policies aimed at monopolising the trade in cloves and nutmegs from the Moluccas. The VOC did not hesitate

Clulow, Adam and Tristan Mostert (eds.), *The Dutch and English East India Companies: Diplomacy, trade and violence in early modern Asia*. Amsterdam: Amsterdam University Press, 2018
DOI: 10.5117/9789462983298/CH01

to enforce its monopolistic aspirations in the Moluccas with violence, but Makassar proved remarkably resilient to these efforts. That it was so successful in resisting Dutch intrusions stemmed from a combination of factors. Makassar was not merely a trade entrepôt; it was also the main political centre of South Sulawesi. The port city was the seat of government of the kingdom of Gowa, which, jointly with the neighbouring kingdom of Tallo, stood at the head of a wider federation of principalities.[1] This federation encompassed not only large parts of South Sulawesi, but also areas on other islands. Gowa fielded formidable armies and was defended by extensive fortifications. It also had an expansive diplomatic reach. The diplomatic connections of Gowa and Tallo reached from the Moluccas to Mecca, including ties with the English and Danish East India Companies and the Portuguese. These networks provided Makassar with political strength and manoeuvrability. Finally, Makassar's extensive international trading contacts provided an influx of technology and knowledge of all kinds, which were adopted with remarkable ease.[2]

For decades, scholars have been intrigued by this military strength, as demonstrated in several large confrontations with the VOC from the 1650s onwards, which make Makassar and the Gowa-Tallo state useful case studies in wider debates on global military history.[3] These military confrontations ultimately came to a dramatic conclusion in the Makassar War of 1666–1669 when the VOC and a host of local allies under the leadership of

---

1   A note on terminology and spelling: In many European sources, the trade entrepôt of Makassar is conflated with the sultanate of Gowa, of which it was also the political centre. This chapter attempts to clearly distinguish between these two. The state of Tallo, located just north of Gowa, as explained below, enjoyed a very close relationship with Gowa at the time (sources from Gowa and Tallo often used the phrase 'only one people but two rulers'), and although one must be careful not to overstate the scope and duration of their political integration (see e.g. Cummings, 'One people but two rulers'), this integration did reach its apex in the early seventeenth century – the young sultan of Gowa, Ala'uddin, was under the tutelage of the senior karaeng of Tallo, Matoaya, during this period, the latter being credited with the achievements of both states in the Gowa and Tallo chronicles. So, whereas I seek to distinguish between the two states where possible, I feel that in some cases it is justified to refer to them jointly as the Gowa-Tallo state. The spelling I employ follows standard practice among South Sulawesi specialists: the city of Makassar, the Makasar and Bugis people, the Makasars, the Bugis. I must thank Campbell Macknight for many valuable suggestions, including but not limited to the terminology and spelling employed here.

2   For a brief history of Gowa, Tallo, and Makassar, see Cummings, *A Chain of Kings*, pp. 1-8; Reid, 'The rise of Makassar' pp. 100-125; Andaya, *The Heritage of Arung Palakka*, esp. Ch. 1. A good introduction to the forts along its coast is Bulbeck, 'Construction history', pp. 67-106.

3   E.g. in Parker, *The Military Revolution*; Parker, 'The artillery fortress'; Charney, *Southeast Asian Warfare*; Andaya, 'De militaire alliantie'; Den Heijer, Knaap, and De Jong, *Oorlogen overzee*.

the charismatic Bugis nobleman Arung Palakka definitively broke Gowan political power over the entrepôt.

By the time of the Makassar War, the VOC and Gowa-Tallo had been in a state of intermittent conflict for more than five decades. Open conflict had first erupted in 1615. Prior to this point, the VOC had actually maintained a lodge in Makassar, alongside many other European trading nations, who refrained from carrying their violent rivalries directly into Makassar itself. But in April 1615, the VOC lodge was abandoned. Before their departure, the Dutch tried to take a number of Gowan dignitaries hostage, killing several in the scuffle and capturing the assistant *shahbandar* and a blood relative of the Gowan sultan alive. In December 1616, the citizens of Makassar avenged themselves when the VOC vessel *Eendracht*, which had arrived directly from the Netherlands and was unaware of the developments of the past two years, arrived at the Makassar roads, and lost sixteen of its crew members when one of their launches was fired at from the shore and stormed. These two incidents ushered in a kind of cold war between the VOC and Makassar, which erupted into armed conflict in 1633–1637, and again throughout the 1650s and 1660s.

But what prompted the conflict in the first place? This is a crucial question but one that much of the literature tends to skip over by not venturing far beyond the basic observation that the conflict stemmed from the question of access to spices from the Moluccas and the right to trade them. F.W. Stapel's 1933 study of the conflict describes the causes as coming down to:

> Similar goals and interests. The Makasars and the Dutch had both traditionally been seafaring nations and traders; both sought to expand their sphere of influence, with force and boldness if necessary. [...] The Company claimed for itself the largest possible share in the spices from Ambon, Banda and the Moluccas; Makassar's trade largely consisted of precisely the purchase and sale of those same spices.[4]

To this basic conclusion he adds the 'open door policy' of the sultan, which allowed free trade in spices at Makassar, whereas the VOC, by contrast, tried to keep these spices from falling into the hands of other Europeans.

More recent scholarship has continued this focus on the 'open door policy'. Anthony Reid's work on Southeast Asia, for example, often features Makassar as a prime example of the kind of cosmopolitan trading port that was such a crucial component of what he termed the Age of Commerce in

---

4   Stapel, *Het Bongaais Verdrag*, pp. 15-16.

Southeast Asia. In Reid's analysis, this period came to an end in the course
of the seventeenth century, in no small part because VOC policy destroyed
the cosmopolitan and open system that lay at its heart. In the Braudelian
approach that underpinned his monumental work *Southeast Asia in the Age
of Commerce*, and which pervades much of his subsequent scholarship as
well, Makassar is mainly presented as a *bandar*, an open and cosmopolitan
port town, and it was this *bandar* character that, according to Reid, put it
at odds with the controlling and monopolising VOC.[5] As he summarised:

> Makassar's prosperity depended on being a spice port open to all comers,
> at a time when the VOC was using every means to assert a monopoly over
> both clove and nutmeg. [...] To the VOC's demand for monopoly Makassar
> insisted on even-handed freedom for all.[6]

But Makassar was more than just an open trading city. It was also the political centre of a regional power that interacted not only with its neighbours
in South Sulawesi but with states throughout the Archipelago.[7] By the end
of the sixteenth century, moreover, the Gowa-Tallo state was expanding
its influence over the spice-producing regions of the eastern archipelago,
rivalling other states that did so. This meant that it came into conflict with
the VOC not simply because it had opened its markets but rather because
it was trying to expand its own political power.

There is a growing literature on how the VOC used diplomacy and violence
as essential tools to achieve its trade goals.[8] In its efforts to get a foothold in
the spice trade and, soon after, to become the sole buyer of these spices, the
VOC concluded the bulk of its earliest treaties with a range of island polities
in the Moluccas. The Company also made its first territorial conquests there.[9]

5   Reid, *Southeast Asia in the Age of Commerce*. More recently; Reid, 'Early Modernity as
Cosmopolis'. Although some of his earlier articles, specifically on Makassar, do give some
attention to politics, both 'domestic' and 'foreign', e.g. Reid, 'The Rise of Makassar' and Reid, 'A
Great Seventeenth Century Indonesian family'.
6   Reid, *A History of Southeast Asia*, p. 136.
7   Andaya, *The Heritage of Arung Palakka*. This study focused on developments within South
Sulawesi and particularly the role of Arung Palakka, the Buginese ally of the Dutch whose role
was pivotal in defeating Makassar in 1666-1669. Although he does dedicate a few remarks to
Gowan expansion overseas and the struggle for access to the spice trade, these hardly feature
in his analysis of the conflict.
8   A call for this kind of approach was made in the inaugural lecture of Blussé, '*Tussen geveinsde
vrunden en verklaarde vijanden*'. It has been taken up by a range of works, including Clulow, *The
Company and the Shogun*.
9   Heeres, *Corpus diplomaticum*.

While the VOC would come to exert a dominant influence, it was initially only the latest party to join the wider geopolitical struggle centred on Moluccan spices. This was a struggle that had a dynamic all of its own. In its attempt to get a hold over the clove-producing regions of the Moluccas, the VOC alliance with Ternate, concluded in 1607, was of particular importance. The sultan of Ternate was nominally the head of state over a great many of the islands, and the VOC could use him as an instrument to strengthen its grip on these regions. This alliance came attached, however, to a set of related consequences within the political constellation of the eastern archipelago, not all of them tied directly to the spice trade, or necessarily beneficial to the VOC.

This chapter will explore the role that the VOC's evolving political and military strategy in the Moluccas had in shaping its relationship with Gowa and Tallo in the period leading up to the first open hostilities in 1615 and 1616. My focus is on the unintended consequences that the VOC's alliance with Ternate had for this relationship. In the process, I aim to highlight a factor that has received little attention but that was crucial in the evolution of the conflict between Gowa-Tallo and the VOC. As the VOC became the 'protector' of Ternate on paper in 1607, and increasingly started taking on this role in subsequent years, this also set the organisation on a path towards rivalry with the Gowa-Tallo state. In drawing attention to the influence of the VOC's relations with Ternate on conflicts with Gowa-Tallo, this chapter aims to move the debate beyond a standard binary that sees VOC as the aggressive interloper determined to monopolise the spice trade pitted against an open port city like Makassar. Rather, I argue that the advent of the VOC did not represent a decisive break with older patterns and suggest that scholars should pay more attention to how Europeans were folded into pre-existing rivalries and tensions. This chapter starts by exploring the rise of Ternate and Makassar, and then continues to trace their developing rivalry and the way the VOC became involved in it.

Ternate and the kingdoms of the Northern Moluccas

Today, the term Moluccas, or Maluku, is used to denote the islands to the east of Sulawesi, up to Papua in the east and Timor in the south. In the early modern period, however, the term applied to what we would now call the Northern Moluccas: the island of Halmahera and the smaller islands directly surrounding it (see Map 1, Southeast Asia). Whereas the political unit of the southern regions of the Moluccas, including the Ambon and Banda islands, was typically the village or a federation of villages, the Northern Moluccas were home to the kingdoms or sultanates of Ternate, Tidore, Gilolo, and Bacan. The most powerful and influential of these were Ternate and Tidore, two states in constant rivalry that were centred in two adjacent small islands (see Figure 2, below), but both with political power that extended far beyond these islands at their core, as large areas throughout the Moluccas, as well as some areas of Sulawesi, were at some point vassals of one or the other.[10]

The first European involvement in the Moluccas immediately became tied up with this political rivalry between Ternate and Tidore. In 1512, a small group of Portuguese that had originally been part of the first Portuguese trading expedition to Banda, was shipwrecked on the Lucipara islands.[11] Rescued by Ambonese fishermen, they were soon invited to the island of Ternate by the sultan, who appears to have hoped that the Portuguese would be an asset in Ternate's conflicts with Tidore, and that an alliance with them would raise his own standing and power. He wrote a letter to the Portuguese king, inviting him to come and buy cloves, nutmeg and mace in Ternate – the island was the original habitat of the clove tree and had trade relations throughout the Moluccas. The sultan would also welcome Portuguese soldiers and weapons, and would allow them to build a fort in his domains. Nine years later, Tidore, along with Gilolo, tried to make a similar arrangement with the Spanish when the two remaining ships of Magellan's expedition, sent out specifically to contest the Portuguese claims to the Spice Islands, passed through the Moluccas. From the very beginning, European competition for access to the spices was thus entwined with political rivalries between the states in the Moluccas.

In the initial phase it was the alliance between the Portuguese and Ternate that stuck. In 1522, the Portuguese, startled into action by the appearance of the Spanish ships, sent a contingent of soldiers under the command of Antonio de Brito to Ternate to begin building a fort on its southern coast. They completed construction in 1523. The following year the Ternatans and their European allies successfully attacked Tidore, burning down the capital Mareku. The Spanish presence in the archipelago, meanwhile, was too intermittent and weak for them to substantially help their Moluccan partners. In spite of limited Spanish help to Gilolo, the Portuguese conquered it in 1534, capturing the sultan and, after his suspiciously untimely death,

---

10   Much of what follows heavily relies on Andaya, *The World of Maluku*. Footnotes have been placed where a specific reference was useful, or where other sources were used.
11   The Lucipara islands are a small group to the west of Banda; the Portuguese were shipwrecked here on their return voyage.

installing a new one that was loyal to them.[12] In 1551, Gilolo, after renewed conflict with Ternate and the Portuguese, would become entirely subservient to Ternate.

Despite these initial successes, the Ternatan alliance with the Portuguese turned out to be a mixed blessing. As the conflicts referenced above show, the Portuguese were a formidable ally, and their support helped Ternate become the most powerful of the Moluccan sultanates. Portuguese traders, like their Muslim counterparts, also brought wealth, some in the form of cloth, iron and luxury goods, to Ternate, reinforcing the position and status of the ruling class in the process. In addition, Leonard Andaya has argued that the clove trade, with the income it provided and the organisation that was required to meet Portuguese demands for timing and preparation of the harvest, accelerated the state-formation process underway in the islands.[13] But relations between the Ternatans and the Portuguese soon turned sour. De Brito's successor, Dom Jorge de Meneses, managed to alienate the ruling class within a very short period with his policies, which included keeping the sultan hostage in the Portuguese fort and executing various Ternatan high officials he suspected of conspiring against him. Under the leadership of the sultan's mother, the Ternatans started starving the fort of food supplies, only lifting the blockade when Meneses was replaced as Captain of Ternate in 1530.

The Meneses captaincy was the start of increasing Portuguese involvement in Ternatan politics, and a resultant surge of Ternatan resistance against this. Subsequent decades saw frequent conflict, and the exile or even death of a number of sultans at the hands of the Portuguese. On one occasion the Ternatan leaders swore to 'destroy all the spice and fruit trees on the islands' so that the Portuguese would have no further interest in the area.[14] Meanwhile, Christianity was taking hold in many areas of the archipelago that the sultan of Ternate laid claim to. The latter usually happened not on the initiative of Portuguese missionaries but that of the population of these areas, who, among other motivations, sometimes saw Christianity as a means of weakening Ternatan control over them.[15] The Muslim Ternatan sultans rightly felt that this served to undermine their power.

---

12   Some Spanish survivors of the Saavedra expedition, which had stranded in Gilolo in 1528, had remained there and apparently helped the sultan with weapons, training and fort building. Andaya, *The World of Maluku*, pp. 121-122.

13   Ibid., pp. 55-57.

14   Ibid., p. 124.

15   This local agency in the spread of Christianity is convincingly demonstrated in Baker, 'Indigenous-driven mission.' Baker also points out that interest in Christianity did not only stem from the elite considerations of political and economic power I emphasise here (although

Things came to a head after 1570 when Sultan Hairun was killed by the Portuguese (and, according to several sources, subsequently cut to pieces and salted in a barrel).[16] His son and successor, Babullah, resolved to drive the Portuguese from Ternate altogether. In this, he would prove to be far more successful than his predecessors. He managed to unite a Muslim coalition against the Portuguese, and proceeded to starve them into submission in their fort. Babullah, moreover, campaigned around the Moluccas, driving out the Portuguese and forcing Christian communities to convert to Islam. In 1575, after what had amounted to a five-year siege and with no prospect of help from the ailing empire, the Portuguese surrendered the fort and were evicted to Ambon. With this surrender, the Portuguese presence in Ternate came to an end. Despite this experience, Europeans remained potentially valuable allies. Interestingly, Tidore would open its doors to the Portuguese soon after. Ternate, for its part, was soon courting new European arrivals in the Moluccas. When Francis Drake sailed through the area in 1579, he had initially intended to sail to Tidore. A Ternatan approached the ships and implored Drake to come to Ternate instead, as he would find a warm welcome there. In contrast, Drake was warned that the Portuguese were in Tidore and that the English could expect nothing there but deceit and treachery. Drake obliged, setting sail for Ternate instead.[17]

Babullah meanwhile started reasserting and extending his power, sending a fleet to the western Ambon islands in 1576, and setting out with a fleet himself in 1580, first to North Sulawesi, and then to Southeast Sulawesi. The campaign ended at Selayar, just below South Sulawesi, where a treaty was apparently made with the Gowan Karaeng.[18] Sultan Babullah was now

---

these certainly played a role), but also from individual religious choices. Of course, these two are not mutually exclusive, as I shall also be arguing below for the conversion to Islam of the elite of Gowa and Tallo.

16   For example, Valentijn, *Oud en Nieuw Oost Indien*; Commelin, *Begin ende voortgangh van de Vereenighde*, pp. 28-41. In the latter van Warwijck tells the Ternatan Sultan Said that the (Spanish) king of the Portuguese (referring to Philip II, the news of whose death shortly before had not yet reached the Indies) had had their Prince (referring to William of Orange) assassinated. The sultan then answers that one of his ancestors had also been killed, and chopped to pieces and salted, in the name of the king of Portugal.

17   Fletcher, *The World Encompassed by Sir Francis Drake*, p. 85.

18   Andaya, *The World of Maluku*, p. 134. Andaya bases himself heavily on Valentijn, *Oud en Nieuw Oost Indien* here, and Valentijn's information largely came from Ternatan lore, so that the reliability of this information is somewhat uncertain. It must be noted that the Gowa Chronicle (Cummings, *A Chain of Kings*, p. 41) makes no mention of this treaty, although it does mention Maluku in the information about diplomatic contacts built up by this ruler: 'It was also this *karaeng* [Tunijalloq, r.1565-1590] who befriended the Javanese, crossed over to Karasanga, to

free of the Portuguese and presided over a self-confident and cosmopolitan Southeast Asian court. The report of Francis Drake's visit to Ternate illustrates this – not only were Drake and his crew impressed by the opulence and state of the court, they also took note of the cosmopolitan character of the sultan's retinue, which included:

> foure [...] Romans, or strangers [Rumi?], who lay as lidgiers [agents or representatives] there to keepe continuall traffique with this people; there were also two Turkes and one Italian as lidgiers; and last of all, one Spaniard who, being freed out of the hands of the Portugals in the recovering of the iland, served him now in stead of a souldier.[19]

Drake was less impressed with the state of Ternate's defences – the sultan had taken up residence in the old Portuguese fort, but Drake's men did not 'find it to be a place of any great force; two onely cannons there they saw, and those at that present moment untraversable because unmounted.'[20] Six years later, however, the Ternate court had apparently improved dramatically on this point. In 1585, the Spanish, now allied with the Portuguese since the Iberian Union of 1580, made an attempt to conquer Ternate, sending a fleet from Manila. The Spanish and a host of local allies, however, found a significantly reinforced fort, with an added ring of walls, new bulwarks and towers, mounted with guns captured from the Portuguese. Spanish sources also describe how some 20 Turkish gunners participated in the defence, using bombs and grenades against the attacking forces. In the end, the Spanish were forced to break off their attack.[21]

Thus, by the end of the sixteenth century, Ternate had become a formidable military power, independent of the Iberian powers, and one that was expanding to include an ever greater number of vassals throughout the eastern archipelago. With an eye to subsequent developments in the seventeenth century, it is worth pointing out that in this period its vassals included the western Ambon islands, where the western peninsula of Seram, Hoamoal, had a Ternatan steward or *kimelaha*,[22] as did the island of Buru,

---

Johor, crossed over to Melaka, crossed over to Pahang, crossed over to Balambangang, crossed over to Patani, crossed over to Banjar, went east to Maluku.'

19   Fletcher, *The World Encompassed by Sir Francis Drake*, pp. 90-91. Incidentally, on Ternate they also met with a Chinese who claimed to have been exiled from the Chinese court and would only be allowed to return when he had discovered some worthwhile information.

20   Fletcher, *The World Encompassed by Sir Francis Drake*, p. 92.

21   Andaya, *The World of Maluku*, p. 137.

22   The Dutch referred to them as 'stadhouders'.

Figure 1   The Ternatan capital of Gammalamma. This print was made on the
            basis of van Warwijck's 1599 visit to Ternate. We see van Warwijck's two
            ships (A) and the sultan's warships (C). The old Portuguese fort, now
            turned into the royal palace, is indicated G. M indicates another fortified
            Portuguese building. O indicates a tower 'with one gun'.

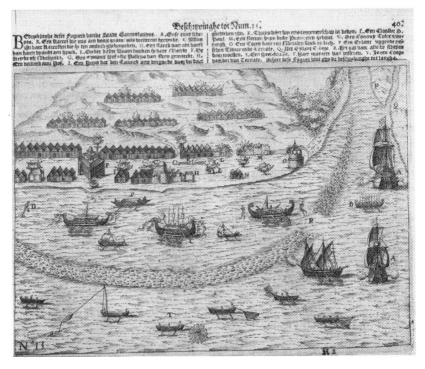

Collection Universiteit van Amsterdam, O 60 641, p. 40.

directly to its west. The smaller islands around them also fell under the
stewardship of either of the two *kimelaha*. In addition, various areas of
Sulawesi had come within the Ternatan sphere of influence – some areas
on its north coast, but also the islands of Southeast Sulawesi, including the
small island kingdom of Buton. The areas claimed by Ternate by the late
sixteenth century even included the island of Selayar – much more to the
west, and right below South Sulawesi. That, of course, was the area where,
during that same period, another Southeast Asian state was thriving and
expanding.

The parallel rise of Makassar

The emergence of Makassar as a trade entrepôt dates back to the mid-sixteenth century, when the principality of Gowa, which had an economy based on wet-rice agriculture, expanded to incorporate a number of surrounding polities. In the 1530s it defeated its neighbouring states, including Tallo, which was an important trading port at the time. Rather than being forcibly transformed into a vassal, Tallo was joined in union with Gowa, laying the foundations for a dual kingdom, a political system that would endure until 1669. Under the rule of Karaeng Tunipalangga (r. 1547–1565), Gowa-Tallo made vassals of most of the polities on South Sulawesi's west coast.[23]

As trade increased, its political centre moved to the coast, creating the entrepôt that we know as Makassar. During the rule of Tunipalangga, the office of *shahbandar*, already created under his predecessor but as part of the duties of one minister, became a separate position. Tunipalangga also gave written guarantees of freedom and rights to the Malay community: a Malay captain called Nakhoda Bonang is mentioned in the Gowa court chronicles as coming to the court bearing gifts and asking for permission to settle in Makassar, setting several conditions that would protect their possessions and livelihood there.[24] The next important Karaeng, Tunijalloq[25] (r. 1565–1590), built a mosque for the Malay community, years before the rulers of Gowa and Tallo would themselves convert to Islam. Tunijalloq, according to the court chronicles, also made active efforts to build up diplomatic ties in the late sixteenth century: in the Moluccas and Timor, as well as with Mataram, Banjarmassin and Johor.[26] In the same period, Portuguese private traders from Melaka became regular visitors to Makassar's harbour.[27] Islam and Christianity, meanwhile, also generated interest in Makassar both among the general population and the political elite, which resulted in the rulers of Gowa and Tallo converting to Islam around 1605.[28]

---

23   *Karaeng* is the Makasar word for ruler. Its Buginese equivalent is *Arung* (as in Arung Palakka). After their conversion to Islam, the rulers of Gowa would style themselves as sultans, but the rulers of Tallo would still be referred to as *karaeng*.

24   Cummings, *A Chain of Kings*, p. 34; Cummings, 'The Melaka Malay diaspora', pp. 107-110.

25   Tunijalloq was not his direct successor, but almost – in 1565 Tunibatta ascended to the throne, then immediately went to war against Bone, and got himself killed. His rule lasted only 40 days.

26   Cummings, *A Chain of Kings*, p. 41.

27   Borges, *Os Portugueses e o Sultanato de Macaçar no Século XVII*, pp. 62-63.

28   The sources are somewhat ambiguous about the exact moment that this occurred. Jacobus Noorduyn, who has dedicated an article to both the motivations for the rulers of Gowa and Tallo

In his examination of religious development, Jacobus Noorduyn has argued that the conversion of the karaengs of Gowa and Tallo in this period, and, in its wake, of the entire state, were the outcome of a period of theological inquiry by the rulers, rather than the consequence of any kind of political or economic opportunism.[29] Regardless, conversion provided further impetus to diplomatic contacts and spurred Makassar's rise as an international trading port, providing a basis for more intensive contacts with other Muslim polities throughout the archipelago, and tying the state into the Islamic networks spanning the Indian Ocean and beyond.[30] It also gave Gowa-Tallo's further expansion a strong impetus, as the conversion signalled the beginning of what are called the 'Wars of Islamisation' on South Sulawesi, during which the Gowa-Tallo alliance converted the Bugis states at the east coast of South Sulawesi by military means, and simultaneously brought them into their sphere of influence. Islam thus functioned as an engine of further expansion and consolidation of the power of the Gowa-Tallo state within South Sulawesi.[31]

At the conclusion of these wars of Islamisation, all the polities in the coastal plains of South Sulawesi had become affiliated to the Gowa-Tallo state. This expansion, however, was not limited to the mainland of South Sulawesi. Gowa-Tallo had also been expanding further afield. By the late sixteenth century, it commanded an impressive navy, using it to expand to Sumbawa and other polities. Around the turn of the seventeenth century, as the Gowa-Tallo state was consolidating its hold over South Sulawesi, it strived to bring several areas on the north coast of Sulawesi, around Manado, under its protection.[32] To its southeast, it sought to turn the island kingdom of Buton into its vassal.[33] These attempts at further expansion set

to convert to Islam and the moment this conversion occurred, holds it to be 1605, rather than the other likely possibility, 1603. Noorduyn, 'De Islamisering van Makassar,' p. 252.

29   Ibid.

30   One might imagine that the rulers of Gowa and Tallo, for instance, would have observed with interest the developments in Ternate, where contacts with the greater Muslim world also translated into military power. Gowa-Tallo would also develop a large Gujarati trading community in the course of the seventeenth century, develop diplomatic contacts with other Muslim states like Mataram and Aceh, and, as we shall see, politically expand into Muslim areas of the Southern Moluccas.

31   Reid, 'A Great Seventeenth Century Indonesian family,' p. 139; Andaya, *The Heritage of Arung Palakka*, p. 33.

32   Andaya, *The World of Maluku*, pp. 84-85.

33   Cummings, *A Chain of Kings*, p. 88, which sums up the conquests under Karaeng Matoaya (r. 1593-1623). Among several places in South Sulawesi and many names I do not recognise with certainty, he mentions e.g. Buton, Wowoni (another island below Southeast Sulawesi), Sula (most

it on a collision course with Ternate, which had recently expanded into these same territories. Gowa-Tallo and Ternate were therefore increasingly fierce rivals, just at the moment that new European powers were entering the eastern archipelago.

The northern European Companies and Spain

As we have seen, the English and Spanish made their first push into the eastern archipelago in the late 1570s and 1580s, with the Dutch following in the 1590s. The first Dutch expedition to reach Asia did not make it beyond Java and Madura. Rather it was the second Dutch expedition that finally reached the Moluccas, after being invited by Ternate when it had called at Ambon. When two ships under the leadership of Wybrant van Warwijck arrived at Ternate, he found the sultan willing to sell cloves to the Dutch, but also keen to secure the Dutch as an ally against the Portuguese. In fact, the sultan was clear that he wanted some of van Warwijck's crew to remain at Ternate, and was very interested to see demonstrations of the firepower of Dutch ships.[34]

One of the men involved in this second expedition wrote the first detailed Dutch description we have of Makassar, and was involved in the first diplomatic contacts. In 1601, Augustijn Stalpaert van der Wiele, one of 20 men who had been left on the Banda islands by this expedition, compiled a report about various trading ports throughout Asia, including Makassar. He described it as an important trading city, where most merchants bound for the Spice Islands would call in order to sell textiles, provision their ships and buy high-quality rice, which was available in abundance and for which one would always find a ready market in the Spice Islands. 'You will also be free of the Portuguese here,' Stalpaert van der Wiele wrote home, 'who do come here every year to conduct quite some trade, but who do not have any fortification here, and come here in junks, not in ships.'[35] He then described how he and his colleagues had already opened up relations with the ruler of Makassar by sending him a letter and an appropriate gift. The ruler had

likely the Sula islands east of Sulawesi, which would also be a bone of contention between the two in the course of the seventeenth century) and several places on Sumbawa.

34   Commelin, *Begin ende voortgangh van de Vereenighde*, pp. 28-41.

35   The report is partly printed in de Jonge, *De opkomst van het Nederlandsch gezag in Oost-Indië*, p. 156; the original, which includes long lists of types of textiles that were in vogue in Makassar, with an indication of the price they would yield, is in VOC 7525, fol. 95. It has been preserved as one of the documents that were sent along on the fleet of Steven van der Haghen, departing for the Indies in 1603, of which copies were kept.

replied that the Dutch should certainly come and trade, but as he was aware they were at war with the Portuguese and wanted to avoid trouble, he would prefer them to send no more than eight men, whose protection he would guarantee. The exact moment the Dutch did send their first merchant to Makassar is unclear, but it would seem that around 1605, Claes Luersen moved from Banda to Makassar to reside there permanently.[36]

By that time, the conflict between the Dutch and the Portuguese had taken on a different character. In 1602, the VOC was founded, uniting the various smaller companies that had equipped the first expeditions to Asia under one umbrella organisation. Both its permanence and its founding charter, which allowed the VOC to conduct politics and defend itself in the name of the Dutch Republic, made it possible for it to develop a political and military strategy in Asia, and it immediately started doing so. In 1603, in response to various reports of incidents involving the Portuguese throughout Asia, the VOC directors decided to take to a more aggressive policy. At the end of 1603, Steven van der Hagen was sent to Asia in command of a heavily armed fleet and with orders to do all possible damage to the Portuguese and Spanish. In Bantam he met with several representatives of the Ambonese polity of Hitu, who asked for his help against the Portuguese.[37] In February 1605, he sailed into the bay of Ambon with ten ships and took the fort without firing a shot. This conquest was the beginning of the VOC's emergence as a territorial power. The southern half of the island of Ambon, as well as areas on several neighbouring islands, had been directly under Portuguese control and had a predominantly Christian population. The VOC now replaced the Portuguese as ruler of these areas.[38]

The increasing Dutch presence in the Moluccas at the expense of the Portuguese prompted the Spanish to take action. In early 1606, a Spanish fleet of five large ships and several dozen smaller vessels, carrying over 1,400 Iberian troops, set sail from the Philippines towards the Moluccas under the leadership of Pedro de Acuña. Rallying the sultanate of Tidore to his

---

36   This, in any case, is compellingly argued in Noorduyn, 'De Islamisering,' p. 260, as the first known Makassar merchant, Claes Luersen, was still in Banda until 1605. Of course, it is possible that someone else occupied the function before that time, or that the merchants were travelling up and down from Banda.

37   Hitu was a polity that consisted of the northern half of the island of Ambon, whereas the Portuguese controlled the southern half. It was Muslim and independent, but was increasingly suffering from Portuguese military encroachment in the first years of the seventeenth century. As there had been contacts between the VOC and the Hituese before, the Hituese sent out representatives to find Dutch support, and found Steven van der Hagen.

38   Den Heijer, Knaap, and De Jong, *Oorlogen overzee*, p. 60.

cause, he proceeded to attack Ternate. This time, the Spanish managed to conquer the old Portuguese fort on the south coast. Acuña left a garrison of 600 soldiers in the fort on Ternate, and another 50 on Tidore, before returning to Manila in May.[39]

The Ternatans, who had been in contact with various English and Dutch fleets over the past few years, turned to them for help. In April 1607, VOC admiral Cornelis Matelief de Jonge met with a Ternatan representative while his fleet was at Ambon. The representative asked for his help in driving the Spanish from Ternate. Matelief gladly obliged, setting sail for Ternate from Ambon on 3 May. Having arrived there, he met with the new Ternatan Sultan Muzaffar (the old one having been deported to Manila by the Spanish), but soon discovered that it would be impossible to take the Spanish fort with his fleet and the limited number of warriors that the sultan would be able to muster. Instead, he sailed around the island and built a fort, which would come to be called Oranje, at Melayu on the east coast.[40] In subsequent years, the VOC would fortify much of the northeast of the island, whereas the Spanish entrenched themselves on the southwestern half.

The VOC alliance with Ternate

Their home island thus divided, the Ternatan royal family and nobility threw in their lot with the Dutch and built up their new capital around the Dutch fort in Melayu on the east coast. A treaty concluded between the new sultan, Muzaffar, and the VOC stipulated that the sultan of Ternate should recognise the Dutch as his 'protector', and gave the VOC a monopoly on buying cloves from the Ternatan territories.[41] This included parts of the Ambon islands that were ruled by the Ternatan stewards, and the monopoly there was reconfirmed in a separate treaty with them two years later.[42] Tidore, conversely, allied itself with the Spanish, and the Northern Moluccas would be the scene of intermittent fighting between these rival coalitions for the next decades.[43]

39   Spate, *Monopolists and Freebooters*, pp. 11-12; Andaya, *The World of Maluku*, pp. 152-153.

40   Akveld, *Machtsstrijd om Malakka*, p. 168.

41   Heeres, *Corpus diplomaticum*, pp. 50-53.

42   Knaap, 'De Ambonse eilanden tussen twee mogendheden,', pp. 51-52.

43   Andaya, *The World of Maluku*, pp. 152-156; Den Heijer, Knaap, and De Jong, *Oorlogen overzee*, pp. 61-67.

Figure 2   The islands of Ternate and Tidore off the coast of Halmahera (here called
            Gilolo Island). North is right. To the far right, we see Ternate, with the
            now Spanish fort of Gammalamma on the left, and the Dutch fort at
            Melayu slightly below it. On Tidore we see fort Marieko, originally built
            by the Spaniards but conquered by the VOC in 1613; the other islands
            further left have various other Spanish and Dutch forts. This map was
            used in many of the Blaeu atlases and dates to c. 1635.

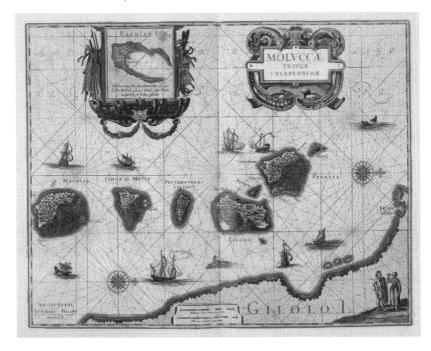

Koninklijke Bibliotheek, The Hague, inv. 1049 B 13.

Aside from the building up of the spice monopoly, of which the conquest
of Ambon and the treaty with Ternate constituted the first serious steps, the
VOC now had an alliance with, and a certain degree of power over, a sultan
in the eastern archipelago. This changed the way the organisation operated. For one, the VOC's alliance with, and its role as 'protector' of, Ternate
meant that it had a stake in various vassalages, conflicts and alliances that
Ternate already maintained. In 1613, for example, the VOC concluded a treaty
with Buton, which fell in the Ternatan sphere of influence. In the treaty,
the Company promised to protect the small kingdom against invasion,
specifically mentioning 'the king of Makassar' as the main threat. The ruler
declared that he had called the Dutch to his kingdom 'to wage offensive

and defensive war against the enemies of the mighty king of Ternate, with whom our friendship shall continue as of old'.[44] The VOC built two small fortifications on Buton and stationed a garrison there. When, two years later, it was decided to lift the permanent presence at Buton (for reasons described below), the ruler expressed his surprise, because if his kingdom would fall to 'the enemy' (presumably Gowa-Tallo), it would be a source of shame for both the VOC and Ternate, of which he was the loyal servant.[45]

Similarly, the VOC conquered the Portuguese fort on Solor in 1613, and found that, whereas the population proclaimed allegiance to the sultan of Ternate, Gowa-Tallo was actively engaged in collecting tribute there. The VOC brought this to an end, sending away the ships from Makassar. In early 1614, Adriaan van den Velde, the Dutch commander on Solor, informed the Governor-General that he had written to the ruler of Gowa, explaining 'that it was not their intention to divert, or draw away from his obedience, any of his subjects, but that, as friends and allies of the king of Ternate, they could not but bring them back under his rule'.[46] He added, however, that they had not received a reply, and that he feared Gowa-Tallo might try to collect the tribute by force and join forces with the Portuguese. The alliance with the sultan of Ternate, and the way it played out in practice, therefore had a negative effect on the VOC's relationship with Gowa-Tallo.

On the other hand, the alliance with a local sultan was in itself a political tool that the VOC quickly learned to use. As a trading company from a European republic, operating in a world where diplomacy was typically conducted between kings, the VOC had no real experience with, or standing in, Asian politics. In its early years VOC officials tried to work around this by presenting themselves as representatives of the 'King of Holland', in some cases bringing images and diplomatic letters of Stadholder Maurice of Orange, with mixed results.[47] In the eastern archipelago, it now had another option: it could conduct 'diplomacy by proxy' through the sultan of Ternate. As we shall see below, the VOC did so with enthusiasm as it was trying to establish a monopoly over spices from this region.

44   Heeres, *Corpus diplomaticum*, pp. 105-108.

45   Coen to patria, 22 October 1615, printed in Colenbrander (ed.), *Jan Pietersz. Coen: bescheiden omtrent zijn bedrijf in Indië*, p. 120.

46   Tiele and Heeres, *Bouwstoffen voor de geschiedenis der Nederlanders in den Maleischen Archipel*, p. 95.

47   VOC diplomacy and the various strategies used by the company in Japan were recently analysed in Clulow, *The Company and the Shogun*. For the attempts to present the Stadholder as their king, see op. cit., 31-39. For similar attempts on Ceylon, see Lunsingh-Scheurleer, 'Uitwisseling van staatsieportretten op Ceylon in 1602,' pp. 165-200.

The developing role of Makassar in the European spice trade

In 1607, the Dutch factory near Makassar (which seems to have been located not in Makassar proper but in Tallo, just to the north) had been temporarily abandoned, not because of conflicts with the ruler but because Claes Luersen, the merchant mentioned earlier, had been cooking the books and, in the eyes of the visiting fleet under Jacques l'Hermite and Paulus van Solt, had been too friendly with the Spanish.[48] The ruler of Tallo[49] professed his sadness at seeing them go, and implored them to come back soon – he would make sure that they could buy all the mace they wanted, and added that gold noble coins[50] were particularly in demand in Makassar. His remark was not an idle one, as the ruler had a trade agent permanently stationed at the Banda islands, and was a consequential commercial presence there.[51]

The Portuguese, who were forced out of the Moluccas in this period, increasingly bought their spices in Makassar. The trading policy of the VOC in Makassar was, however, a different one. It preferred to buy the spices in the Moluccas directly, particularly as its monopoly was slowly taking shape in the wake of the conquest of Ambon, the treaty with Ternate, and, in 1609, a treaty with some of the *orangkayas* on Banda Neira. Makassar was prominent among several port towns where it would buy the rice that was brought to the Moluccas as a trade good, with which the spices were then bought – under trading conditions and for prices that the Dutch were increasingly trying to control.

The new VOC merchant, Samuel Denijs, who arrived in Makassar in 1609, proved not especially effective in securing rice. His extant correspondence from 1610 to 1612 paints a tragicomic picture of successive failures and setbacks. The price of the rice that he was supposed to send to the Moluccas happened to be unusually high in these years, because of bad harvests and

48   He had, for instance, been adding debts of local rulers that did not exist. When Paulus van Solt travelled around the area to seek information about these debts, and it became clear that there were none, he remarked that falsely accusing local rulers of being in debt would have been a very dangerous job, if it weren't for the fact that the Makasars were such 'kind and friendly people.' Commelin, *Begin ende voortgangh van de Vereenighde*, pp. 81-82. Commelin does not mention Luersen by name, but various VOC documents do, including a mention of van Solt's 'examinatie' of him in VOC 1053 (unfoliated).

49   This would have been Karaeng Matoaya (r. 1593–1623). The description in Commelin gives the impression that the first Dutch lodge was actually in Tallo, rather than in Gowan-ruled Makassar. What is certain is that the new merchant, Samuel Denijs, who arrived in 1609, constructed a new lodge in Makassar itself.

50   'Rozenobels'.

51   Commelin, *Begin ende voortgangh*, p. 82.

the Wars of Islamisation mentioned above. After the conclusion of these wars by late 1610, Sultan Ala'uddin prohibited the export of rice in order to prevent famine among the Bugis, 'who he has recently subjugated, who have become Moorish, and who were nearly starving.'[52] The letters also betray a total dependence on local shipping and trade that stands in stark contrast to the monopolistic ambitions that the VOC was developing in the Moluccas. The provision of Ambon and Banda with supplies from Makassar took place exclusively in local ships, and Denijs was dependent on local captains planning to sail there. In the absence of VOC ships providing him with fresh capital, he often had to rely on local credit, his creditors including karaeng Matoaya of Tallo. Most of the cargoes of rice, arrack, salted buffalo meat and fish he was able to send off never reached their destination: in 1610, five junks carrying provisions for Banda and Ambon were all turned back by the monsoon, and part of the cargo was spoiled by seawater getting into the hold. In 1611, another junk bound for the (Northern) Moluccas was shipwrecked on a reef, and the entire cargo was lost.[53] Meanwhile, he had to stand idly by as the Portuguese, arriving from Melaka each year, dumped large amounts of textiles onto the Makassar market for low prices, bringing down the value of his own trade goods, and buying the spices that both Makasar and Javanese ships were bringing in, which sometimes sold for a better price than what the VOC paid in the Moluccas themselves. Denijs had no instructions to buy these up himself, and in any case did not have sufficient funds to do so.[54] In addition, the rulers of Gowa and Tallo demanded all sorts of diplomatic gifts from the Company, including a small gun for the Gowan royal ship, *kris* (Southeast Asian daggers), various textiles and porcelain. The fact that two *bahar* of mace, which Claes Luersen had accepted from the sultan of Gowa, and in exchange for which he was to deliver chainmail armour and a small gun, had apparently gone missing, was a continuing annoyance to the court and a worry to Denijs.[55]

In July 1613, the English opened a factory in Makassar, which soon developed into their base of operations for their own trade in the Spice

---

52   VOC 1053, Makassar folder (unfol.), letter of Samuel Denijs to Jacques l'Hermite in Bantam, 19 October 1610.

53   VOC 1053, Makassar folder (unfol.), letter of Samuel Denijs to the Directors in the Netherlands, 12 July 1612.

54   Ibid.

55   This is a recurring topic throughout the letters, but handily summarised in VOC 1053, Bantam folder (unfol.), Hendrick Brouwer to Directors in the Netherlands, 27 June 1612. I wish to thank independent historian Menno Leenstra for his help locating some of these early archival references to Makassar.

Islands. Their use of the Makassar harbour was very similar to that of the Dutch: they mostly bought rice there, selling it for spices in the Moluccas.[56]

Trading in the Spice Islands, however, was becoming increasingly difficult for the English even before they built their lodge in Makassar, as VOC control in the Moluccas increased. The VOC increasingly asserted its right to be the sole buyer of spices, forcing the *orangkaya* on the Banda islands into concluding trade treaties with it and using its influence over Ternate to increase their grip on areas like Western Seram in the Ambon islands. The people living there, apparently unhappy with the increasing Dutch control that was the consequence of being vassals of Ternate, also clandestinely sold spices to the English.[57] In 1615, the villagers at Cambello invited the English to build a lodge there – the Dutch, upon noticing this, approached with a ship and started firing on the village. Cambello was defended by a fortification, and the inhabitants approached the English, telling them that they would give the fort, along with 'the whole island,' to the English if they would but help against the Dutch.[58] The incident shows that areas officially under Ternatan control chafed at increasing Dutch control, and attempted to turn elsewhere for political protection. All the same, the English eventually had to retreat on this occasion. The EIC was unable to stand up to the VOC's increasingly aggressive stance, backed up with growing military power.

The English ship with which this expedition had been undertaken, the *Concord*, then returned to Makassar, where, to their surprise, the crew found the Dutch lodge abandoned and the English one guarded by only one man. While they had been away, the facts on the ground had changed at Makassar.

European rivalry at the Makassar roads

'Arriving here at Macasser I find our people to be run away, all but one lame man who, more honester than the rest, stayed [...]', a surprised George Ball wrote to Bantam, the day after reaching Makassar on 23 June 1615.[59] Although his letter is not especially detailed, it explains that the English factor had become too close with the Dutch by siding with them against the Spanish, and that the English were also complicit in the killing and abduction of

---

56 Bassett, 'English trade in Celebes', pp. 1-4.
57 For example, in 1613, as described in Jourdain, *The Journal of John Jourdain*, pp. 247-273.
58 Foster, *Letters Received,* III, p. 134.
59 Ibid., p. 287.

several Makasar dignitaries, so that the sultan now wished for the English to leave entirely.

A letter by Jan Pieterszoon Coen, who would later become VOC Governor-General, gives more details about the eruption of violence between different groups of Europeans. In April 1615, a small flotilla of Spanish ships had attacked the VOC ship *Enkhuizen* as it approached the Makassar roads.[60] The ship repelled the attack with difficulty, losing eleven men in the process. Fearing more Spanish aggression, and worried that the sultan, who had been away from the city when the attack happened, was no longer willing or able to protect them, the Dutch decided to abandon their lodge, as did the English, who were given passage on the Dutch ship. As preparations to leave were made, the crew of the ship tried to take hostage a number of local dignitaries who had come on board in the wake of the attack. A skirmish broke out, in which nine of these dignitaries, including one of the sultan's sons, died. Two others, the assistant *shahbandar* and another blood relative of the king, were captured alive. They were taken along as the ship departed from Makassar.[61]

George Ball, the EIC merchant, found that the sultan had not taken the incident lightly and was now resolved to ban 'all Christians' from Makassar. It took all of Ball's negotiation skills to convince him to exempt the English, and he was allowed to leave George Cockayne as a factor in Makassar.[62] The latter wrote to his superiors two months later that the sultan was mobilising his defences in anticipation of an all-out war with the VOC, and that:

all the whole land is making [...] bricks for two castles this summer to be finished; in the armoury is laid ready 10,000 lances, 10,000 cresses

60 Interestingly, George Ball might have been partly responsible for the incident in the first place. On its way out from Makassar, the *Concord* had taken a small Spanish frigate on 18 February. The Spanish had subsequently been seeking compensation from the English through Sultan Ala'uddin of Gowa. When the sultan proved unwilling to get involved and subsequently left town, the Spanish apparently decided to get their compensation single-handedly by attacking the Dutch and English lodges. (In spite of the escalating situation in the Moluccas, the Dutch and English were technically still on friendly terms.) Right around that time, the *Enkhuizen* came in sight, and the Spanish, who wanted to avoid the ship making contact with the lodges, immediately launched an improvised attack. Colenbrander, *Bescheiden Coen*, pp. 120-122; Foster, *Letters Received,* III, p. 286.

61 Coen to directors, 22 October 1615, in Colenbrander, *Bescheiden Coen*, pp. 121-122.

62 Foster, *Letters Received,* III, pp. 286–289. Interestingly, another English letter (John Skinner in Makassar to Adam Denton, 12 July 1615) reports that this also applied to the Portuguese, who 'are commanded hence and are the most part gone...' (Foster, *Letters Received,* III, p. 134). Later, they were evidently also allowed back in, and in the longer term would turn out to be the largest beneficiaries of the conflict between the VOC and Makassar. Cf. Borges, *Os Portugueses e o Sultanato de Macaçar*, pp. 82-83.

with bucklers to them, spaces [a type of lance] as many, pieces 2422: 800 quoyanes of rice [roughly one million kilograms] for store; all this is to entertain the Flemings.[63]

Diplomacy by proxy, escalating conflict

The Governor-General and Council, however, had already decided to retreat from Makassar even before the *Enkhuizen* episode took place, for reasons that had little to do with fear of Spanish aggression. Before word of the incident had reached Governor-General Reynst, he had already sent out commissioners to close the lodge, and request that the sultan cease all trade with the Spice Islands. This decision was closely connected to the evolving monopoly policy in the Moluccas.

In August 1613, the Governor-General had appointed Hans de Hase as Inspector-General, and given him the task of making a financial and general inspection round of all the VOC's posts. The reports and advice he submitted in the course of his commission testify to how overstretched the VOC had already become. They would prove pivotal in a shift to concentrate on the Moluccas. De Hase started with a tour of the Moluccas. He did not like what he found, writing that the Moluccan posts were severely understaffed and undersupplied. After continuing on to the other posts of the eastern archipelago in December 1613, he found most of them unprofitable and useless, noting, for instance, that the freshly-conquered Fort Henricus on Solor would probably not be able to become profitable because the VOC had been unable to completely remove the Portuguese from the area. Continuing to Buton, he noted that there was 'absolutely nothing to trade there, and the two bastions have only been established to please the king,' whom, for reasons he did not divulge, he considered 'the biggest liar of all the Oriental kings.'[64] Being first and foremost a financial inspector and seeing no point in a trading post for political purposes, he recommended the lodge be closed as soon as possible.

Moving on to Makassar, he found that Samuel Denijs had died, that the lodge was in disorder and the ledgers 'in complete disarray.'[65] The situation was so bad that, like van Solt seven years earlier, he had to enquire from the Company's debtors themselves how much they owed, as it could not be

---

63   Foster, *Letters Received*, III, pp. 151-152.
64   Hans de Hase to Directors, 12 August 1614, VOC 1057, fol. 65r and v.
65   Hans de Hase to Directors, 12 August 1614, VOC 1057, fol. 65v.

grasped from the books. He left a new merchant, who he hoped would 'take better care,' but also recommended the lodge be closed. Not only was it 'a money drain, rather than the breadbasket it is reputed to be;' abandoning the lodge would also clear the way for attacking junks from Makassar, who were trading in the Moluccas, but which 'we do not dare attack [...] due to our lodge.'[66] He came to similar conclusions with respect to Gresik on East Java , which was also unprofitable and was also sending its own junks to Banda.[67]

De Hase's recommendations were heard, and the lodges in Buton, Makassar and Gresik, as well as Fort Henricus on Solor, were all abandoned in the course of 1615. The commissioners sent to close the lodge at Makassar, unaware of what had happened there, found it already abandoned. All that was left for them to do was to deliver the VOC's request to halt trading with the Moluccas. In a return letter to them, the sultan famously replied: 'God made the land and the sea, divided the land among the people, and gave the sea in common. It has never been heard that anyone has been prohibited from navigating the sea. If you would do it, you would take the bread out of the mouths of people. I am a poor king.'[68]

All of this means that the VOC had already decided to withdraw from Makassar and the *Enkhuizen* incident served only to hasten the breakdown of the relationship with Gowa. The break itself would have been an inevitable consequence of policies the VOC put into effect in that period, aimed at concentrating the Company's resources on the Moluccas, and freeing its hands to take a more aggressive stance there. While this was happening, the Dutch were making regular use of their Ternatan ally to maintain and strengthen their grip on the spice-producing regions. In the same letter in which Cockayne informed his superiors of the military preparations, he also mentioned that he had heard the Dutch were now attempting to get Western Seram back under their control by using the authority of the

66   Hans de Hase to Directors, 12 August 1614, VOC 1057. The Gentlemen XVII agreed, and made similar recommendations on 6 May 1615. By the time their letter arrived in Asia, the High Government had already gone ahead and closed these lodges. Colenbrander, *Bescheiden Coen,* p. 315.
67   In the early seventeenth century, Gresik, along with several other smaller port towns in the area, stood under the strong political and religious influence of the nearby hilltown of Giri. This latter town was the home of a Muslim religious leader and his followers, who were influential in the Southern Moluccas, with Gresik in a sense functioning as its port. The relation between Gresik and the Southern Moluccas therefore combined political and religious dimensions. For details see Kemper, 'The White Heron,' forthcoming (with thanks to the author for allowing me to read it ahead of publication).
68   Colenbrander, *Bescheiden Coen,* p. 122.

sultan of Ternate and referring the conflict to him.[69] A letter by Coen to the Netherlands confirms that the Dutch were using Ternatan representatives to resolve the matter. The same letter also informed the directors that the people of the Banda island of Ai had now sued for peace by sending representatives to the Ternatan sultan.[70]

The next year, two Dutch yachts visited Makassar, bringing a letter written 'on the initiative of the Hon. [Governor-General Reael], but in the name of the king of Ternate,' making use of the higher standing that a sultan would have in diplomacy with Makassar.[71] No Dutch representatives dared come ashore and the sultan was in no mood to accept the letter, but it is telling that the VOC now tried to conduct diplomacy with the Gowan sultan through the sultan of Ternate. In this way, a European overseas organisation attempted to conduct diplomacy through a local proxy. It would continue to make use of the same template on subsequent occasions.[72] The correspondence between the VOC and the EIC, meanwhile, did not require any proxy: in early 1616, the VOC sent a warning letter informing the English they would keep them from the Moluccas with violence if necessary.[73]

VOC officials, who had hoped to use the two hostages from Makassar secured during the April 1615 conflict as a means of collecting outstanding debt in Makassar, released them by the end of 1616 but had no interest in reopening trade relations. 'Coming to a lifeless friendship [*doode vrientschap*] with Makassar would not be so bad, but all the same it would not at all be advisable to once again open a lodge there,' as Coen formulated it.[74] Right around the same time, however, it became apparent that the incident of 1615 had not been forgotten. In December 1616, the VOC ship *Eendracht* arrived at Makassar. On its way from the Cape to Batavia, this ship had gone too far east, becoming the first European ship to land at the west coast of Australia.[75] Then turning north, it ended up in Makassar, unaware of the events of

---

69   Foster, *Letters Received,* III, pp. 150-153.

70   Colenbrander, *Bescheiden Coen,* p. 120.

71   Ibid., p. 225.

72   A particularly well-documented example is the visit of commissioner Arnold de Vlamingh van Oudshoorn in 1651. In his diary and report, De Vlamingh describes in vivid detail the importance attached to the letter of a fellow sultan, his grasp of Southeast Asian diplomacy, and the way the VOC manages to make this work in its favour. Mostert, '"Ick vertrouwe, dat de werelt hem naer dien op twee polen keert",' pp. 87-88.

73   For example, Colenbrander, *Bescheiden Coen,* p. 147, also pp. 74-75.

74   Letter of 10 October 1616, in Colenbrander, *Bescheiden Coen,* p. 226.

75   They also left what is believed to have been the first European object on the Australian coast: a tin pewter dish in which they inscribed the details of their visit to the coast. This dish is now in the Rijksmuseum collection (inv. nr. NG-NM-825).

the last year and a half. The junior merchant was sent ashore in a launch, accompanied by a small crew, to go to the Dutch lodge, but found only the English. Meanwhile, word of the arrival of a Dutch ship spread through Makassar, and the Gowan sultan personally came to the beach with some two thousand armed men. He allowed the Dutch to leave but made clear that they should not come back. The crew rowed away and, afraid the sultan would change his mind, hid in one of the English ships anchored offshore before rowing back to the *Eendracht* under cover of darkness. Before they reached the *Eendracht* the next day, however, another boat had already been sent ashore to look for them. This time, the Makasars shot on sight and then stormed the boat, killing all its sixteen crew members.[76] Friendship, lifeless or otherwise, was not going to develop any time soon.

Conclusion

In this chapter, I have tried to give a detailed answer to the question why conflict broke out between the VOC and Gowa-Tallo in 1615 and 1616, paying specific attention to the role of the political interaction between various polities in the Moluccas, in which the sultanate of Ternate was of great importance. The fact that, in the early seventeenth century, Gowa and Tallo became a military and diplomatic power, in competition with other Muslim states further east, was of great consequence for the relationships between Gowa-Tallo and the VOC. As the VOC became the 'protector' of Ternate on paper in 1607, and increasingly started to actively assume that role in subsequent years, this already set it on a path towards rivalry with Gowa and Tallo.

Of course, the relationship with Ternate was intimately connected to the monopoly policy elsewhere. Ternate, itself a clove-producing region, indirectly ruled the western areas of the Ambon islands and was an ally in making war on the spice-producing areas not controlled by the Dutch (like Spanish Ternate and Tidore). The alliance with the Ternatan sultan also gave the Dutch a way of exerting more political influence in the eastern archipelago by conducting 'diplomacy by proxy'. Ternate, all in all, was indispensable to the Dutch monopoly policy. In the period leading up to 1615, when the VOC also started a policy of keeping other Asian traders, such as those from Makassar and Javanese ports like Gresik, out of the Spice

---

76   J.W. IJzerman, 'Het schip "De Eendracht" voor Makasser in december 1616,' containing as an appendix the report of Joannes Steins, the junior merchant in charge of the first launch.

Islands, and aware it could not have it both ways, it decided to abandon its lodge there. Breaking off the trade relationship with Makassar was a conscious decision on the part of the VOC – the 1615 *Enkhuizen* incident merely accelerated the process.

The emphasis on Makassar as a *bandar* in much of the existing literature therefore only tells part of the story. Whereas the rulers of Gowa and Tallo did try to keep Makassar as an open port based on early modern notions of free trade, they stood at the head of an expanding empire, not just an open marketplace. Trade was politics, not just for the Europeans but also for Gowa and Tallo, and spices were secured through existing networks that were political as much as economic.

Recognising Gowa-Tallo as one of the states in competition for power in, and access to, the eastern archipelago also helps us understand later developments in the conflict. The first major conflict between the VOC and Gowa-Tallo would be sparked in 1633 by the latter's siege of Buton. This was the consequence of the role of Ternate's ally and protector that the VOC had taken up in the existing political constellation of the eastern archipelago. In addition, Ternate, an influential court in the late sixteenth century, would have become less attractive in the marketplace of political patronage (particularly for spice-producing regions wary of Dutch encroachment) due to its role in the Dutch monopoly policies. This played out in the western Ambon islands, where the inhabitants, unhappy with increasing Dutch control, started looking for alternatives. As Tidore was tied up with the European rivalries as well, and Gresik, a Javanese centre of religious authority influential in the Spice Islands, was cut off in this period, Gowa-Tallo, with its strong military and increasing prestige, became an increasingly attractive alternate political and religious authority. It is therefore not surprising that in the course of subsequent conflicts, various territories in for example the western Ambon islands would seek to place themselves under Gowan protection. This would become a main cause of the war between the VOC and Gowa-Tallo that broke out simultaneously with a revolt in the Ambon islands in 1653–1656.[77]

In these later events, the pattern that we have seen develop here would play out in various ways. The VOC could not achieve its policies in the Moluccas without the help of its allies, in this case first and foremost the sultan of Ternate. By playing a political role and making alliances, however, the organisation was pulled into a pre-existing geopolitical game in the Moluccas. Although the VOC soon became a very consequential and

---

77   Mostert, "'Ick vertrouwe, dat de werelt", p. 86.

successful player in this game, it was not always able to set and change the rules.[78] Thus, its local alliances and political activities, while indispensable, came at a cost: they sucked the Dutch into local geopolitics, shaping their relationships and policies in ways they might not have foreseen or wished for. In the course of its subsequent history, as the VOC became a political player in other areas as well, similar patterns would recur.[79]

The summary way in which the causes of the conflict between the VOC and the Gowa-Tallo state are often described tends to set up an overly simplistic binary between 'a spice port open to all comers' and the VOC using 'every means to assert a monopoly over both clove and nutmeg.'[80] Such binaries act to obscure the chronology and causality of events. Although spices were certainly being traded in Makassar in the early seventeenth century, it was at the time mainly a rice port, where various traders, including Europeans, would buy rice before going to the Spice Islands to buy spices there directly. Only after the watershed events of the 1610s would the market for spices in Makassar increase so much that the city became the main non-Dutch spice port in the archipelago for both Asian and European traders. It is possible to go further, then, by arguing that at least up until the early 1640s VOC policies were responsible for the rise of Makassar, rather than its decline, as they inadvertently caused all the forces opposing the Dutch monopolies to concentrate there.

78   A similar point was recently made by Jennifer Gaynor, framing the Spice Wars as largely driven not by European interests but by the rivalry between Makassar and Ternate, as these 'competed for coastal dominance, maritime superiority and influence in the central and eastern archipelago'; Gaynor, *Intertidal History*, p. 65. I agree with the overall point, although Gaynor may be overstating it when she writes, for example, that the Dutch were 'not aware, it seems, that [Makassar and its allies] had their own motives for waging war, regardless of European rivalries' (p. 78, and very similarly p. 84, where she separates Ternatan and VOC military ambitions) in the mid-seventeenth century. This, in my opinion, separates to a too large degree European and local interests, which had become inextricably intertwined by then.

79   A surprisingly similar pattern, for example, developed one decade later in the Formosan plains, where the various villages also played various 'foreign powers' against each other in their rivalries. Andrade, 'The Mightiest Village.'

80   Reid, *A History of Southeast Asia*, p. 136.

Works cited

Akveld, Leo, *Machtsstrijd om Malakka: reis van VOC-admiraal Matelief naar Oost-Azië, 1605-1608* (Zutphen: Walburg Pers, 2013).

Andaya, Leonard, *The Heritage of Arung Palakka: a History of South Sulawesi in the 17th century* (The Hague: Verhandelingen KITLV 91, 1981).

Andaya, Leonard, 'De militaire alliantie tussen de VOC en de Buginezen', in *De Verenigde Oost-Indische Compagnie tussen oorlog en diplomatie*, ed. Gerrit Knaap and Ger Teitler (Leiden: KITLV Press, 2002), pp. 283–308.

Andaya, Leonard, *The World of Maluku: Eastern Indonesia in the Early Modern Period* (Honolulu: University of Hawai'i Press, 1993).

Andrade, Tonio, 'The Mightiest Village: Geopolitics and Diplomacy in the Formosan Plains, 1623-1636', in *Pingpu zu qun yu Taiwan lishi wenhua : lunwen ji*, ed. Pan Inghai and Chan Su-chuan (Taipei: Academia Sinica Press, 2001).

Baker, Brett Charles, 'Indigenous-driven mission: reconstructing religious change in sixteenth-century Maluku' (PhD thesis, Australian National University, 2012).

Bassett, D.K., 'English trade in Celebes 1663-1667', *Journal of the Malaysian Branch of the Royal Asiatic Society*, 31 (1954): 1–39.

Borges, Maria do Carmo Mira, *Os Portugueses e o Sultanato de Macaçar no Século XVII* (Cascais: Câmara Municipal, 2003).

Bulbeck, David, 'Construction history and significance of the Makassar fortifications', in *Living Through Histories: Culture, History and Social Life in South Sulawesi*, ed. Kathryn Robinson and Mukhlis Paeni (Canberra/Jakarta: RSPAS, Australian National University, 1998), pp. 67–106.

Charney, M.W., *Southeast Asian Warfare, 1300-1900* (Leiden: Leiden University Press, 2004).

Clulow, Adam, *The Company and the Shogun: The Dutch Encounter with Tokugawa Japan* (New York: Columbia University Press, 2014).

Colenbrander, H.T., ed., *Jan Pietersz. Coen: bescheiden omtrent zijn bedrijf in Indië*, I (Amsterdam: M. Nijhoff, 1919-23).

Commelin, Isaac, *Begin ende voortgangh van de Vereenighde Nederlandtsche geoctroyeerde Oost-Indische compagnie. Vervatende de voornaemste reysen, by de inwoonderen der selver provintien derwaerts gedaen* (The Hague: 1646).

Cummings, W., *A Chain of Kings: The Makassarese chronicles of Gowa and Talloq* (Leiden: Leiden University Press, 2007).

Cummings, W., 'Only one people but two rulers: Hiding the past in seventeenth-century Makasarese chronicles', in *Bijdragen tot de Taal-, Land- en Volkenkunde* 155:1 (Leiden: KITLV press, 1999), 97-120.

Cummings, W., 'The Melaka Malay Diaspora in Makassar, c. 1500-1669', *Journal of the Malaysian Branch of the Royal Asiatic Society*, 71:1 (Kuala Lumpur: Malaysian Branch of the Royal Asiatic Society, 1998), pp. 107-121.

Fletcher, F., *The world encompassed by Sir Francis Drake, being his next voyage to that to Nombre de Dios formerly printed etc.* (London, 1628).

Foster, William, *Letters Received by the E.I.C. from its servants in the East*, Vol. 3 (London: Royal Collection Trust, 1897).

Gaastra, Femme, *Geschiedenis van de VOC* (Zutphen: Walburg Pers, 2009).

Gaynor, Jennifer L., *Intertidal history in island Southeast Asia: submerged genealogies and the legacy of coastal capture* (Ithaca, NY: Cornell University Press, 2016).

Heeres, J.E., *Corpus diplomaticum Neerlando-Indicum : verzameling van politieke contracten en verdere verdragen door de Nederlanders in het Oosten gesloten, van privilegebrieven aan hen verleend, enz.* I, (Den Haag: Martinus Nijhoff, 1907).

Heijer, Henk den, Gerrit Knaap, and Michiel de Jong, *Oorlogen overzee: militair optreden door compagnie en staat buiten Europa, 1595-1814* (Amsterdam: Boom, 2015).

IJzerman, J.W., 'Het schip "De Eendracht" voor Makasser in december 1616', *Bijdragen tot de Taal-, Land- en Volkenkunde* 78 (1922): 343–372.

Jonge, J.K.J. de, *De opkomst van het Nederlandsch gezag in Oost-Indië: verzameling van onuitgegeven stukken uit het oud-koloniaal archief*, Vol. 3 (1865).

Jourdain, John, *The Journal of John Jourdain (1608-1617), Describing His Experiences in Arabia, India and the Malay Archipelago*, ed. William Foster (London: Hakluyt Society, 1905).

Kemper, Simon C., 'The White Heron called by the Muezzin: Shrines, Sufis and Warlords in Early Modern Java', in *Challenging Cosmopolitanism: Coercion, Mobility and Displacement in Islamic Asia*, ed. Michael Feener and Joshua Gedacht (Edinburgh: Edinburgh University Press, forthcoming).

Knaap, Gerrit, 'De Ambonse eilanden tussen twee mogendheden: De VOC en Ternate, 1605-1656', in *Hof en Handel: Aziatische vorsten en de VOC, 1620-1720*, ed. Elsbeth Locher-Scholten and Peter Rietbergen (Leiden: KITLV Press, 2004), pp. 35-58.

Lunsingh-Scheurleer, Pauline, 'Uitwisseling van staatsieportretten op Ceylon in 1602', in *Aan de overkant: Ontmoetingen in dienst van de VOC en WIC, 1600-1800*, ed. L. Wagenaar (Leiden: Leiden University Press, 2015).

Mostert, Tristan, '"Ick vertrouwe, dat de werelt hem naer dien op twee polen keert": de VOC, de rijksbestuurder van Makassar en een uitzonderlijk grote globe', in *Aan de overkant: Ontmoetingen in dienst van de VOC en WIC, 1600-1800*, ed. L. Wagenaar (Leiden: University of Leiden Press, 2015), pp. 77–96.

Noorduyn, Jacobus J., 'De Islamisering van Makassar', *Bijdragen tot de Taal-, Land- en Volkenkunde* 112 (1956): 247–266.

Parker, Geoffrey, *The Military Revolution: Military innovation and the rise of the West* (Cambridge: Cambridge University Press, 1988).

Parker, Geoffrey, 'The artillery fortress as an engine of European overseas expansion', in *City Walls: The Urban Enceinte in Global Perspective, 1480-1750*, ed. James D. Tracy (Cambridge: Cambridge University Press, 2000), pp. 386–417.

Reid, Anthony, 'The Rise of Makassar', in Reid ed., *Charting the shape of Early Modern Southeast Asia* (Singapore: ISEAS, 2000), pp. 100–125.

Reid, Anthony, 'A Great Seventeenth Century Indonesian family: Matoaya and Pattingalloang of Makassar', in Reid ed., *Charting the shape of early modern Southeast Asia* (Singapore 1983), pp. 126–154.

Reid, Anthony, *Southeast Asia in the Age of Commerce 1450-1680*, Vol. 2, *Expansion and crisis* (New Haven: Yale University Press 1993).

Reid, Anthony, 'Early Modernity as Cosmopolis: Some suggestions from Southeast Asia', in *Delimiting modernities: conceptual challenges and regional responses*, ed. Sven Trakulhun and Ralph Weber (London: Lexington Books, 2015), pp. 123–142.

Reid, Anthony, *A History of Southeast Asia: Critical Crossroads* (Malden, MA: Wiley-Blackwell, 2015).

Spate, O.H.K., *The Pacific Since Magellan*, Vol. 2, *Monopolists and Freebooters* (London: Croom Helm, 1983).

Stapel, F.W., *Het Bongaais Verdrag: de vestiging der Nederlanders op Makassar* (Groningen/Den Haag: Wolters, 1922).

Tiele, P.H., and J.E. Heeres, *Bouwstoffen voor de geschiedenis der Nederlanders in den Maleischen Archipel*, I (The Hague: Martinus Nijhoff, 1886).

Valentijn, François, *Oud en Nieuw Oost Indien* (Franeker: Van Wijnen, 2002, orig. 1724-1726).

Contact details

Tristan Mostert, Leiden University
t.mostert@hum.leidenuniv.nl

2   Diplomacy in a provincial setting

The East India Companies in seventeenth-century Bengal and Orissa*

Guido van Meersbergen

Abstract

This chapter introduces the perspective of 'provincial diplomacy' as a means to analyse the political and commercial relationships between the Mughal Empire and the EIC and VOC. Its focus on interactions at the provincial level of the imperial administration moves against the common tendency to concentrate exclusively on diplomatic proceedings at the central court. The first section examines Ralph Cartwright's mission (1633) to the *nawab*'s court in Cuttack (Orissa) to argue that provincial diplomacy was on the whole characterised by mutuality, not cultural misunderstanding. The second section charts the VOC's entanglement in Mughal imperial politics during the war of succession (1657-1659) to show how successive governors of Bengal gradually incorporated the Company into the Mughal political landscape.

Keywords: Provincial diplomacy, East India Companies, Mughal Empire, Bengal

On 22 October 1634, the clerk responsible for keeping the diary drawn up in Batavia Castle (*Dagh-Register gehouden in't Casteel Batavia*) diligently summarised the latest intelligence about trade in the Bay of Bengal. His employer, the *Vereenigde Oostindische Compagnie*, had just commenced trading operations in the Mughal provinces of Bengal and Orissa, and a

* The research for this chapter was funded by a Leverhulme Trust Early Career Fellowship (ECF-2016-477). I wish to thank the editors of this volume for their valuable comments on earlier versions.

Clulow, Adam and Tristan Mostert (eds.), *The Dutch and English East India Companies: Diplomacy, trade and violence in early modern Asia*. Amsterdam: Amsterdam University Press, 2018
DOI: 10.5117/9789462983298/CH02

barque arriving that day carried initial snippets of information concerning the first Dutch factory in the region, recently established in the small port town of Hariharpur.[1] So far trade had been slack, hampered by a shortage of merchandise and high prices. This unpromising yet otherwise rather ordinary entry took a surprising turn, however, when discussing another recent entrant into the Bengal trade, the English East India Company.[2] The building of an English factory in Hariharpur had commenced with the consent of the *nawab* (provincial governor) of Orissa, but, according to Dutch reports, once the structure was nearly completed, the *nawab* had it entirely 'destroyed and pulled down again'.[3] The reason given for this reversal of fortunes was that 'a certain English merchant named Mr. Cartrijcq' and 'the wife of a prominent Moor there residing' were found to be 'having carnal conversation through a large hole in the wall of said lodge'. To make things worse, when Cartwright left on Company business to nearby Balasore, he had attempted to take the married woman with him.[4]

While we cannot be certain of its accuracy,[5] the story of the amorous encounter, and of Ralph Cartwright's alleged arrest, imprisonment, and payment of a thousand rupees to obtain his release, was deemed credible by Batavia's administrators.[6] Although it seems inconsequential at first, the Cartwright episode captures a larger truth about the East India Companies in seventeenth-century Mughal India. As this chapter argues, the Companies' global operations depended to an important extent on what I term 'provincial diplomacy', a mode of political negotiation structured through political and social interactions between Company agents and lower-tier officials in the empire's frontier regions. Such exchanges mainly took place

---

1   Van der Chijs et al. eds., *Dagh-Register Batavia 1631-1634*, p. 415; see also pp. 241-242.

2   The East India Companies referred to the wider trading region encompassing the Mughal *subahs* (provinces) of Bengal, Bihar, and Orissa collectively as "Bengal". While constituting different administrative units of the Mughal Empire, at times the *subahdar* of Bengal also governed Bihar and/or Orissa. Prakash, *The Dutch East India Company and the Economy*, p. 24.

3   *Dagh-Register Batavia* 1631-1634, p. 415.

4   Ibid.

5   There is substantial reason to doubt the accuracy of the report, as its source cannot be traced back to Dutch letters still extant today, and surviving English records make no mention of the episode. Foster, *The English Factories in India 1634-1636*; Nationaal Archief, The Hague, access number 1.04.02: Vereenigde Oostindische Compagnie (VOC) (hereafter: NL-HaNA, VOC), inventory number 1113, ff. 314-331.

6   Above all, the story resonated with the recent track record of disputes with local governments in port towns such as Surat and Masulipatnam. Numerous examples of such low-level conflict are discussed in: Subrahmanyam, *The Political Economy of Commerce*.

at provincial courts, including Rajmahal and Dhaka, as well as in port towns such as Hugli. Given the centrality of interpersonal relations on the ground, controversial conduct such as that attributed to Ralph Cartwright could make or break diplomatic arrangements. Provincial diplomacy was essential to the operations of the Companies because the interests and attitudes of local government representatives were just as significant, if not more so, for the everyday practice of trade on the ground as imperial commands in the form of *farmans*; a situation that stemmed in part from the considerable degree of autonomy enjoyed by Mughal officials in the eastern provinces.[7] Port towns and provincial courts were also, in quantitative terms, the sites where most of the diplomatic action happened.[8] My focus in this chapter on negotiations at the local and provincial levels of the Mughal administration argues against the common tendency to concentrate attention exclusively on diplomatic proceedings at the highest seat of power. This trend is nowhere clearer than in the steady stream of publications focused on the embassy of Sir Thomas Roe to the court of Jahangir (r. 1605-1627).[9] While of course important, such an emphasis on what was happening in the imperial centre can only illuminate part of the intricate relationship between diplomacy, trade, and violence that shaped the Companies' presence in South Asia. Sustained attention to provincial and local sites of political negotiation is needed to fill in the picture.

By calling attention to diplomacy in provincial settings, this chapter seeks to advance two further goals. First, it aims to bring East India Company history into closer conversation with the flourishing field of early modern diplomatic history.[10] Second, it addresses the ways in which the Companies became integrated into local political contexts. Borrowing from a range of disciplines, 'New Diplomatic History' has called attention to the prominent role of social networks, cultural practices, and non-state and non-elite actors

---

7   Farhat Hasan has shown that the EIC's trading privileges in Bengal relied not on imperial *farmans* but on decrees issued by a series of provincial governors. Local officials even consciously contravened imperial edicts to encourage English investment and promote their own trading interests: Hasan, 'Conflict and Cooperation'.

8   The exact scope of provincial diplomacy has yet to be established. For an initial examination of the interrelatedness of diplomacy at the provincial and central levels, see Van Meersbergen, 'Kijken en bekeken worden'.

9   Roe attended Jahangir's court between December 1615 and September 1618. Recent studies of the embassy include: Mitchell, *Sir Thomas Roe and the Mughal Empire*; Barbour, *Before Orientalism*; Subrahmanyam, 'Frank Submissions'; Flüchter, 'Sir Thomas Roe vor dem indischen Mogul'; Das, 'Apes of Imitation'; Chida-Razvi, 'The Perception of Reception'; Mishra, 'Diplomacy at the Edge'.

10   For a recent overview, see Sowerby, 'Early Modern Diplomatic History'.

in the development of early modern diplomatic exchange.[11] In the process, our notion of early modern diplomacy has been markedly expanded. No longer viewing diplomacy as the exclusive preserve of high politics bounded by a Eurocentric chronology, scholars have also begun to take account of the many contributions of non-European actors to the wider development of diplomatic institutions and practices.[12] While the contours of a 'diplomatic turn' are increasingly evident in scholarship on the VOC and EIC, neither these organisations nor the Asian polities they interacted with have thus far played more than a minor role in the renewal of diplomatic history.[13]

My discussion of Company diplomacy in the Mughal provinces of Bengal and Orissa combines exploration of diplomacy at 'sub-state levels' with the recent interest in 'sub-state diplomatic actors' such as trading companies.[14] I start by examining the foundations of the relationship between the Companies and the Mughal administration in Bengal and Orissa through a focus on Ralph Cartwright's mission to the provincial court in Cuttack (Katak) in 1633.[15] Addressing questions of diplomatic communication and cultural commensurability, this section argues that provincial diplomacy was characterised far more by immediacy than by cultural distance.[16] The next section argues that the Companies gradually became incorporated into the Mughal political landscape as a result of localised conflicts in which provincial authorities sought to exploit European naval power. It does so by charting the VOC's entanglement in Mughal imperial politics during the mid-century war of succession (1657-1659) and its immediate aftermath, as successive Mughal governors of Bengal sought to co-opt the Company's military resources. In this way, it mirrors some of the patterns sketched out

---

11   An early example of this trend is Watkins, 'Toward a New Diplomatic History'.

12   See the articles in the special issues Van Gelder and Krstić, eds., 'Cross-Confessional Diplomacy and Diplomatic Intermediaries', and Osborne and Rubiés, eds. 'Diplomacy and Cultural Translation in the Early Modern World'. This perspective is also present in the argument, if less so in the subject matter, of Black, *A History of Diplomacy*.

13   Of course, predating and separate from the New Diplomatic History, there exists a rich and growing body of scholarship on VOC and EIC embassies. Important early studies include Wills, *Embassies and Illusions*, and Blussé, *Tussen Geveinsde Vrunden*.

14   Osborne and Rubiés, 'Introduction: Diplomacy', pp. 313, 319. Philip Stern has stressed the role of Companies as state actors in their own right; see Stern, *The Company-State*. Compare the view of William A. Pettigrew, who maintains that trading corporations were subject to higher state authority but stresses that they 'proved more agile transnational interlocutors than the states who authorised them'; Pettigrew, 'Corporate constitutionalism', p. 490.

15   Bruton, *Newes from the East-Indies*.

16   For these themes, see Subrahmanyam, *Courtly Encounters*; Ghobrial, *The Whispers of Cities*; Burschel and Vogel, *Die Audienz*.

by Peter Good's chapter in this volume; although here the focus is on the role played by provincial officials.

Enter the Companies

The account of Cartwright's mission to the *nawab*'s court in Cuttack, written by the English quartermaster William Bruton and published in London in 1638, offers a useful starting point for an analysis of how Company diplomacy functioned in a provincial setting. Bruton's detailed description of Cartwright's mission provides a picture of what may well have been a typical diplomatic encounter at a provincial court, and allows us to contrast it to diplomatic proceedings at the seat of imperial power in capital cities such as Agra and Delhi. Compared to the better-known English and Dutch embassies to the Mughal imperial centre – including Roe's mission to the court of Jahangir (1615-1618) and Dircq van Adrichem's embassy to the court of Aurangzeb (1662) – diplomatic engagements at the lower rungs of the imperial hierarchy stand out for their more strikingly ad hoc character, decentralised decision-making, and informal rituals of interaction.[17] They were also more specific in focus. To a far greater degree than diplomacy at the imperial court, provincial diplomacy dealt directly with the regulation of, and disputes arising from, site-specific political and commercial interactions. In the case of Cartwright's 1633 journey to Cuttack, what was at stake were English rights to trade freely within the *nawab*'s domains and the containment of both the EIC's potential for violent action and the harmful consequences to local trade of Anglo-Portuguese conflict.

The Mughal Empire, founded in 1526, came to comprise most of northern India during the reign of Akbar (r. 1556-1605). The Sultanate of Bengal was conquered in 1575-1576 and the annexation of Orissa followed in 1593, although imperial authority in the region remained hotly contested until the 1610s.[18] Once incorporated into the empire, the Mughal province (*subah*) of Bengal was governed by a viceroy or provincial governor (*subahdar*) appointed by the emperor. Orissa was made into a separate province in 1607, although it continued to fall under the authority of the governor of

---

17   Foster, *The Embassy of Sir Thomas Roe*; Kempers, *Journaal van Dircq van Adrichem's Hofreis*. About the latter, see Van Meersbergen, 'The Dutch Merchant-Diplomat in Comparative Perspective', pp. 147-165.
18   Eaton, *The Rise of Islam and the Bengal Frontier*; Flores, *Nas Margens do Hindustão*, pp. 153-157, 181, 307.

Bengal, his deputy, or someone recommended by him.[19] Reflecting its importance as one of the empire's richest provinces, the government of Bengal was only entrusted to noblemen of the highest rank, including imperial princes such as Shah Shuja (1639-1660) and other relatives of the reigning emperor such as Aurangzeb's maternal uncle, Shaista Khan (1664-1678, 1679-1688). Traditionally regarded as a highly centralised empire, recent studies have argued for the relative autonomy of Mughal government in the provinces and its crucial reliance on the participation of local power holders.[20] They have also stressed the vital importance of political and military support networks centred on princely households as a means by which members of the dynasty strengthened their own power bases.[21] The point was picked up by contemporary European observers, who commented that some Mughal governors in the provinces ruled as if they were kings themselves.[22]

Seventeenth-century Bengal retained the character of a frontier region, and internal resistance from subordinate chieftains as well as armed conflicts against neighbouring Assam and Arakan (comprising parts of modern-day Bangladesh and Myanmar) continued during the reigns of Shah Jahan (r. 1628-1658) and Aurangzeb (r. 1658-1707).[23] Bengal was also the home of largely autonomous groups of Portuguese mercenaries and private traders, whose activities in the region predated the arrival of the Dutch and English Companies by about a century. Their presence created a precedent for the government's dealing with Europeans. Due to their involvement in slave raiding, Portuguese freemen caused recurrent moments of tension in the relationship between the *Estado da Índia* and the Mughal state.[24] In 1632 matters came to a head when Qasim Khan, then *subahdar* of Bengal, attacked Hugli, the principal Portuguese settlement in the region. His successful siege asserted Mughal control over the Ganges delta and curbed the political threat the defiant 'Franks' (*firangis*) posed to imperial authority.[25] While Portuguese influence in Bengal before 1632 or the extent of

19   Saran, *The Provincial Government of the Mughals*, pp. 65-67, 162.
20   See in particular Hasan, *State and Locality in Mughal India*. For the view stressing centralisation, see Ali, *Mughal India*.
21   Faruqui, *The Princes of the Mughal Empire*.
22   Illustrative in this respect is William Bruton's consistent use of 'king' to refer to the *nawab* of Orissa. See also the remark of Pieter Hofmeester, VOC envoy in Dhaka in 1672, that at the provincial court it was openly stated that Shaista Khan was king in Bengal: Constantin Ranst and Council of Hugli to Batavia, Hugli, 8 September 1672, NL-HaNA, VOC 1288, ff. 50r-54r.
23   For the latter, see: Choudhuri, 'An Eventful Politics of Difference and its Afterlife.'
24   Subrahmanyam, *The Portuguese Empire in Asia*, p. 157; Flores, *Nas Margens do Hindustao*, p. 374.
25   Subrahmanyam, *The Portuguese Empire*, pp. 176-177; Flores, *Nas Margens do Hindustao*, pp. 372-375.

Figure 3 The VOC factory in Hugli-Chinsurah. Hendrik van Schuylenburgh, 1665.

Collection Rijksmuseum SK-A-4282.

its decline afterwards should not be overstated, the fall of Hugli nevertheless served to expedite the establishment of English and Dutch factories in the region from 1633 onwards.[26] The Companies certainly did not lack encouragement from local authorities, who welcomed additional outside parties as means of expanding economic activity within their districts and boosting tax income.[27] It was such 'promises [...] for Traffick, and to be Custome-free' which encouraged John Norris, the EIC's Agent on the Coromandel Coast, to dispatch Ralph Cartwright's party to Orissa.[28]

Having set out from Masulipatnam aboard an Indian junk hired for the occasion, Cartwright, William Bruton, and six other Englishmen arrived in the small town of Harishpur Garh at the mouth of the Mahanadi river delta on 21 April 1633.[29] Cartwright, Bruton, and a third EIC agent soon travelled onwards by river bark and by land to Cuttack, the capital of the Orissa *subah*, but not before fending off a surprise attack from the Pipli-based *nachoda*

26 Prakash, *The Dutch East India Company*, p. 36. Compare: Subrahmanyam, *Improvising Empire*, p. 127.

27 Prakash, *The Dutch East India Company*, p. 43.

28 Bruton, *Newes from the East-Indies*, p. 3.

29 This identification is based on: Bowrey, Temple ed., *A Geographical Account of Countries Round the Bay of Bengal*, p. 129, n. 1.

(captain) of a Portuguese-owned frigate.[30] In parallel to Cartwright's journey, the captain of this vessel, now detained by the English, also made his way to Cuttack to plead his case. Arriving in Hariharpur, the three Englishmen were received by a nobleman named Mirza Momein, who accompanied them on their last day's travel to the court of his master (referred to as 'the King' in Bruton's account). Although Bruton's text fails to mention the *nawab*'s name, it is likely that it would have been Mu'taqad Khan, a close confidant and possibly a foster brother of Shah Jahan, who served two stints as *subahdar* of Orissa during the latter's reign, the first commencing in 1632.[31]

On 1 May 1633, scarcely twelve hours after his arrival in Cuttack, Cartwright's first of six audiences took place in the *darbar* (audience hall) of the stately palace built for the last Hindu ruler of Orissa, Mukunda Deva (r. 1559-1568).[32] Attended by some 40 to 50 courtiers besides a hundred armed guards, the *nawab* maintained a sumptuous court which duly impressed Bruton. His detailed descriptions of the palace and the spatial configuration of the *darbar* underline the fact that provincial courts were essentially smaller versions of the royal household, with similar business conducted as in the emperor's *Diwan-i-Am* or Hall of Public Audience.[33] Bruton's depiction of courtiers sitting cross-legged around the *nawab* and the English representative engaging in unmediated interaction with the ruler, however, suggests a level of proximity much greater than at Shah Jahan's heavily scripted public audiences, where few Company envoys enjoyed the honour of being received, and opportunities for direct communication were extremely limited.[34] Having been introduced by Mirza Momein, Cartwright bowed before the *nawab*, kissed his foot, and was directed to sit down beside the *nawab*'s brother. Next, the visitors offered up their somewhat modest assortment of gifts, consisting of 20 pounds each of cloves, mace,

---

30   Bruton, *Newes from the East-Indies*, pp. 4-5.
31   Shāh Nawāz Khān and 'Abdull Hayy, H. Beveridge (trans.), *The Maāthir-ul-Umarā*, II, pp. 347-350. Regarding the identity of the nawab, Bruton only mentions that the incumbent succeeded Baqir Khan. M. Athar Ali's standard work states that Mu'taqad Khan (also known as Mirza Maki) was appointed *subahdar* of Orissa in AH 1041/AD 1631-1632: Ali, *The Apparatus of Empire*, p. 117. Dismissing the accuracy of Mughal chroniclers, C.R. Wilson has claimed that the *nawab* in question must have been Muhammad Agha Zaman Tihrani, who is known to have served in this capacity during the 1640s: Wilson ed., *The Early Annals of the English in Bengal*, I, p. 8. The case for Muhammad Agha Zaman's brief term in office between Baqir Khan and Mu'taqad Khan is unconvincingly made by: Nair, *Bruton's Visit to Lord Jagannatha 350 Yers [sic] Ago*, pp. 105-108.
32   Wilson, ed., *The Early Annals of the English in Bengal*, I, p. 4, n. 2.
33   Blake, *Shahjahanabad*, pp. 96-97; Richards, *The New Cambridge History of India I.5*, p. 61; Eaton, p. 160.
34   This marked a sharp contrast with Jahangir's reception of Thomas Roe a generation earlier.

and nutmeg, small quantities of damask and cloth, a gilded mirror, a rifle and a double-barrelled pistol.[35]

Apparently without prior negotiations or indeed the composition of a written petition, Cartwright (or rather his interpreter) proceeded to explain the English requests to the *nawab* and his counsellors, who conferred to discuss the matter on the spot. Together with the speedy arrangement of Cartwright's reception, this direct handling of state affairs offers clear indications as to the impromptu nature of provincial diplomacy. Even more striking, certainly when compared to the rigid protocol of diplomatic audiences at the imperial court, is that during his second appearance at the *darbar* Cartwright not only had the audacity to walk out in the midst of proceedings (or so Bruton claimed), but also faced no consequences for doing so.[36] Further evidence of the heightened degree of immediacy in this courtly encounter is provided by the absence of references to interactions with scribes and lower-tier administrators, the two-way dialogue between Cartwright and the *nawab*, and the fact that the latter publicly authorised the *parwana* (decree) with his own seal in the presence of the English. What is more, when the *nawab* hosted a banquet for the principal noblemen under his command, he invited Cartwright to eat with the Muslim courtiers, summoned the Englishman to sit beside him, and personally clad him with a robe of honour. The significance of this personalised act of investiture was not lost on Bruton, who emphasised that the *nawab* 'with his own hands did put it upon our Merchant'.[37] Commonly referred to by its Arabic name of *khil'at* (or *kel'at*), the granting of robes of honour was widespread in South Asia and adjacent regions as an important public ritual in which a superior gifted a subordinate with a special mark of favour as a means to establish or reaffirm bonds of loyalty and service.[38] With this ceremonial gesture the *nawab* symbolically incorporated the English representative into his client network – a concrete reminder both of the continuity of languages of political authority between the imperial centre and provincial courts and of the close entanglement between diplomatic relationships and interpersonal ties.

The Company's request to trade in Orissa and the *nawab*'s decision to confiscate the Portuguese-owned vessel which the English had meant to seize for themselves were conclusively dealt with during Cartwright's third

---

35   Bruton, *Newes from the East-Indies*, pp. 13-14.

36   Ibid., pp. 17-18.

37   Ibid., p. 22.

38   Gordon, ed., *Robes of Honour*; Floor, "Kel'at," *Encyclopædia Iranica*, XVI/2, pp. 226-229; available at www.iranicaonline.org/articles/kelat-gifts (accessed 13 January 2017).

audience. It is by looking at these negotiations that the purposes of provincial
diplomacy become more apparent. Persian merchants attending the court
were invited to provide intelligence about English trading activities, the
Company's maritime strength, and its practice of seizing Indian ships not
carrying a pass issued by the English, Dutch, or Danish. Given the tendency
of all European participants in Indian Ocean trade to employ maritime force
as a means to back their commercial ambitions, there is certainly something
to be said for Bruton's suggestion that it was the potential economic damage
which the EIC could inflict by hampering commercial activity in Orissa that
induced the *nawab* to grant Cartwright the desired exemption from custom
duties and license to build a factory.[39] Concern about English maritime
strength certainly underpinned the *nawab*'s insistence that the English
not seize any vessel belonging to the *nawab* or his subjects, nor attack any
other ship within the boundaries of Orissa regardless of its origins. Asserting
control over a potentially unruly outside element was also at work in the
nawab's demand that disputes between the English and his subjects were
to be judged by himself, which came with the veiled admonition that the
English were expected to 'behav[e] themselves as Merchants ought to doe'.[40]
Contemporary Mughal edicts concerning the VOC confirm this picture. A
parwana granted in 1636 by the *subahdar* of Bengal, Islam Khan Mashadi,
stipulated that the Dutch should not hinder the Portuguese trading in Hugli
and that they were not allowed to export gunpowder and saltpetre nor carry
away Bengali slaves or workmen.[41] In the same year, Shah Jahan issued a
farman that sought to limit the Dutch presence in Bengal to no more than
30 unarmed men at a time.[42]

    While the threat of maritime force thus clearly played a role, Bruton's
explanation ignores the larger benefits that accrued to the Mughal administration as a result of its commercial policy vis-à-vis the Europeans.
Cartwright agreed to provide English assistance to the *nawab*'s subjects
when finding the latter 'in distresse either by foule Weather, or in danger
of Enemies', and to supply them with hardware and victuals in case of
need.[43] Islam Khan decreed that local officials should have the first right to
inspect and buy any exotic rarities imported by the VOC. And Shah Jahan
roundly proclaimed that the Dutch were to be shown all favour because

---

39   For a discussion of these dynamics involving the Danish Company in the same region, see:
Wellen, 'The Danish East India Company's War against the Mughal Empire, 1642-1698'.
40   Bruton, *Newes from the East-Indies*, p. 19.
41   Heeres and Stapel eds., *Corpus Diplomaticum Neerlando-Indicum*, I, p. 283.
42   Ibid., p. 289.
43   Bruton, *Newes from the East-Indies*, p. 19.

their trade would further enrich Bengal, enlarge his income, and bring profits to local administrators.[44] The challenge for Mughal officials in the maritime provinces was to profit economically from the largely mutually beneficial relationship they forged with European traders, while reining in the potentially harmful effects of the latter's presence in their domains. Often this meant exploiting competition between parties as well as identifying the right horse to back. During Cartwright's stay in Cuttack, one Mir Qasim, governor of the coastal town of Balasore, initially spoke on behalf of the Pipli-based *nachoda*. Then, upon observing the turn of events, he shifted his support to the English, presented Cartwright with various gifts, and successfully induced the merchant to settle the EIC's second factory in Orissa under his jurisdiction. Especially when customs duties had been assigned or farmed to a local official, the latter had every incentive to increase the volume of trade in the relevant district as a means to achieve higher returns on his investment. More generally, the imperial administration looked favourably upon European trade because it channelled much-needed quantities of precious metals into the Mughal economy.[45]

Recounting the final audience at Cuttack on 8 May 1633, Bruton describes how 'our Merchant (reverently) took his leave of the King, and the King (with his Nobles) did the same to him, wishing him all good successe in his affaires in his Countrey'.[46] The picture that emerges in accounts such as these is of a provincial diplomacy characterised by mutuality and apparently unhindered by any serious form of cultural barrier. Save for a stock reference to Cartwright's initial refusal to kiss the *nawab*'s foot, the Englishmen's participation in Mughal court ceremonial is nowhere problematised or made to appear less than self-evident. Indeed, the remark that the *nawab* and Cartwright were able to communicate in 'Moores language' – presumably referring to the colloquial Hindustani spoken in northern India, and here contrasted to the formal Persian used during court proceedings – serves to underline the impression that the principal actors in this encounter were conversant in the same diplomatic idiom.[47] This seeming reciprocality in the communicative sphere was mirrored by the forging of mutually beneficial commercial relations. Still, so shortly after Qasim Khan's startling attack on Hugli, few European observers would have failed to recognise that, ultimately, the terms of the diplomatic relationship were principally set by

---

44   *Corpus Diplomaticum* I, pp. 282-283, pp. 286-287.
45   Prakash, 'The Dutch East India Company in Bengal', pp. 273-274.
46   Bruton, *Newes from the East-Indies*, p. 24.
47   Ibid., pp. 14, 19.

the *nawab* and the state power he represented. It was this message that in 1634 found its way into the Batavia *Dagh-register* in the form of the perhaps apocryphal story about the fate of the newly-built English Hariharpur factory.

Co-opting the Companies

In charting the establishment of diplomatic arrangements between representatives of the East India Companies and governors of the easternmost Mughal provinces during the 1630s, I have discussed the precarious balance between European attempts to exploit maritime power and the push by local authorities to rein it in. From the middle of the seventeenth century onwards, a succession of extraordinarily powerful *subahdars* of Bengal – the Mughal Prince Shah Shuja (1639-1660), the entrepreneur and general Mir Jumla[48] (1660-1663), and the senior nobleman and uncle to the emperor, Shaista Khan (1664-1678, 1679-1688) – introduced a new element into the relationship, namely the demand for money, material, and military support to be used to advance their geopolitical ends. Shaista Khan's requests to the VOC's High Government (*Hoge Regering*) in Batavia for naval support in the run-up to his campaign against Chittagong and Arakanese territories further east during the mid-1660s are well known, described by Om Prakash as the VOC's first 'major involvement' in a military operation carried out by the Mughal government against a neighbouring state or insubordinate vassal.[49] Yet this was by no means the first occasion at which the imperial administration sought to co-opt the VOC's maritime power. Similar requests of naval assistance against Arakan had been made by Shah Shuja in 1657 and Mir Jumla in 1660; again appeals issued by the provincial authorities, not the central government.[50] Furthermore, proposals discussed during Van Adrichem's 1662 embassy to Delhi included a joint Mughal–Dutch attack on the Portuguese stronghold of Daman – a plan put forward by Aurangzeb but soon thereafter abandoned – as well as the emperor's

48   Since entering Mughal service in 1656, this merchant-entrepreneur and former general and chief minister of Golconda, born as Muhammad Sayyid Ardestani, bore the title Mu'azzam Khan. I will refer to him by the title he held in Golcondan service and under which he is generally known, that of Mir Jumla.

49   Prakash, *The Dutch East India Company*, p. 49. The VOC's effective contribution to taking Chittagong was negligible as it only sent two small ships which moreover arrived at the port more than eight months after the Mughal expeditionary force had completed its siege.

50   Coolhaas, Van Goor, Schooneveld-Oosterling, and s'Jacob eds., *Generale Missiven* III, pp. 189-190; Dagh-Register Batavia 1661, p. 6.

request for Dutch assistance in capturing Shah Shuja, his elder brother, who had gone missing after his flight to Arakan at the end of the Mughal war of succession.[51]

This proposal, although it seems eccentric at first glance, was a natural continuation of the role forced upon the VOC over the course of the conflict, when the Company first became embroiled in imperial politics. The ad hoc exaction of material or military support from Company representatives in Bengal and elsewhere during the civil war and its aftermath is significant as it foreshadowed the more institutionalised forms of co-optation of European naval power that developed in later years. The best known examples of this are the convoying duties which Aurangzeb imposed on the Dutch, English, and French in the 1690s and 1700s in an attempt to extend protection to his subjects engaged in maritime trade and hold the European Companies responsible for losses in the event of piracy on the high seas.[52] Furthermore, these examples fit a larger pattern of formidable Asian states drawing naval assistance from the Companies, visible at different points during the seventeenth century in relations with Safavid Iran, Tokugawa Japan, and Qing China.[53] The next section traces this process of incorporation by focusing on the VOC's role as a political actor in Mughal Bengal in the period leading up to and immediately following Aurangzeb's consolidation of power. It was in the provinces rather than the court where the key action played out as VOC agents based in different parts of the empire had to deal locally with a host of conflicting political demands emanating from powerful officials representing the various warring parties.

The main events of the Mughal succession conflict can be swiftly summarised. By the late 1650s, Shah Jahan's four adult sons – Dara Shukoh (1615-1659), Shah Shuja (1616-1660?), Aurangzeb (1618-1707), and Murad Bakhsh (1624-1661) – each possessed personal client networks and extensive experience in provincial governance. When the reigning emperor fell ill in September 1657, Dara Shukoh, the heir-apparent and the only one among the princes present at court, quickly assumed command of

51 Bernet Kempers, *Journaal van Dircq van Adrichem's Hofreis*, p. 16. The idea of a joint Mughal-Dutch attack on Daman was first suggested by Shah Jahan in 1635 and was raised again by Aurangzeb in 1639. The scheme was revived in the 1650s, only to be definitely abandoned after Van Adrichem's mission. *Generale Missiven* I, pp. 528-530; *Generale Missiven* II, p. 46, p. 730, pp. 799-800; *Generale Missiven* III, p. 104, p. 334.
52 Prakash, *The Dutch East India Company*, pp. 50-52; Prakash, *The New Cambridge History of India II.5*, pp. 144-146.
53 Matthee, *The Politics of Trade in Safavid Iran*, p. 106; Wills, 'Trade and Diplomacy with Maritime Europe, 1644-c. 1800', p. 188; Clulow, *The Company and the Shogun*, pp. 95-97.

Figure 4   Portrait of *nawab* Shaista Khan (d. 1694). Mid-18th century.

day-to-day management of the empire.[54] Upon hearing about their father's indisposition, both Murad Bakhsh (*subahdar* of Gujarat and Malwa) and Shah Shuja (*subahdar* of Bengal, Bihar and Orissa) took the step of crowning themselves emperor. Shah Shuja led his troops in the direction of Agra, to be repelled near Varanasi by an imperial army sent by Dara Shukoh. Around the same time, Aurangzeb marched north from his government in the Deccan and joined forces with Murad Bakhsh.[55] At the decisive battle of Samugarh on 29 May 1658, their combined armies defeated the imperial troops under Dara's command, putting their elder brother to flight. In the

54   Faruqui, *The Princes of the Mughal Empire,* pp. 38-40, 242-243.
55   Richards, *The New Cambridge History of India I.5,* pp. 158-160.

weeks that followed Aurangzeb occupied Agra and confined Shah Jahan to the fort. He subsequently imprisoned Murad Bakhsh and took possession of Delhi. The victorious prince spent the next two years in the pursuit and eventual defeat of his two remaining rivals. Dara Shukoh was betrayed into Aurangzeb's hands and executed in August 1659, yet Shah Shuja continued the war effort from Bengal. After a string of defeats the prince eventually sought refuge in Arakan, where he is believed to have been killed in late 1660 after falling out with the Arakanese king.[56]

The effects of these events were felt by the Company, since the crisis of imperial power at the centre caused authority to fragment locally. In Bengal, Bihar, and Orissa, until the imperial army under Mir Jumla succeeded in driving out Shah Shuja, administrative control was temporarily divided between the prince's officers and those of the new Mughal governor. Internal rebellion and aggression along the eastern borders further destabilised the region.[57] The co-existence of two contesting power blocks along a rapidly shifting frontier posed pressing challenges to VOC merchants in the region. While the Company's official policy was one of neutrality, in practice it proved impossible to maintain this position because the warring parties treated the Dutch as a welcome source of money and weaponry.[58] This became most clear as the military balance shifted. Shah Shuja was dealt a crushing blow at Varanasi in February 1658. Later that year the prince undertook a second westward advance from Patna which was halted by Aurangzeb's troops in January 1659 at the battle of Khajwa. In April 1659, the remnants of Shah Shuja's retreating army were forced to abandon Rajmahal and withdraw to the eastern bank of the Ganges. However, aided by the strength of the Bengal flotilla, a turn of military fortunes took place during the summer months as Shah Shuja's riverine forces managed to retake Rajmahal and advance against Mir Jumla. Successive confrontations continuing into 1660 once more forced Shah Shuja on the defensive, until, hopelessly outnumbered and with Aurangzeb's generals in hot pursuit, he fled from the eastern capital of Dhaka in May 1660.[59]

Shah Shuja's recovery of Hugli on 2 July 1659 drew the VOC into the heat of the conflict. Forces loyal to the Mughal prince, who had governed Bengal as *subahdar* since 1639, plundered the town, killed its governor and other

56 Ibid., pp. 160-162. See also the very detailed account of the Mughal succession war in: Sarkar, *History of Aurangzib, Mainly based on Persian Sources*, vol. I, pp. 172-387, and vol. II, pp. 1-288.

57 Chatterjee, *Bengal in the Reign of Aurangzib 1658-1707*, pp. ix, pp. 16-19; Ray, *Orissa under the Mughals*, pp. 50-52.

58 For the official stance of neutrality: *Generale Missiven* III, p. 303.

59 Sarkar, *History of Aurangzib*, II, pp. 129-161, 237-288.

magistrates, and apprehended several administrators and merchants for their support to Mir Jumla. Among those detained were two VOC employees, the merchant Dirck Essinghs – acting as factory chief in the absence of *directeur* Mattheus van den Broeck – and the Indian broker Bhola Ram.[60] After being forced to witness the decapitation of five dignitaries, the two men were threatened with the same punishment because the local VOC representation had, on the one hand, delivered five pieces of cannon to Mir Jumla and, on the other, refused to provide ships to the governor loyal to Shah Shuja. The Company had moreover turned down the prince's request for a loan of 100,000 rupees.[61] The prompt recovery of Hugli by the imperial army enabled Essinghs and Bhola Ram to escape unharmed, yet further difficulties ensued for the Company's personnel in Dhaka. On 26 August 1659, troops belonging to Shah Shuja's son Buland Akhtar attacked the Dutch factory, took 51,000 guilders in cash and goods, imprisoned the merchants François Santvoort and Harmen Voorburgh and two Dutch assistants, and killed one of their Indian servants.[62] In an attempt to extort greater sums of money, the Dhaka merchants were told that the VOC servants in Hugli had been massacred and that they could expect to meet the same fate. The charge levelled against the Company was that the director of its trade in Bengal had not only gone off to visit Mir Jumla in his army camp but had also supplied him with eighteen pieces of cannon, two ships, and 300,000 rupees in cash.[63]

While the extent of their assistance was inflated, there was indeed plenty of reason to suspect that the Dutch were siding with Aurangzeb's general, whom Van den Broeck was visiting when the take-over of Hugli took place.[64] As years of experience had taught the various European traders, Mir Jumla was uniquely able to exert pressure due to his extensive political and mercantile influence. At this point in time the VOC owed the *nawab* over 500,000 guilders borrowed to finance its Coromandel trade, with a further 400,000 rupees received in Bengal in exchange for

60   I am following the spelling used in Prakash, 'The Dutch East India Company', pp. 286-287. In VOC sources, the broker's name is usually spelled 'Bolleram'.

61   *Generale Missiven* III, p. 290; Prakash, 'The Dutch East India Company', p. 281.

62   Santvoort and Voorburgh remained under arrest until 24 October 1659. They were first allowed to leave Dhaka in February 1660 after paying for their release. The assistants, Tido Geestdorp and David van den Hemel, would remain as hostages in Dhaka for several more months: *Generale Missiven* III, pp. 311, 341-342.

63   *Generale Missiven* III, 302.

64   Van den Broeck in a letter to Batavia extolled the good treatment received from Mir Jumla and expressed his wish to see Shah Shuja's downfall sooner rather than later: *Generale Missiven* III, p. 267.

uncoined Japanese silver. The latter transaction enabled Dutch trade to proceed at a time when the mint in Rajmahal had ceased operation as a consequence of the war, another example of the importance of good relations with the *nawab*.[65] Add to this the awkward circumstance that in 1658 the VOC had detained 25 elephants belonging to Mir Jumla, and it becomes clear that the Dutch in Hugli were not in a position to turn down the general's demands for cannon, gunpowder and gunners, despite being aware of the likely repercussions for their colleagues still residing under Shah Shuja's jurisdiction.[66] Using threats to bring Dutch trade in Bengal to a standstill, and having issued orders to that effect to his subordinate officers, Mir Jumla obtained cannons, gunpowder and sulphur from the Dutch ships anchored at Hugli. When, in December 1659, Shah Shuja made another temporary advance, Mir Jumla moreover made good use of the presence of Dutch ships for the safekeeping of seven chests of silver.[67] In total the Company supplied at least eleven pieces of iron cannon and six bronze cannons to be deployed in the war, part of which it received back in 1661 and part of which remained among Mir Jumla's possessions when the latter died in 1663.[68]

Requests for men and materiel continued to mark the relationship between the VOC and Mir Jumla after the end of the succession war. In September 1660, Mir Jumla detained Dutch ships to pressure the Company into supplying assistance in his pursuit of Shah Shuja, while also demanding the service of a Dutch galliot for his expedition to establish imperial authority over Hijli, a small island in the Ganges estuary.[69] Dutch sources claim that it was indeed the support offered by the yacht *Ougly* and its commander, Jan van Leenen, which secured the eventual conquest of the island.[70] Mir Jumla further leased Dutch shipbuilders, mariners, and the surgeon Gelmer Vosburg. This episode offers a helpful insight into the mechanics of the VOC's diplomacy in Bengal. To begin with, because of his proximity to Mir Jumla, the Company regarded Vosburg as best placed to carry out day-to-day dealings with the *nawab*. In addition, Batavia expected the Dutch resident

---

65   *Generale Missiven* III, p. 299; Stapel, ed., *Pieter van Dam's Beschryvinge van de Oostindische Compagnie*, II.2, p. 8. A sum of Rs. 150,000 paid by the VOC in 1672 was calculated as f. 210,000, or 1.4 guilders to the rupee: *Generale Missiven* III, p. 826. The exchange rate fluctuated, and around 1700 a silver rupee equalled 24 Dutch stivers, or 1.2 guilders: Van Dam, *Beschryvinge*, II.3, p. 101.

66   *Generale Missiven* III, pp. 291, 301.

67   *Generale Missiven* III, pp. 300-302, p. 340.

68   *Dagh-Register Batavia 1661*, p. 389; *Dagh-Register Batavia 1663*, p. 664.

69   *Dagh-Register Batavia 1661*, p. 6.

70   Ibid., pp. 241, 315.

in Dhaka to visit Mir Jumla once a week. Finally, *directeur* Van den Broeck was expected to maintain contact through regular correspondence and the occasional gift, providing a good example of the division of labour in provincial diplomacy.[71] Over and above these interactions, Mir Jumla also corresponded with the VOC's Governor-General in letters conveyed through the Company's factors in Bengal, a communication that again involved the issue of cannons.[72] Only if and when matters could not be resolved locally did the VOC take its grievances to the emperor, as happened with its claim for compensation for the attack on the Dhaka factory which Van Adrichem unsuccessfully put forward during his embassy to Delhi.[73]

In closing, it is helpful to return briefly to Shaista Khan's Chittagong campaign. The viceroy's dispatch of an envoy to Batavia was significant from a diplomatic-history point of view because it involved a rare instance of a seventeenth-century Mughal emissary travelling to the capital of a European Company-state. Whilst exchanges of ambassadors took place between Mughal emperors and Goa, such reciprocity was absent in relations between the imperial court and the East India Companies. The fact that the *subahdar* reached out on his personal initiative once more underlines that provincial diplomacy comprised a relatively independent sphere. On 3 March 1665, the envoy, one Khwaja Ahmad, presented his master's gifts and letter at Batavia Castle. The Dutch reaped great benefit from their trade in Bengal, Shaista Khan wrote, yet they simultaneously traded in the lands of his enemies, the Magh pirates from Arakan. He threatened the Company that if it did not close its Arakan factory and support his expedition with ships and cannons, the Dutch would be forced not only to leave Bengal but to cease their operations throughout the empire.[74] While the *Hoge Regering* did decide to close its lodge in Arakan, it initially put off naval assistance on the grounds that the *nawab*'s request lacked sufficient practical detail. The governing council only consented in July 1666 after a second envoy sent by Shaista Khan had delivered a *farman* authorised by Aurangzeb.[75]

---

71   Ibid., p. 239.

72   See for instance: *Dagh-Register Batavia 1661*, pp. 480-482.

73   Bernet Kempers, *Journaal van Dircq van Adrichem's Hofreis*, p. 187.

74   *Dagh-Register Batavia 1665*, pp. 42-45.

75   Ibid., pp. 191-192; Resolutions of Batavia Castle, 27 July 1665, Arsip Nasional Republik Indonesia (ANRI), Archive of the Governor-general and Council of the Indies (K66a), inventory number 877, ff. 251-257. When the Hoge Regering finally decided to send the yachts *Landsmeer* and *Purmerlandt* to Chittagong, news of Shaista Khan's victory against Arakan had already reached them: Resolutions of Batavia Castle, 2 July 1666, ANRI, K66a, 878, f. 243.

Of particular interest are Batavia's reasons for not establishing direct contact with the emperor to discuss his viceroy's demands: 'we have considered that the *nawab* in Bengal resides far from the court, and that if we forward the letter he sent us to His Majesty, and if [Shaista Khan] ends up being reprehended for it, [...] he and his subaltern governors will make us feel the consequences in Bengal, while our complaints, as we have experienced repeatedly, will not carry much weight at court.'[76] Doubtful of the efficacy of diplomacy at the central level of the Mughal administration, and cognisant of the fact that Company trade throughout Bengal depended on political cooperation from the *subahdar* and his subordinate officials, the *Hoge Regering*'s reasoning embodied the rationale behind provincial diplomacy as the VOC saw it. The Company continued to focus diplomatic efforts at the sub-state level, which was considered cheaper and less troublesome than diplomacy at the imperial court, while the attendant forms of political incorporation by the Mughal government of Bengal were deemed a price well worth paying for the substantial commercial benefits reaped from this prosperous region.

Conclusion

This chapter has dealt with the topic of provincial diplomacy through a focus on two episodes that highlight different aspects of the political and commercial relationship between the seventeenth-century East India Companies and the Mughal state. It has argued that the provincial setting is a vital albeit often neglected site to explore the place of the Companies in the Mughal political landscape, and that diplomacy offers an appropriate lens through which to analyse the complex politics of trade and violence that shaped Mughal–European interactions. Many of the diplomatic arrangements that set the parameters for such interactions were worked out along the empire's maritime frontier rather than at the centre, thus challenging notions of centre and periphery with regard to diplomatic decision-making. This chapter has attempted to promote an integrated perspective on Company diplomacy that moves beyond an exclusive focus on formal embassies to the imperial court, by drawing attention to the importance of the Companies' more frequent communication with provincial governments and the everyday practice of political interactions in port towns.

76   Resolutions of Batavia Castle, 27 July 1665, ANRI, K66a, 877, ff. 257-258.

As shown by my reading of William Bruton's *Newes from the East-Indies*, the perspective of provincial diplomacy invites explorations of cross-cultural encounters on the basis of a category of Asian-European interactions that were regular and on the whole characterised by proximity rather than cultural distance. Whereas an older historiography has portrayed early Anglo–Mughal encounters as meetings between different diplomatic systems hampered by semiotic disparities, Ralph Cartwright's reception by the *nawab* of Orissa instead points towards individuals operating within a common sphere of trade and politics according to established routines of interaction.[77] Furthermore, both case studies examined in this chapter underline the fundamental importance of Asian agency in shaping diplomatic interactions and arrangements. Initial trade agreements reached in the 1630s aligned with the economic and political interests of the provincial Mughal elites, while military upheaval during the late 1650s and early 1660s accelerated the co-opting of the Companies by the provincial Mughal authorities. Both go to show just how much the Companies depended on Indian political and commercial cooperation to advance their trade.

As a closer look at the VOC's position in mid-century Bengal makes clear, the perspective of provincial diplomacy is also useful in scrutinising diplomacy's blurred edges. When did a trading relationship shade into one of political vassalage, and when should we forego the prism of inter-state relations and think in terms of domestic frameworks for political solicitation instead? Answers to these questions will provide better insight into the diverse ways in which the Companies came to be incorporated into existing political structures across Asia. In much the same way that economic historians have positioned the role of East India Company trade within global networks of production and consumption, the study of Company diplomacy has the potential to highlight how macro-processes of global integration took shape through cross-cultural interactions in a variety of local sites.[78] Such future work is likely to accentuate the vital importance of the incentives, constraints, and power differentials encountered in various local contexts in shaping diplomatic relationships, and through the latter, the Companies' larger commercial and political presence in early modern Asia.

77   A classic formulation of the incommensurability thesis is: Cohn, *Colonialism and its Forms of Knowledge*, p. 18.
78   A recent collection situating the Companies within global consumer networks is: Berg, Gottman, Hodacs, and Nierstrasz, eds., *Goods from the East, 1600-1800*.

Works cited

Ali, M. Athar, *Mughal India: Studies in Polity, Ideas, Society, and Culture* (Oxford: Oxford University Press, 2006).

Ali, M. Athar, *The Apparatus of Empire: Awards of Ranks, Offices and Titles to the Mughal Nobility (1574-1658)* (Bombay: Oxford University Press, 1985).

Barbour, Richmond, *Before Orientalism: London's Theatre of the East, 1576-1626* (Cambridge: Cambridge University Press, 2003).

Berg, Maxine, Felicia Gottmann, Hanna Hodacs, and Chris Nierstrasz, eds., *Goods from the East, 1600-1800: Trading Eurasia* (Houndmills: Palgrave Macmillan, 2015).

Bernet Kempers, A.J., ed., *Journaal van Dircq van Adrichem's Hofreis naar den Groot-Mogol Aurangzēb 1662* (The Hague: Martinus Nijhoff, 1941).

Black, Jeremy, *A History of Diplomacy* (London: Reaktion Books, 2010).

Blake, Stephen P., *Shahjahanabad: The Sovereign City in Mughal India, 1639-1739* (Cambridge: Cambridge University Press, 1991).

Blussé, Leonard, *Tussen geveinsde vrunden en verklaarde vijanden* (Amsterdam: Koninklijke Nederlandse Akademie van Wetenschappen, 1999).

Bowrey, Thomas, Sir Richard Carnac Temple, ed., *A Geographical Account of Countries Round the Bay of Bengal 1669 to 1679* (Cambridge: Hakluyt Society, 1905).

Bruton, William, *Newes from the East-Indies: Or, A Voyage to Bengalla, one of the greatest Kingdomes under the High and Mighty Prince Pedesha Shasallem, usually called the Great Mogull* (London: Okes, 1638).

Burschel, Peter, and Christine Vogel, eds., *Die Audienz: Ritualisierten Kulturkontakt in der frühen Neuzeit* (Cologne: Böhlau Verlag, 2014).

Chatterjee, Anjali, *Bengal in the Reign of Aurangzib 1658-1707* (Calcutta: Progressive Publishers, 1967).

Chida-Razvi, Mehreen M., 'The Perception of Reception: The Importance of Sir Thomas Roe at the Mughal Court of Jahangir', *Journal of World History* 25, no. 2-3 (2014): 263-284.

Chijs, J.A. van der, et al., eds., *Dagh-Register gehouden int Casteel Batavia vant passerende daer ter plaetse als over geheel Nederlandts-India*, 31 vols. (The Hague/ Batavia: Martinus Nijhoff, 1887-1931).

Choudhury, Rishad, 'An Eventful Politics of Difference and its Afterlife: Chittagong Frontier, Bengal, c. 1657-1757', *The Indian Economic and Social History Review* 52, no. 3 (2015): 271-296.

Clulow, Adam, *The Company and the Shogun: The Dutch Encounter with Tokugawa Japan* (New York: Columbia University Press, 2014).

Cohn, Bernard S., *Colonialism and its Forms of Knowledge: The British in India* (Princeton: Princeton University Press, 1996).

Coolhaas, W.Ph., J. van Goor, J.E. Schooneveld-Oosterling, and H.K. s'Jacob, eds., *Generale Missiven van Gouverneurs-Generaal en Raden aan Heren XVII der Verenigde Oost-Indische Compagnie*, 13 vols. (The Hague: Martinus Nijhoff, 1960-2007).

Das, Nandini, '"Apes of Imitation": Imitation and Identity in Sir Thomas Roe's Embassy to India', in *A Companion to the Global Renaissance: English Literature and Culture in the Era of Expansion*, ed. Jyotsna G. Singh (Oxford: Wiley-Blackwell, 2009).

Eaton, Richard M., *The Rise of Islam and the Bengal Frontier, 1204-1760* (Berkeley: University of California Press, 1993).

Faruqui, Munis D., *The Princes of the Mughal Empire, 1504-1719* (Cambridge: Cambridge University Press, 2012).

Floor, Willem, "Ḳelʿat," *Encyclopædia Iranica*, XVI/2, pp. 226-229; available at www.iranicaonline.org/articles/kelat-gifts.

Flores, Jorge, *Nas Margens do Hindustão: O Estado da Índia e a expansão mogol ca. 1570-1640* (Coimbra: Coimbra University Press, 2015).

Flüchter, Antje, 'Sir Thomas Roe vor dem indischen Mogul: Transkulturelle Kommunikationsprobleme zwischen Repräsentation und Administration', in *Im Schatten der Macht. Kommunikationskulturen in Politik und Verwaltung 1600-1950*, ed. Stefan Haas and Mark Hengerer (Frankfurt: Campus, 2008), pp. 119-143.

Foster, William, ed., *The Embassy of Sir Thomas Roe to India, 1615-1619: As Narrated in his Journal and Correspondence* (London: Humphrey Milford, 1926).

Foster, William, *The English Factories in India 1634-1636. A Calendar of Documents in the India Office, British Museum and Public Record Office* (Oxford: Clarendon Press, 1911).

Gelder, Maartje van and Tijana Krstić, eds., 'Cross-Confessional Diplomacy and Diplomatic Intermediaries in the Early Modern Mediterranean', *Journal of Early Modern History* 19, no. 2-3 (2015): 93-259.

Ghobrial, John-Paul, *The Whispers of Cities: Information Flows in Istanbul, London, and Paris in the Age of William Trumbull* (Oxford: Oxford University Press, 2013).

Gordon, Stewart, ed., *Robes of Honour: Khil'at in Pre-Colonial and Colonial India* (New Delhi: Oxford University Press, 2003).

Hasan, Farhat, 'Conflict and Cooperation in Anglo-Mughal Trade Relations during the Reign of Aurangzeb', *Journal of the Economic and Social History of the Orient* 34, no. 4 (1991): 351–360.

Hasan, Farhat, *State and Locality in Mughal India: Power Relations in Western India, c. 1572-1730* (Cambridge: Cambridge University Press, 2004).

Heeres J.E., and F.W. Stapel, eds., *Corpus Diplomaticum Neerlando-Indicum: Verzameling van Politieke Contracten en verdere Verdragen door de Nederlanders in het Oosten gesloten, van Privilegiebrieven, aan hen verleend, enz.*, 6 vols, (The Hague: Martinus Nijhoff, 1907-1955), Vol. I.

Matthee, Rudolph P., *The Politics of Trade in Safavid Iran: Silk for Silver, 1600-1730* (Cambridge: Cambridge University Press, 1999).

Meersbergen, Guido van, 'Kijken en bekeken worden: Een Nederlandse gezant in Delhi, 1677-1678', in *Aan de Overkant: Ontmoetingen in dienst van de VOC en WIC (1600-1800)*, ed. Lodewijk Wagenaar (Leiden: Sidestone Press, 2015), pp. 201-216.

Meersbergen, Guido van, 'The Dutch Merchant-Diplomat in Comparative Perspective: Embassies to the Court of Aurangzeb, 1660-1666', in *Practices of Diplomacy in the Early Modern World c.1410-1800*, ed. Tracey Sowerby and Jan Hennings (New York: Routledge, 2017), pp. 147-165.

Mishra, Rupali, 'Diplomacy at the Edge: Split Interests in the Roe Embassy to the Mughal Court', *Journal of British Studies* 53, no. 1 (2014): 5-28.

Mitchell, Paul, *Sir Thomas Roe and the Mughal Empire* (Karachi: University of Karachi, 2000).

Nair, P. Thankappan, *Bruton's Visit to Lord Jagannatha 350 Yers [sic] Ago: British Beginnings in Orissa* (Calcutta: Minerva Associates, 1985).

Osborne, Toby, and Joan-Pau Rubiés, 'Introduction: Diplomacy and Cultural Translation in the Early Modern World', *Journal of Early Modern History* 20, no. 4 (2016): 313-330.

Pettigrew, William A., 'Corporate Constitutionalism and the Dialogue between the Global and the Local in Seventeenth-Century English History', *Itinerario* 39, no. 3 (2015): 487-501.

Prakash, Om, 'The Dutch East India Company in Bengal: Trade Privileges and Problems, 1633-1712', *The Indian Economic and Social History Review* 9, no. 3 (1972): 258-287.

Prakash, Om, *The Dutch East India Company and the Economy of Bengal 1630-1720*, (Princeton NJ: Princeton University Press, 1985).

Prakash, Om, *The New Cambridge History of India II.5: European Commercial Enterprise in Pre-Colonial India* (Cambridge: Cambridge University Press, 1998).

Ray, B.C., *Orissa under the Mughals: From Akbar to Alivardi, a fascinating Study of the Socio-Economic and Cultural History of Orissa* (Calcutta: Punthi Pustak, 1981).

Richards, John F., *The New Cambridge History of India I.5: The Mughal Empire* (Cambridge: Cambridge University Press, 1993).

Saran, P., *The Provincial Government of the Mughals 1526-1658*, 2nd ed. (London: Asia Publishing House, 1973).

Sarkar, Jadunath, *History of Aurangzib, Mainly based on Persian Sources*, 5 vols. (Calcutta: M.C. Sarkar & Sons, 1912-1924), Vols. 1 & 2.

Shāh Nawāz Khān, Nawwāb Samsām-Ud-Daula, and Abdul Hayy , *The Maāthir-ul-Umarā: Being Biographies of the Muhammadan and Hindu Officers of the Timurid Sovereigns of India from 1500 to about 1780 A.D.*, trans. H. Beveridge, 2 vols. (Calcutta: Asiatic Society of Bengal, 1911-1952), Vol. 2.

Sowerby, Tracey A., 'Early Modern Diplomatic History', *History Compass* 14, no. 9 (2016): 441-456.

Stapel, H.W., ed., *Pieter van Dam's Beschryvinge van de Oostindische Compagnie*, 7 vols. (The Hague: Martinus Nijhoff, 1927-1954), Vol. 2.

Stern, Philip J., *The Company-State: Corporate Sovereignty and the Early Modern Foundations of the British Empire in India* (Oxford: Oxford University Press, 2011).

Subrahmanyam, Sanjay, *Improvising Empire: Portuguese Trade and Settlement in the Bay of Bengal 1500-1700* (Delhi: Oxford University Press, 1990).

Subrahmanyam, Sanjay, *The Political Economy of Commerce: Southern India 1500-1650* (Cambridge: Cambridge University Press, 1990).

Subrahmanyam, Sanjay, 'Frank Submissions: The Company and the Mughals between Sir Thomas Roe and Sir William Norris', in *The Worlds of the East India Company*, ed. H.V. Bowen, Margarette Lincoln, and Nigel Rigby (Woodbridge: The Boydell Press, 2002), pp. 69-96.

Subrahmanyam, Sanjay, *Courtly Encounters: Translating Courtliness and Violence in Early Modern Eurasia* (Cambridge, MA: Harvard University Press, 2012).

Subrahmanyam, Sanjay, *The Portuguese Empire in Asia, 1500-1700: A Political and Economic History*, 2nd ed. (Chichester: John Wiley & Sons, 2012).

Watkins, John, 'Toward a New Diplomatic History of Medieval and Early Modern Europe', *Journal of Medieval and Early Modern Studies* 38, no. 1 (2008): 1-14.

Wellen, Kathryn, 'The Danish East India Company's War against the Mughal Empire, 1642-1698', *Journal of Early Modern History* 19, no. 5 (2015): 439-461.

Wills, John E., Jr., 'Trade and Diplomacy with Maritime Europe, 1644-c. 1800', in *China and Maritime Europe, 1500-1800: Trade, Settlement, Diplomacy, and Missions*, ed. John W. Wills Jr. (Cambridge: Cambridge University Press, 2011).

Wills, John E., Jr., *Embassies and Illusions: Dutch and Portuguese Envoys to K'ang-hsi, 1666-1687* (Cambridge MA: Harvard University Press, 1984).

Wilson, C.R., ed., *The Early Annals of the English in Bengal, being The Bengal Public Consultations for the First Half of the Eighteenth Century*, 3 vols. (London: W. Thacker & Co., 1895-1917), Vol. 1.

Contact details

Dr Guido van Meersbergen, University of Warwick
g.van-meersbergen@warwick.ac.uk

3 Contacting Japan

East India Company Letters to the Shogun

Fuyuko Matsukata

Abstract

This chapter describes the struggles of diplomatic embassies from East India Companies in the seventeenth century to incorporate themselves into the Japanese diplomatic sphere, focusing on their practices rather than their world views. The Dutch East Indies Company (VOC) failed to maintain diplomatic correspondence in 1627 and decided to rely on the merchants in Hirado. Along with the Tokugawa state formation around 1640 the Dutch merchants in Japan transformed into 'pseudo-subjects' of the Tokugawa state. Even after that East India Companies sent letters to the shogunate, but the shogunate treated the envoys not as diplomatic embassies but as merchants coming to petition for trade.

Keywords: Diplomacy, state letter, pseudo-subjects

The primary reason why the two East India Companies came to Asia was of course to trade. In order to establish trading networks and to resolve conflicts in Asia, however, the Dutch and English East India Companies dealt in both violence and diplomacy. The purpose of this chapter is to describe how European newcomers in Asia interacted with Asian diplomatic structures.[1] This question was first asked 20 years ago by the influential

1   The research for this chapter was supported by JSPS KAKENHI Grant Number JP15H03236. An earlier version of the paper was presented in Japanese as '17-seiki-chūyō Yōroppa seiryoku no Nihon kenshi to kokusho' [Embassies and state letters sent from the European powers to Japan in the middle of the seventeenth century], in *Nichiran kankeishi wo yomitoku* [Deciphering the Dutch-Japanese Relations] (Kyoto: Rinsen Shoten, 2015), and also as a presentation in the 26th EAJRS (European Association of Japanese Resource Specialists) conference held in Leiden in September 2015.

Clulow, Adam and Tristan Mostert (eds.), *The Dutch and English East India Companies: Diplomacy, trade and violence in early modern Asia*. Amsterdam: Amsterdam University Press, 2018
DOI: 10.5117/9789462983298/CH03

historian of the Dutch East India Company, Leonard Blussé, to whom this volume is dedicated.[2] In a groundbreaking analysis, he considered how the headquarters of the VOC in Batavia, once referred to as the 'Queen of the Orient', 'invented' its own diplomatic rituals in interaction with a range of rulers across the Indonesian archipelago.[3] Blussé explained that written correspondence and more specifically letters between rulers played a prominent role in the often vertical nature of Asian diplomatic relations. This was in contrast to the European reliance on ambassadors who were dispatched as negotiating agents. In a recent study, Adam Clulow has examined the encounter between the VOC and the Tokugawa government with a focus on diplomacy. His main concern was to criticise the so-called '1492 Schema' of history, a term pulled from the work of Tonio Andrade who has also contributed to this volume.[4] Like Blussé, he describes two different types of worldview by examining multiple examples of conflicts and misunderstandings between the VOC and the shogunate.[5]

At the same time, scholars working within East Asian history have examined Tokugawa diplomatic relations. Ronald Toby has argued against the traditional understanding of the term *sakoku* (national isolation) by examining the intra-Asian relations of the Tokugawa *bakufu*. His main point is that the legitimacy of the Tokugawa authority was partially based on its recognition by neighbouring states, especially Korea. He depicts a Tokugawa world order of hierarchical relations, in which the shogunate recognised a peer in Korea, looked upon Ryukyu as an inferior vassal state, and deemed China to be at the lowest rung of its hierarchy of partners.[6] In Japanese academia, scholars have studied the vertical relationships in East Asia, focusing on the phraseology of diplomatic documents.[7] Arano Yasunori argues that we should refer to the external relations of the Tokugawa period as '*kaikin-kaichitsujo taisei*' (the maritime ban and tributary system) rather than calling it a 'closed country'.[8] In this way, he emphasises the similarity between the policies used by the Chinese and Japanese governments.[9]

2   Blussé, 'Amongst Feigned Friends and Declared Enemies', p. 155.

3   Blussé 'Queen among Kings', p. 187.

4   Andrade, 'Beyond Guns, Germs, and Steel', p. 167.

5   Clulow, *The Company and the Shogun*, pp. 218-220.

6   Toby, *State and Diplomacy in Early Modern Japan*, pp. 229-230. The basic idea of the tribute system is perhaps best expressed in Fairbank, *The Chinese World Order*.

7   E.g. Toby, 'Kinsei shotō tai-Min no ichi gaikō monjo'.

8   Yamamoto Hirofumi proposed a counterargument in his *Sakoku to kaikin no jidai* , especially pp. 252-257.

9   It is true that the Ming and Qing courts required specific official documents such as *biao* 表 (tributary memorial for the Emperor), *zhao*詔 (proclamation mandate of the Emperor), *chi*勅

This chapter asks a straightforward question: to what extent were diplomatic letters in Asia always vertical? In other words, does it make sense to evaluate diplomatic relations as horizontal or vertical? My question is motivated in part by what appears to be the Eurocentric nature of such a division. In answering it, I propose a modification of past scholarship. While I agree with Blussé's argument that letters played a significant role in diplomatic interactions in Asia, the persistently vertical nature of Asian diplomacy is far less clear.[10] And I suggest that we should be careful of making assumptions about two distinct European and Asian world orders.[11] In this chapter, I attempt to explain conflicts and misunderstandings by focusing on the practices and manners of diplomacy, with an emphasis, following Blussé, on letters as the core of Japanese foreign relations.

The Tokugawa shogunate, or *bakufu*, conducted written correspondence with Korea, the Ryukyu Kingdom, and a number of Southeast Asian countries.[12] Letters exchanged with Korea were composed in Chinese with an emphasis on equality, or rather to suggest a mutual relationship unquestioned between the two monarchs. In contrast, correspondence with the Ryukyus was written first in Chinese and then in Japanese, and clearly expressed an unequal relationship between the Tokugawa Shogun and the Ryukyuan king. As for Southeast Asian rulers, their diplomatic letters to the shogunate were composed in Chinese, but the nature of reciprocal relations expressed in them was unclear as to hierarchy, partially because skill in writing formal Chinese was usually limited.[13]

Within the Indonesian archipelago, the VOC government in Batavia forged its relations with indigenous kings and lords by regularly exchanging letters during its two hundred years' existence from 1602 to 1800.[14] Scholars of Thai history have paid attention to '*prarachasan*' (or king's letters) exchanged between Siam and its Burmese and Vietnamese neighbours during the

(imperial command of the Emperor), or *die*牒 (low level memoranda) from foreign rulers. These various terms more clearly express the hierarchical structure than *shu*書 (letter) or *shangshu* 上書 (memorial to the throne).

10   Blussé does make an exception for Southeast Asia, where Malay rulers (as in post-Westphalian Europe) addressed each other on basis of equality even if at times they attempted to bluff their correspondents.

11   In his recent work with Lauren Benton, Clulow has argued for commonality between Asian and European diplomatic structures. Benton and Clulow, 'Legal Encounters and the Origins of Global Law', p. 82.

12   E.g. Kitagawa and Okamoto, 'Correspondence between Cambodia and Japan'.

13   Ibid.

14   Blussé, 'Queen among Kings'.

eighteenth and nineteenth centuries.[15] The monarchs of Siam and Persia also corresponded with each other during the seventeenth century.[16] Masuda Erika has tried to bridge the gap between the Sino-centric sphere and the world of Southeast Asia by examining the correspondence between Chinese emperors and Siamese kings. She points out that missives from the latter were full of expressions suggesting equal relationships, but that these were subsequently transformed into hierarchical terms in the Chinese translations that were presented to officials in China.[17] In this way, letters changed depending on their audience.

For the purposes of this chapter, I will refer to diplomatic letters in Asia as 'state letters'.[18] I suggest that what might be called 'letter diplomacy' was characterised by its flexibility. Permanent and resident ambassadors facilitated a multilateral diplomatic exchange, but letter diplomacy could keep relations essentially bilateral. A letter could be, and frequently was, manipulated in translation as it travelled. We should not forget that shifting circumstances along the designated route might prompt carriers to alter official documents, in some cases to aid delivery. The letter might be deliberately mistranslated by a mediator at the port or court of the recipient. In their work, Japanese researchers have revealed many examples of such manipulations.[19]

While more work based on Asian and European sources is needed, I suggest that letter diplomacy was used, and expected, to bridge different world orders and mutual misunderstandings, especially when there was considerable geographical and cultural distance between the sender and the recipient. Yet, even if they were not always vertical, diplomatic practices in Asia remained difficult for European newcomers in the region to grasp. In Asian letter diplomacy the ambassadors who delivered these documents did not have the same status, agency or voice as in European diplomacy, but they

15   Koizumi, 'Ratanakōshin-chō 1-sei ōki Shamu no taigai kankei'; Koizumi, 'The "Last" Friendship Exchanges between Siam and Vietnam, 1879-1882'.
16   Embassies were sent from Siam to Persia in 1669, 1679 and 1682, and a delegate was sent from Persia to Siam in 1685. Morikawa, 'Safāvī-chō no tai-Shamu shisetsu to Indo Yō'.
17   Masuda, 'Rama 1-sei no Taishin Gaikō'; Masuda, 'The Fall of Ayutthaya'.
18   This terminology was used by Ronald Toby as, it seems, a direct translation of the Japanese word kokusho (Toby, pp.178-183). The original meaning of kokusho (or kuoshu in Chinese pronunciation) would be 'royal letter'. However, letters from the Dutch or Spanish Governors-General were sometimes called kokusho. The various forms of official correspondence, such as biao, zhao, chi, zi, or die, remain in need of further elucidation.
19   Tashiro, Kakikaerareta kokusho; Hashimoto, Itsuwari no Gaikō Shisetsu; Shimizu, Kinsei Nihon to Ruson, pp. 140-171; Sannō, 'Shindai Chūki ni okeru Sūrū to Chūgoku no aida no monjo ōrai'.

could still sometimes carry out negotiations beneath the surface. This happened even if they were not regarded as representatives who could express the views of their superiors but were merely treated as 'letter bearers'.[20]

This chapter describes the struggles of diplomatic embassies from various European powers in the seventeenth century to incorporate themselves into the Japanese diplomatic sphere, focusing on their practices rather than their world views.[21] Here it should be noted that their envoys often did not come from Europe, but rather from headquarters of the East India Companies in Asia.

For the shogunate, generally speaking, royal letters did not explicitly mention trade, because they were meant to discuss 'royal business'. In order to clarify this issue, let us see how a Tokugawa high official replied to the Dutch *opperhoofd* of Deshima when the latter asked whether the VOC should send a new ambassador to thank the shogun for the hospitality shown by the shogunate to the crew members of a VOC ship:

> Why should their [the Dutch] ambassador come to express gratitude for the fact that the Dutch Company's merchants live and prosper in Japan? Such business does not merit an ambassador; we only deem of substance kings and potentates, when they speak of royal business – and not of merchant business – and when they request assistance or offer assistance in war. Sending another envoy [by the VOC] will only result in trouble.[22]

This response shows that the Tokugawa councillor understood 'royal business' to consist only of asking for or offering military assistance. I suggest that it might also have included the celebration of a counterpart's enthronement, the announcement of one's own enthronement, or the establishment of peace.

An embassy from the Dutch Governor-General in 1627

In 1609, the VOC began to trade with Japan. After the Company established its base at Tayouan on the island of Formosa (Taiwan) in 1624, it came into conflict with Japanese traders and samurai who had been visiting the island

---

20   Letter from the Governor-General, Pieter de Carpentier to the *opperhoofd* in Hirado, Cornelis van Nijenroode, 17 November 1625, Overgekomene brieven en Papieren, jaar 1626, boek II: FF, Archives of Verenigde Oostindische Compagnie (VOC) (1.04.02), Nationaal Archief (NA) 1087, The Hague.

21   Nagazumi Yōko mentioned this topic in her pioneering work, *Kinsei shoki no gaikō*, pp. 114-125.

22   Quoted in Blussé, 'Amongst Feigned Friends and Declared Enemies', p. 167.

for years. In order to request the Tokugawa government to stop issuing vermilion-seal trading passes to Japanese junks sailing to Taiwan, in 1627 the Dutch Governor-General of Batavia sent the newly appointed governor of Formosa, Pieter Nuyts, to Japan. The Dutch envoy carried letters from the Governor-General addressed to the retired shogun, Tokugawa Hidetada, and his successor, Shogun Iemitsu.[23]

Nuyts was initially welcomed in Japan with the same kind of ceremony accorded to envoys from Korea. His entourage of 290 persons travelled to Edo with 78 horses, of which 70 were provided at the expense of the shogun. After arriving in the capital Nuyts was subjected to a detailed interrogation and was asked who had sent him and where he came from. After waiting two weeks without an audience with the shogun, Nuyts expressed his frustration, particularly since he did not understand the reason why his embassy had been rejected. As a result, he left Edo without even having gained permission from Tokugawa officials to leave.[24]

Nuyts pretended in his report to Batavia that the shogun had not been willing to receive him as an ambassador, and therefore had made negotiations impossible. What really happened is that Tokugawa officials could not accept him as an envoy because that would have implied that the shogun would have recognised the Dutch Governor-General in Batavia as being of equal status. In the words of Tokugawa officials:

The letters were written by a vassal of Java in *kanamajiri* [proper Japanese]. Java is equal to Holland. As the people of Holland have no letters [i.e. do not know how to write], they had a Javanese write it. [The king of] Holland should not write to the king of Japan directly, much less a vassal of Java [...]. The letter is impolite. It was decided that they should come again through the mediation of Matsura [the daimyo of Hirado] if they want to show true sincerity.[25]

23 The letters are not extant. The Dutch translations dated 10 May 1627 are kept in Batavia's Uitgaand Briefboek 1627, VOC (1.04.02) 854, NA, The Hague.
24 For details, see 'Journael van de reyse gedaen bij Pieter Nuijts ende Pieter Muijser oppercoopman, als ambassadeurs aen den Keyser en rijcxraden van Japan van den 24 July 1627 tot 18 Febr. 1628', Overgekomen Brieven uit Batavia, jaar 1629, boek II. OO, VOC (1.04.02) 1095. See also Katō, *Bakuhansei kokka no seiritsu to taigai kankei*, pp. 140-42, and Clulow, *The Company and the Shogun*, pp. 67-94.
25 'Ikoku Nikki', by Konchi'in Sūden, dated the 17th day of the 9th month of Kan'ei 4, *Ikoku Ōfuku Shokanshū & Zōtei Ikoku Nikki Shō* pp. 223-24.

While the author seems to have been poorly informed as to the relationship between Java and Holland, it is obvious that the understanding of the Japanese authorities was that the sender of the letter was merely a subordinate of the Oranda *yakata* [Superior of the Dutch].[26]

There was one further point where the Dutch and Japanese were at cross purposes. The letters carried by the ambassador stated that the Governor-General had sent Pieter Nuys with gifts both in order to thank Japan for 28 years of Tokugawa kindness to the Dutch, and to congratulate the shogun on his accession to the throne. Sending a letter to congratulate a new king upon his enthronement did follow Asian practices but the last sentence of the document introduced Nuyts as a representative or a negotiator. In fact, Nuyts insisted he was an official diplomatic representative with a commission to negotiate over the question of Dutch sovereignty in Taiwan.

Adam Clulow recently examined why Nuyts failed to be recognised as a formal ambassador. I agree with his overall argument that the failure was not only due to Nuyts' arrogant personality but also because of the differences in diplomatic customs that came into play. However, I would also stress that the main problem centred not on the status or dignity of the Governor-General but rather on the question as to whether he was an independent ruler. Both Dutch and Japanese sources reveal that there was a long discussion between Tokugawa leaders and Nuyts concerning who sent the letters and who was really in charge of the Dutch residing in Japan. Nuyts answered that the Governor-General had the same sort of authority as the lord of Holland. As a result, Tokugawa authorities believed that Holland and Java were equals and that the letter was sent by a subordinate of Java. This implied that the leader who dispatched Nuyts, the Governor-General at Batavia, was merely a subordinate of someone in Holland or Java, and this interpretation provided the basis for the rejection of Nuyts' embassy. If Tokugawa authorities failed to form a clear understanding of the political system of the Dutch, this may have been the fault of Nuyts' inept way of answering questions.

Forming Tokugawa pseudo-subjects in the 1630s

After the Nuyts embassy, the relationship between the Dutch and *bakufu* leaders worsened on account of further disputes between Nuyts and visiting

---

26   *Oranda yakata* does not necessarily mean the Prince of Orange. 'Oranda' in this context means 'the Dutch people', and *yakata* is used in the *sengoku* sense of a daimyo of high rank.

Japanese merchants about trade in Taiwan. As a result of all this the Japanese government imposed an embargo on all trade with the Dutch, so that the VOC saw its trade with Japan come to a full stop. In 1632 when trade was resumed, the Governor-General in Batavia decided to no longer send envoys but to rely only on the merchants stationed in Hirado. While this was happening, the *bakufu* was building up an innovative system of trade relations (in the nineteenth century called *tsūsho-no-kuni* 通商国, or a state conducting commercial relations) to accept foreign merchants without having to maintain correspondence with foreign rulers. This stemmed not only from the failure of the Dutch embassy but also from the fact that the Ming government was losing its power, which meant that the *bakufu* could no longer find a counterpart in China to address.[27] Europeans regarded the Chinese and Dutch merchants in Nagasaki separately, as members of the Chinese diaspora or agents of the Dutch trading empire respectively. However, the Tokugawa did not distinguish between the two communities: both were accepted as merchants without the need for correspondence on the state level.

The construction of this system ran parallel with the domestic process of the creation of 'Tokugawa subjects', as distinguished from native 'Japanese' subjects.[28] It should be understood that the domestic legitimacy of the Tokugawa government derived largely from its military power. Rituals and symbols supported the idea that the Tokugawa house was protecting Japan. The shogunate had to 'shadow box' with supposed enemies – which should appear neither too weak nor too strong – in order to demonstrate that the shogunate could ward off any threat to Japan. Although the shogun did not interfere with the rule of the daimyo (vassals) in their own dominions, the centrally conducted anti-Christian policy formed a unique exception, as under this 'national' policy, people had to be registered individually.

In the midst of this crackdown on Christianity, Chinese and European trading networks in Japan posed a potential problem to the shogunate. Rigid measures were taken: the Portuguese were expelled from Japan, and mestizo children born out of Japanese-European unions were ordered to leave Japan and forbidden to return. The Chinese were divided into two categories. Resident Chinese would be treated in the same way as indigenous people in

---

27   Matsukata, 'Countries for Commercial Relations'.

28   In Japanese academia, the concept of *bakuhansei kokka* has been dominant for several decades. Early modern Japan consisted of one state but with twin authorities, namely the shogun and the *tennō*. See e.g. Takano, *Kinsei Nihon no kokka kenryoku to shūkyō*, pp. i-xiv. Here I propose another image, one of two overlapping states, crowned with the shogun and the *tennō*.

Japan, and non-resident Chinese could no longer permanently reside in the country.[29] But, the Tokugawa continued to allow the Dutch and the Chinese, as well as some merchants and sailors from Southeast Asia, to visit Nagasaki for trade as long as they strictly obeyed the anti-Christian policy under the supervision of the Nagasaki magistrates. The VOC promised to do so, and told its personnel to comply with all necessary rules in Nagasaki. Reporting foreign news (*fūsetsugaki*) to the shogun, especially on Christian powers, was required of the Dutch, and consequently they provided news concerning the outside world to the Nagasaki magistrates.[30] This arrangement transformed Chinese and Dutch merchants into 'pseudo-subjects' of the Tokugawa state, allowed to operate in Japan. At the same time, the shogunate severely curtailed its subjects ability to leave the country. It stopped issuing trading passes to its own people and banned Japanese junks from going abroad. As such, the VOC and rulers of Southeast Asian kingdoms such as Vietnam or Siam no longer had to accept Japanese junks into their ports. This marked a contrast with earlier periods in which Japanese merchants abroad had been as active as their foreign counterparts in Japan, thus ending the country's two-way maritime traffic.

Importantly, these measures did not cause a decline in the status of VOC personnel in Japan. On the contrary, it was confirmed and given its proper place within the pecking order of Japanese society. I therefore do not agree with Katō Eiichi, who argues that the VOC became a vassal of the shogun. Japanese society was, at least officially if not in practice, mobilised along military lines even in peace.[31] The shogun, the daimyo, and their vassals all held the status of samurai (i.e. fighters). Other Tokugawa subjects like peasants or townspeople served to provide logistics, maintenance of roads and bridges, and building siege works and fortresses. In my opinion, the Dutch in Japan served the shogunate in an intelligence capacity by providing reports on the outside world and therefore functioned in an ambiguous space between direct fighting and civilian logistical support. The Dutch served the shogun in the suppression of the Shimabara rebellion in 1637-1638 by providing a ship, *De Rijp*, when they were asked to do so. These actions suggest that the Dutch may have been briefly able to obtain formal *samurai* or ruling rank at that time, but ultimately the Dutch did not want to bear the cost and the shogunate held little interest in granting such a privilege. In

---

29   Matsui, 'The Legal Position of Foreigners in Nagasaki during the Edo Period'; Arano, 'Nihon-gata kai chitsujo no keisei'.

30   Matsukata, *Oranda fūsetsugaki to kinsei Nihon*, pp. 39-40.

31   Takagi, *Nihon kinsei kokkashi no kenkyū*, pp. 1-4, pp. 127-135, pp. 321-322.

any case Shimabara marked the one and only time that the Dutch provided military service during the Tokugawa period.

The 1649 Dutch Embassy from Holland

In 1643 a VOC ship, the *Breskens*, was dispatched to explore the geographical position of the reputed Gold and Silver Islands, which were said to be located off the northern coast of Japan. When some crew members came ashore in Nanbu (today's Iwate prefecture, on the northern Pacific coast of Honshu) to fetch water, they were captured and then brought to Edo. After being interrogated they were finally delivered to the Dutch chief in Nagasaki. On the latter's suggestion the VOC administration in Batavia decided to send an envoy to the shogun to thank the Tokugawa leader for his tolerant attitude concerning the *Breskens* crew.

Reinier Hesselink has provided a detailed analysis of these events in his book, *The Prisoners from Nambu*.[32] He argues that the Governor-General and François Caron, the former chief of the VOC Hirado factory, deceived the shogun by sending an ambassador without credentials signed in Holland to thank him for his lenient attitude towards the captured crew members. I argue instead that the shogun did not expect an ambassador with credentials precisely because there was no such tradition of credentialed representatives in Japan. This can be clearly seen in the letter from the Governor-General and the 'old Japan hand' Caron to the Nagasaki magistrates written in Japanese. The Japanese version is lost, but a Dutch copy is extant in the archives of the Dutch factory.[33] In the Japanese context, this letter is both a *hōsho* 奉書 (a letter written on behalf of a superior) and a *hirōjō* 披露状 (a letter addressed to a subordinate in lieu of the true, higher-ranking addressee). In this case, the Governor-General wrote on behalf of his superiors in Holland. In turn he addressed the Nagasaki magistrates, not the shogun. In other words, this letter could function as a missive from the superiors of the Dutch to the shogun. Furthermore, the chief of the Nagasaki factory, not the envoy, presented the letter.[34] The letter stated that the superiors of the Governor-General had been informed of the *Breskens* incident and

32   Hesselink, *Prisoners from Nambu*.
33   Dutch translation of letter from the Governor-General, Cornelis van der Lijn, to the Nagasaki magistrates, of 27 July 1649. Archives of Dutch Factory Japan (NFJ) (1.04.21) 282, NA, The Hague,.
34   Letter from the Governor-General van der Lijn to the *opperhoofden* in Japan, Dirq Snoek and Antonij van Brouckhorst, of 27 July 1649 in *Historical Documents in Foreign Languages Relating to Japan: Diaries Kept by the Heads of the Dutch Factory in Japan*, Vol. 11, Appendix IV, pp. 207-252.

asked him to send a letter of gratitude in their place because they could not compose a proper letter in Japanese for the shogun:

> Five years ago, some Dutchmen were arrested near Nanbu in Japan [...]. They were absolved by extraordinary mercy of the Emperor [the shogun] and sent back to their homeland. Our superiors in Holland heard of the incident and became most thankful. They discussed how to express their thanks for this special benefit by sending a special envoy. The gentlemen were willing to attach a letter expressing gratitude, but were anxious whether or not the manner of the letter would be appropriate and modest enough to be directed to the Emperor. They were also concerned whether a Dutch text would be acceptable in Japan because of their ignorance [of Japanese custom]). Therefore, they ordered me [the Governor-General] to compose a letter in the most appropriate manner. According to the order, I, with this letter, respectfully ask your favour and help in appropriately dispatching the envoy to the Emperor.

Who were these superiors? In the Japanese context, this issue could remain vague. In fact, the Nagasaki magistrates forwarded the letter to Edo without querying who the Dutch superiors actually were, and only asked this question after they received a positive answer from the Tokugawa headquarters. The envoy answered that his superiors were the States-General of the Dutch republic, although his instructions specified that he should pretend that he was sent by the *Heeren XVII*, the Directors of the VOC.[35] In any case, the Tokugawa shogun had no interest in securing a credentialed ambassador as there was no such tradition in Japan.

Contrary to what Hesselink has argued, it was actually not the shogun but the envoy Frisius that was deceived. The instructions for Frisius do not mention the letter addressed to the Nagasaki magistrates, although the letter went together with him to Japan on board of the ship *Robijn*.[36] The delivery of the letter was mentioned in the instructions for the chief of the Dutch factory in Nagasaki, Antonij van Brouckhorst, who had arrived in

---

35   Dachregister van 't voornaemste voorgevallende ende gepasseerde in 't legaetschap aen de Keyserlijke Mayesteit des rijcx van Japan. Overgekomene brieven en papieren, jaar 1651, boek I bis:NNN bis, VOC (1. 04.02) 1176, NA, The Hague.

36   A letter of instructions (*Instructie*) of the Governor General and Council of the Indies addressed to the ambassador Petrus Blockhovius, dated 27 July 1649, in *Historical Documents in Foreign Languages Relating to Japan: Diaries Kept by the Heads of the Dutch Factory in Japan*, Vol. 12, Appendix, pp. 243-263. Petrus Blockhovius was initially appointed as ambassador, but after his death Frisius took his place. This is detailed in Hesselink's study.

Japan from Tayouan just before the letter. Van Brouckhorst could boast of a long career in Japan and Vietnam, while Frisius was a newcomer who had just arrived from Europe.

Louis XIV's Letter

In 1664, Jean-Baptiste Colbert re-established the French East India Company and invited the now-former VOC official François Caron to join it. After joining the French Company, Caron in 1667 was to carry as ambassador a letter from King Louis XIV to the shogun, but he never managed to reach Japan. He made it as far as Surat in India but had to return to Europe due to differences with his French colleagues. The letter, which was probably drafted by Caron himself, introduced France and briefly explained why the king had selected Caron as his ambassador and why he proposed the opening of free trade with France.[37] The letter could be called a credential rather than a state letter because its main purpose was to introduce the position of Caron as ambassador. In contrast to the Dutch and English Companies which were established by merchants and later formalised by the government, the French Company was established by policymakers at the royal court. Thus the French East India Company could prepare a true royal letter. Caron also carried instructions referencing Japanese customs unfamiliar to French policymakers and based upon his own experience and knowledge.[38] These instructions mention his experience in 1627 as a member of the failed mission led by Nuyts.

The *Return* incident of 1673

After leaving Japan in 1623, the English East India Company (EIC) planned to reopen the Japan trade on the basis of its good relationship with the

---

37   Au Souverain, et Très-haut Empereur et Régent du Grand Empire du Japon, dont les sujets sont très soumis et obéissants, le Roi de France souhaite une longue et heureuse vie et beaucoup de prospérité en son Règne.in *Le Puissant Royaume du Japon*, pp. 228-30. I would like to thank Segawa Yūta and Shimanaka Hiroaki for their assistance with the translation from French into Japanese.

38   'Instruction pour François Carron, Envoyé du Roi de France et de Navarre, à l'Empereur du Japon, pour lui délivrer la lettre et le present de Sa Majesté, et suivant laquelle il se conduira pour l'exécution des affaires projetées et qui lui sont commises'. *Le Puissant Royaume du Japon*, pp. 231-240.

Zheng regime in Taiwan. A ship, the *Return*, left England in 1671 and Simon
Delboe, the EIC official aboard, was instructed to establish a new factory
in Japan and to become its chief. The VOC had anticipated the designs
of the EIC, and informed Tokugawa authorities of the marriage between
Charles II of England and Catharine, a Portuguese princess.[39] The *Return*
arrived in Nagasaki in June 1673. When Japanese officials asked Delboe
why he had been dispatched, he explained that he brought the king's letter
to the 'Emperor of Japan', i.e. the shogun, in order to conduct commerce in
Japan.[40] However, the letter was not handed over to the Nagasaki authorities, although the substance of the petition was probably written down in
Japanese and sent to Edo.

   In other words, the Tokugawa authorities treated Delboe not as an ambassador but as a merchant, mainly because he came to ask for trade. It is useful
to quote the king's letter here:

> Yours abounding in gold, silver, & copper, being of great use for the car-
> rying on of commerce & trade, and our kingdoms affording such great
> varieties & quantities of woolen cloths & stuffs fit for the clothing of all
> sorts of persons, which not only tend to the great health & fortifying the
> spirits & delight of them that wear them, especially in such climates as
> your empire, but are much more lasting & cheaper than other clothing,
> which causes so many countries to desire them that our merchants do
> vend exceeding great quantities thereof [...].[41]

The letter itself indicates that officials in the EIC's headquarters had little
understanding about the Japanese. It did not even pretend to celebrate the
shogun's accession or inform the Japanese side about the accession of their
king. From the Japanese point of view, this looked like the correspondence
of a merchant and not a king. As the *Return* came to request permission for
trade, it should be treated merely as a merchant ship. This did not close off
the opportunity for further negotiation, but rather enlarged it. In fact, the
Nagasaki magistrate, Okano Magokurō, seriously considered accepting the
EIC as a trading partner and asked the Dutch about the possibility of sharing
Deshima. In Japan, Tokugawa subjects maintained the right of petition,
although they had to proceed step by step in any appeals.

---

39   Nagazumi, '17-seiki kōhan no jōhō to tsūji'.
40   'Iapan Diary 1673,' of 29 June 1673, in *Experiment and Return*, pp. 90-91.
41   *Experiment and Return*, p. 20. I have updated the spelling here to reflect modern conventions.

In the end, the *bakufu* did not accept the English, because they could not rely on their compliance with Tokugawa prohibitions of Christianity. After the *Return* incident, no European embassies visited Japan for more than a hundred years before the arrival of Adam Laxman from Russia in October 1792.

Conclusion

In the middle of the seventeenth century, some emissaries from European powers visited Japan, most of whom were sent by officials based in Asia, such as the Dutch Governor-General in Batavia. After the failure of Pieter Nuyts' mission, Dutch-Japanese trade came to a halt for several years. When it reopened, the Tokugawa's framework for accepting the Dutch emerged from the idea of seeing them as 'pseudo-subjects' without correspond-ence on the state level. This process paralleled the creation of Tokugawa subjects that included prohibitions of Christianity. The VOC administration in Batavia accepted the system because it saved them the cost of sending diplomatic envoys and it also preserved the right of petition, even though many troublesome regulations had to be endured by the organisation's personnel on Deshima.

France and England dispatched emissaries and letters in 1667 and 1673 respectively, but the former did not reach Japan and the latter accomplished nothing. French and English efforts failed in part because their position in the China Seas was less established than that of the Dutch and they lacked sufficient understanding of East Asian diplomatic customs. The European Companies expected their letters to function as credentials and their envoys to negotiate trade, but the shogunate operated under a different set of rules. As a result, the *bakufu* treated the emissaries not as diplomatic embassies but as merchants coming to petition for trade because it did not recognise their documents as 'state letters'. To date, historians have attributed the failure of European 'petitions' to the Tokugawa prohibition of Christianity. To this, I would add that from the Tokugawa point of view, the *bakufu* could decide arbitrarily whether or not to accept a 'petition' because it was not an inter-state but a domestic matter.

Foreign relations around Japan in the seventeenth century were based on 'letter diplomacy'. In letter diplomacy, the letter bearer was neither a negotiator nor a representative. Correspondence functioned to maintain mutual relations. The correspondence itself, including the form of the letter, determined the relationship between states. In fact, the members of the envoy party often engaged in commercial negotiations, but negotiations could never serve as the main task of the dispatched party.[42] So what did actually happen when Europeans entered into this framework? Both Asian states and European powers struggled to adapt to the new circumstances, but until the nineteenth century, Europeans had to compromise with Asian customs, at least in the case of Japan. That said, European newcomers wanted to negotiate and conclude mutual treaties because they did not have a place within the existing diplomatic network. For European merchants in the Asian seas it was impossible to repeatedly ask for royal letters in order to promote their commerce. When European envoys reached Nagasaki, Japanese officials asked them if they wanted to negotiate as merchants or if they wanted to be treated as diplomatic embassies. They naturally chose the first option. For the Tokugawa government, too, it was easier to treat Europeans as merchants. In his work, Clulow has suggested that the Dutch lost their diplomatic prerogatives after the failure of Nuyts, but I would argue instead that the Dutch simply stopped sending embassies with diplomatic prerogatives. The Dutch chief was at no stage a diplomatic representative.

By way of conclusion, I do not want to suggest that Europeans were realists and Asians formalists. For example, after the Meiji Restoration in 1871, the Iwakura Mission visited Europe hoping to negotiate for the revision of the unequal treaties. At this time, European states did not move to negotiate with the embassy. Rather, it can be argued that they welcomed the mission simply in order to confirm the illusion of a Eurocentric world order.

The *bakufu* created a new framework to accept Dutch merchants without formal correspondence. Such acceptance could be considered a privilege, because the Governor-General of the VOC, for example, did not have to accept any Japanese junks in Batavia or Taiwan. The privilege depended on the *bakufu*'s certainty that it could control VOC agents, especially when it came to Christian prohibitions. That certainty was based on the ongoing relationship between the Tokugawa and the VOC. It was harder to extend it to newcomers. When the Russians came to Japan in the eighteenth and nineteenth centuries, the *bakufu* discussed seriously if it would accept the Russians or not, but in the end formulated concrete policies not to accept any newcomers. Later the Japanese called the policy *sakoku* or 'seclusion policy'.[43] Moreover, the fact that the Tokugawa shoguns did not conduct commercial negotiations with the Dutch did not mean that they had no

---

42 My comments are limited to East Asia and do not extend to similar forms in other parts of the early modern world.

43 Fujita, *Kinsei kōki no seijishi to taigai kankei*, pp. 3-20.

Figure 5   The reply from the senior council of the shogunate to the letter of King Willem II (1845).

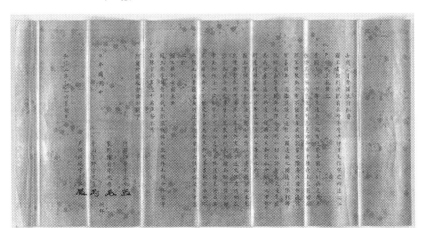

Ministerie van Buitenlandse Zaken 2.05.01/3147a, Nationaal Archief, The Hague, 2.05.01 (Archive of the Ministry of Foreign Affairs), inv. nr. 3147a.

interest in trade. They took measures to control foreign trade in Nagasaki via the Nagasaki magistrates and the Nagasaki *kaisho* (the shogun's trading office conducted by the merchant groups of Nagasaki). Trade was regulated by 'contracts' between the Dutch and the Nagasaki *kaisho* signed by shogunal interpreters in Nagasaki instead of by commercial treaties.

In 1844, the Dutch King William II sent a letter to the Tokugawa shogun, recommending that he open up the country in order to allow international trade and to avoid conflict with Great Britain[44]. In their reply, the council of the Tokugawa government stated that they would maintain the status quo in foreign relations, recognising Korea and Ryukyu as 'Countries of Diplomatic Correspondence (*Tsūshin-no-Kuni*通信国)', and China and the Netherlands as 'Countries of Commercial Relations (*Tsūshō-no-Kuni*)'.[45] This served as an excuse for the fact that the shogun himself did not reply to the king, and furthermore refused any future letters from the Dutch sovereign. The shogunate had attempted to explain its policy to foreigners from the end of the eighteenth century, but this response to Holland serves as the clearest portrait of the Tokugawa framework of foreign relations yet.[46]

44   Matsukata, 'Reevaluating the "Recommendation to Open the Country"'.
45   Archives of Ministry of Foreign Affairs (2.05.01) 3147a, NA, The Hague.
46   Matsukata, 'Countries for Commercial Relations', Fujita, op. cit.

When Commodore Matthew Perry came to Uraga in 1853, he brought two letters from President Millard Fillmore both carrying the same date, i.e. 13 November 1853.[47] One, explaining the peaceful aim of Perry's dispatch, has been called a state letter in Japan. It functioned as a state letter, allowing Perry to be accepted as a diplomatic envoy in Japan. The other has been ignored in Japan but it was a credential for Perry to open another way of diplomacy. When the *bakufu* permitted him to negotiate, a new age of Japanese diplomacy started.

Works cited

Andrade, Tonio, 'Beyond Guns, Germs, and Steel: European Expansion and Maritime Asia, 1400-1750,' *Journal of Early Modern History,* 14 (2010), pp. 165-186.

Arano, Yasunori, 'Nihon-gata Kai Chitsujo no Keisei' [Formation of the Japanocentric World Order], in Asao Naohiro et al., eds., *Nihon no Shakaishi* [Social History of Japan], Vol. 1 (Tokyo: Iwanami Shoten, 1987).

Benton, Lauren and Clulow, Adam, 'Legal Encounters and the Origins of Global Law,' in *Cambridge History of the World, Volume 6* (Cambridge University Press, 2015), p. 82.

Blussé, Leonard, 'Amongst Feigned Friends and Declared Enemies', in Sølvi Sogner. ed., *Making sense of Global History: the 19th International Congress of the Historical Sciences, Oslo 2000, commemorative volume* (Universitetsforlaget, 2001).

Blussé, Leonard, 'Queen among Kings: Diplomatic Ritual at Batavia', in Kees Grijns and Peter Nas, eds., *Jakarta-Batavia: Socio-Cultural Essays.* Verhandelingen van het Koninklijk Instituut voor taal-, land- en volkenkunde 187 (Leiden: KITLV Press, 2000).

Clulow, Adam, *The Company and the Shogun: The Dutch Encounter with Tokugawa Japan* (New York: Columbia University Press, 2014).

Experiment and Return: Documents concerning the Japan Voyage of the English East India Company, 1671-3, transcribed & ed., with an introd., by Roger Machin (Kyoto: The Richard Cocks Society, 1978).

Fairbank, John K., ed., *The Chinese World Order: Traditional China's Foreign Relations* (Cambridge: Harvard University Press, 1968).

---

47   Unter Miller, ed., *Treaties and Other International Acts of the United States of America,* Vol. 6, pp. 526-528; Tōkyō Daigaku Shiryō Hensanjo, ed., *Dainihon komonjo: Bakumatsu gaikoku kankei monjo*, Vol. 1, Appendices I & II, pp. 1-6.

Fujita, Satoru, *Kinsei Kōki no Seijishi to Taigai Kankei* [*Political History and Foreign Relations of the Latter Half of the Edo Period*] (Tokyo: University of Tokyo Press, 2005).

Hashimoto, Yū, *Itsuwari no Gaikō Shisetsu: Muromachi-jidai no Nicchō Kankei* [*Diplomatic Envoys Faked: Japanese-Korean Relations in the Muromachi Period*] (Tokyo: Yoshikawakōbunkan, 2012).

Hesselink, Reinier H., *Prisoners from Nambu: Reality and Make-Believe in Seventeenth-Century Japanese Diplomacy* (Honolulu: The University of Hawai'i Press, 2002).

Ikoku Ōfuku Shokanshū & Zōtei Ikoku Nikki Shō [*Correspondence with Foreign Countries and Enlarged Extracts from Diary over Foreign Affairs*] translated and annotated by Naojiro Murakami (Tokyo: Sun'nansha 1929, reprint Yūshōdō Shoten, 1966, pp. 227-231.

Katō, Eiichi, *Bakuhansei Kokka no Seiritsu to Taigai Kankei* [*Formation of the Tokugawa Regime and its Foreign Relations*] (Kyoto: Shibunkaku Shuppan, 1998).

Kitagawa, Takako and Okamoto Makoto, 'Correspondence between Cambodia and Japan in the Seventeenth and Eighteenth Centuries', *Memoirs of the Research Department of the Toyo Bunko*, No. 73 (2016).

Koizumi, Junko, 'Ratanakōshinchō 1-sei Ō-ki Shamu no Taigai Kankei: Kōiki Chi'ikizō no Kentō ni muketa Yobiteki Kōsatsu [Siamese Inter-State Relations from a Regional Perspective: A Note on the Letters Exchanged between Siam and its Neighbouring States in the First Reign of the Rattanakosin Period], *Toyō Bunka Kenkyūjo Kiyō*, No. 154 (2008).

Koizumi, Junko, 'The "Last" Friendship Exchanges between Siam and Vietnam, 1879-1882: Siam between Vietnam and France-and Beyond', *Trans-Regional and National Studies of Southeast Asia*, 4-1 (2016): 131-164.

Caron, François. *Le Puissant Royaume du Japon: La description de François Caron (1636),* introduction & notes de Jacques & Marianne Proust (Paris: Chandeigne, 2003).

Masuda, Erika, 'Rāma 1-sei no Taishin Gaikō [Foreign Policy toward Ch'ing by Rama I]', *Tōnan Ajia: Rekishi to Bunka* [*Southeast Asia: History and Culture*] (1995): 25-48.

Masuda, Erika, 'The Fall of Ayutthaya and Siam's Disrupted Order of Tribute to China (1767-1782)', *Taiwan Journal of Southeast Asian Studies*, 4(2) (2007): 75-128.

Matsui, Yōko, 'The Legal Position of Foreigners in Nagasaki during the Edo Period,' in Haneda Masashi, ed., *Asian Port Cities 1600-1800: Local and Foreign Cultural Interactions* (Singapore: NUS Press, 2009).

Matsukata, Fuyuko, 'Countries for Commercial Relations (*Tsūshō-no-Kuni*): The Tokugawa Struggle to Control Chinese in Japan', *Maritime Worlds around the China Seas: Emporiums, Connections and Dynamics* (Taipei: Academia Sinica, forthcoming).

Matsukata, Fuyuko, *Oranda Fūsetsugaki to Kinsei Nihon* [*Dutch Reporting of World News During the Tokugawa Period: 1641-1859*] (Tokyo: University of Tokyo Press, 2007).

Matsukata, Fuyuko, translated by Adam Clulow, 'Reevaluating the 'Recommendation to Open the Country': The King of the Netherlands 1844 letter to the Tokugawa Shogun,' *Monumenta Nipponica*, 66-1 (2011).

Miller, Unter, ed., *Treaties and Other International Acts of the United States of America*, Vol. 6 (Washington: United States Government Printing Office, 1942), pp. 526-528.

Morikawa, Tomoko, 'Safāvī-chō no tai-Shamu Shisetsu to Indo Yō: "Sureiman no Fune" no Sekai', *Shihō* No.46 (2013).

Nagazumi, Yōko, '17-seiki Kōhan no Jōhō to Tsūji [Intelligence and Interpreters in the Seventeenth Century]', *Shigaku* 60-4 (1991).

Nagazumi, Yōko, *Kinsei Shoki no Gaikō* [*Diplomacy in Early Modern Japan*] (Tokyo: Sōbunsha, 1990).

Sannō, Masayo, '*Shindai Chūki ni okeru Sūrū to Chūgoku no Aida no Monjo Ōrai: Jawī Monjo to Kanbun Shiryō kara* [Diplomatic Correspondence between Sulu and China in the Mid-Qing Period: A Comparison between Jawi and Chinese Documents]', *Tōyō Gakuhō*, 91-1 (2009).

Shimizu, Yūko, *Kinsei Nihon to Ruson: 'Sakoku' Keiseishi Saikō* [*Early Modern Japan and Luzon: History of* 'Sakoku' *Formation Revisisted* (Tokyo: Tōkyōdō Shuppan, 2012).

Takagi, Shōsaku, *Nihon Kinsei Kokkashi no Kenkyū* [A Description of Early Modern State of Japan] (Tokyo: Iwanami Shoten, 1990).

Takano, Toshihiko, *Kinsei Nihon no Kokka Kenryoku to Shūkyō* [*The State and Religion of Early Modern Japan*] (Tokyo: University of Tokyo Press, 1989).

Tashiro, Kazui, *Kakikaerareta Kokusho: Tokugawa Chōsen Gaikō no Butai Ura* [*State Letters Revised: Background of Tokugawa-Korean Relations*] (Tokyo: Chūōkōronsha, 1983).

Toby, Ronald, 'Kinsei Shotō tai-Min no Ichi Gaikō Monjo Shohon no Keifu: Gosha, Godoku, Goki no Keifu to Nihon Gata Kai Ron [The textual fate of a Letter to Ming China: A Genealogy of copyist errors, misreadings and misprints and the 'Centrality of Japan' debate]', *Tōkyō Daigaku Shiryō Hensan-jo Kenkyū Kiyō* [*Research Annual of the Historiographical Institute*] 13 (Historiographical Institute, the University of Tokyo, 2003).

Toby, Ronald, *State and Diplomacy in Early Modern Japan* (New Jersey: Princeton University Press, 1984).

Tōkyō Daigaku Shiryō Hensanjo, eds., *Dainihon Komonjo: Bakumatsu Gaikoku Kankei Monjo*, Vol. 1, Reprint (Tokyo: University of Tokyo Press, 1972).

Tōkyō Daigaku Shiryō Hensanjo, eds., *Historical Documents in Foreign Languages Relating to Japan: Diaries Kept by the Heads of the Dutch Factory in Japan* (Original Texts) Vol. 11-12 (Tokyo: University of Tokyo Press, 2007-2013).

Yamamoto, Hirofumi, *Sakoku to Kaikin no Jidai* [*The Age of Seclusion and Maritime Ban*] (Tokyo: Azekura Shobō, 1995).

Contact details

Matsukata Fuyuko, c/o Historiographical Institute, University of Tokyo, 7-3-1 Hongo, Bunkyo-ku, Tokyo 113-0033 Japan
Tel.: +81-3-5841-5985 (direct)
Fax: +81-3-5841-5956
fuyuko@hi.u-tokyo.ac.jp
GZL11232@nifty.com

Part 2

Trade

4   Surat and Bombay

Ivory and commercial networks in western India

Martha Chaiklin

Abstract

The west coast of India and the east coast of Africa were linked through an exchange of cotton textiles for ivory. This trade was instrumental in the rise of Surat as a trading centre. Scholars have debated when the commercial centre of northwest India shifted from Surat to Bombay, with dates ranging from the beginning of the eighteenth century to the beginning of the nineteenth century. This chapter argues that Surat remained an important commercial entrepôt well into the nineteenth century because indigenous patterns of trade and consumption of ivory were tenacious and not easily altered by British attempts to shift activity to Bombay.

Keywords: ivory, Surat, Bombay, trade, bangles, boxwork

In the treasure trove of archaisms resides the term 'Bombay boxwork'.[1] Although not listed in the *Oxford English Dictionary*, it is nevertheless sprinkled throughout nineteenth-century sources. According to *Hobson-Jobson*, the classic Anglo-Indian dictionary originally published in 1886, it was 'a well-known manufacture'.[2] Bombay boxwork is a 'trade name' for wooden objects – boxes most famously, but desks, card cases, book stands and other wooden objects too – elaborately overlaid with micro-mosaic made from contrasting woods, horn and ivory, both natural and stained red or green.[3] This elaborate marquetry is formed from rods of various materials bound together with glue

---

1   A 'Bombay box', however, is a campaign box – a box with drawers and carrying handles on the sides that rests on a stand. The mail packet to the Bombay Presidency was also called the Bombay Box.

2   Yule and Burnell, *Hobson-Jobson*, p. 104.

3   *The Imperial Gazetteer of India*, The Indian Empire, Vol. III, p. 192, uses this phrase.

Clulow, Adam and Tristan Mostert (eds.), *The Dutch and English East India Companies: Diplomacy, trade and violence in early modern Asia*. Amsterdam: Amsterdam University Press, 2018
DOI: 10.5117/9789462983298/CH04

Figure 6   Bombay boxwork glovebox c. 1867.

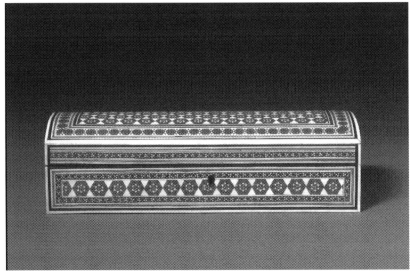

© Victoria and Albert Museum, London.

and then sliced into veneers that are affixed to a wooden base. Motifs are outlined in tin, silver or brass wire.[4] According to the Anglo-Indian official and craft historian George Birdwood, writing in the late nineteenth century, the technique originated in Shiraz (but it is also associated with Isfahan) in Persia, and was brought to Sindh, and finally to Surat and Bombay, in the late eighteenth century.[5] Birdwood appears to have underestimated the timing of the transfer, however, as descriptions exist for this type of object in Bombay from the mid-eighteenth century.[6] Beautiful yet reasonably priced, there was

4   Persian work uses yellow metal while Indian uses silver or tin. Pope and Ackerman, *A Survey of Persian Art from Prehistoric Times to the Present*, p. 2625.

5   See for example, Birdwood, *The Industrial Arts of India*, 2:39-40. Birdwood says it was transmitted from Bombay to Surat, and many other sources appear to have relied on him. By contrast *Hobson-Jobson* says transmission was from Surat to Bombay. If Moses (see note 6 below) is accurate, a Surat-to-Bombay transmission seems more likely, and according to *Report on the Administration of the Bombay Presidency*, p. 122, Surat was the centre of production. Birdwood relied on oral histories taken from artisans in Bombay but does not appear to have done the same in Surat. In Persia it was called *khambat bandi*, literally 'Cambay bound', in reference to the wires that surround the motif. Thanks to Peter Good for the translation.

6   The earliest reference I have uncovered to date is a description by Moses, *Sketches of India*, pp. 63-64. The estimate of late eighteenth century may stem from the flood of craftsmen who left Sindh in the unrest that preceded the establishment of Talpur rule in 1783. See Kennedy, *Narrative of the Campaign of the Army of the Indus in Sind and Kaubool in 1838-1839*, 1:105-106.

Figure 7   Components of Bombay boxwork. Before 1880.

© Victoria and Albert Museum, London.

great demand for them among Westerners.[7] In the 1870s at least, hundreds of workmen in Bombay were employed creating these objects.[8]

Today Bombay boxwork has largely disappeared from our consciousness. The craft itself is underrated, based mainly on an assumption that these objects were merely tourist art. That this was not the case is clear from the variety and, often, quality of extant examples and their relationship to architectural and other ornamentation. To contemporaries, this was considered such a representative craft of India that many objects adorned with this technique were sent to the major international exhibitions. A prize medal was even awarded to Atmaram Valeram of Bombay for his box at the Great Exhibition of 1851.[9] The appreciation of its quality can also be seen in the large, elaborate box produced for Queen Victoria on her Diamond

Some, such as Amin Jaffer, date the technique even earlier, as early as the late sixteenth century, but it is not clear whether the objects he identifies are merely micro-mosaic or specifically this technique. See Jaffer, *Luxury Goods from India*, pp. 19-21, 30-31.

7   Mrs Postans, 'Western India in 1838', *The Metropolitan Magazine*, Vol. 8 No. 103 (November 1839), p. 313. Some suggested that the use of materials was wasteful, but as Mrs Postans points out, this technique produces a detailed pattern relatively simply and rapidly.

8   *General Report on the Administration of the Bombay Presidency*, p. 375.

9   The inlaid items were in high demand at the fair. Rodrigues, 'Art Furniture and Household Decoration in the Nineteenth Century Bombay, p. 3.

Jubilee.[10] So-called Sindh-work appealed to Europeans precisely because it was perceived to be more authentic than objects supposedly degraded by their contact with Europeans.[11] Another cause for confusion is that this type of work is now generally called *sadeli*. This may or may not have been the original term (for example a work from 1871 calls it *mooltan*)[12] but, according to Sir George Watt, 'the expression was early made to embrace carved wood or ivory boxes' or any combination of the two, 'so long as they are made in Gujarat'.[13] There are several noteworthy aspects to Watt's statement. First, it is the oldest mention of the term *sadeli* that I have found in Western literature. Second, Bombay is not in Gujarat. Thus, the use of this Indian term has obscured a unique process by presenting a generic category including all kinds of carving and inlay. While Birdwood has been relied on as an authority, contemporary sources give many conflicting accounts about the spread of this technique, with reports indicating variously Bombay, Surat or the Punjab. There is no clear evidence to definitively establish the origins of Bombay boxwork in India, but when compared to ivory trade patterns, the developmental histories of Surat and Bombay and the migration patterns of Parsees (the most likely transmitters from Persia), Surat seems the likely candidate.

The tangled history of Bombay boxwork provides a concrete expression of the wider story of Surat and Bombay, each in its time the most important port on the west coast of India for the East India companies.[14] The designation 'Bombay' for this technique was a result of the decline of Surat and the rise of Bombay, a development that in turn represents the successful imposition of British power over earlier indigenous trading patterns. When exactly this transfer of power occurred is widely debated among scholars, with estimates ranging from the death of Aurangzeb in 1707 to the 1730s to the end of the

---

10   Wales, *Souvenirs from the Diamond Jubilee of Queen Victoria,* p. 57. It is not clear whether it was ever actually presented. However, the Parsi community of Surat and the cities of Bombay and Surat both presented her with cases of carved or inlaid ivory. For example; *International Exhibition St. Louis, 1904.*

11   Markovits, *The Global World of Indian Merchants,* p. 116. Markovits does not specifically mention *sadeli,* but it was known to have been produced in Hyderabad.

12   Balfour, *The Cyclopaedia of Indian and Eastern and Southern Asia 1,* p. 575. This refers to Multan in the Punjab region of present-day Pakistan. Some scholars, like Louiza Rodrigues, place its origins there. Rodrigues, 'Art Furniture', 1. Yet another name used was 'Bombay mosaic'. See *Review of some of the Principal Acquisitions during the year 1931,* p. 45. It was also produced in Ahmedabad.

13   Watt, *Indian Art at Delhi,* p. 156.

14   Although the city has officially been renamed Mumbai, it is still widely referred to as Bombay and since this name appears in the sources as well, it will be used here.

eighteenth century.[15] Chronological precision is important because the shift from Surat to Bombay represents a milestone for the British Empire. In recent years, scholars have argued persuasively for the continuing importance of Surat. As Ghulam Nadri has noted, the rise of Bombay did not mean the end of Surat.[16] The question as to when Bombay rose and Surat fell depends to a large extent on whether we are looking at political, commercial or military power. In this chapter, I argue that Surat and other port cities proved remarkably resilient even after the arrival of European trading companies like the Dutch and English East India Companies and the rise of colonial entrepôts like Bombay, and that this can be seen clearly in the persistence of indigenous trading patterns oriented around ivory. A key component for Bombay boxwork, ivory is typically ignored or relegated to a list of trade commodities in these ports. This is in part because scholars tend to rely on European sources which do not always reflect local conditions. Yet ivory was a significant reason why the commercial centre of power remained in Surat long after British political and military power had shifted to Bombay, and even after the VOC had collapsed completely. The ivory trade did transfer from Surat to Bombay but it took some two hundred years for the British Empire to triumph over traditional trade patterns.

A tale of two cities

The histories of Surat and Bombay are intertwined, but this story begins in Surat. From the late sixteenth century through to at least the early eighteenth century Surat was, as François Bernier called it, 'that famous and rich port of the Indies'.[17] It was a vital stop along key trading routes that spanned much of the globe. According to one early scholar, 'Surat proved to be the gateway to European domination in India'.[18] Although insignificant until the sixteenth century, it surpassed earlier centres like Cambay, which declined largely because extreme silting of the bay made access increasingly

---

15   See e.g. Rothermund, *Asian Trade and European Expansion* for support for the death of Aurangzeb; Das Gupta *The World of the Indian Ocean Merchant,* for the 1730s.

16   Nadri, 'Revisiting the "Decline of Surat"'.

17   Bernier, *Travels in the Mogul Empire*, p. 188.

18   Gokale, *Surat in the Seventeenth Century*, p. 147. This opinion is seconded by Metha, *Indian Merchants and Entrepreneurs in Historical Perspective*, p. 33. The Companies never established a presence of similar significance in the region, although ports like eighteenth-century Mandvi in Kachh, for example, were certainly important to indigenous traders and as part of the VOC network that supported their factory in Surat. See Nadri, 'Exploring the Gulf of Kachh'.

difficult for large oceangoing vessels.[19] The Dutch and English East India Companies arrived in Surat at roughly the same time, the first decade of the seventeenth century, but neither was able to establish stable factories until the 1620s. For the Dutch, Surat was not as politically important on the west coast as Kochi, but it was significant nonetheless as a vital link in trade networks. Because textiles were so important to the inhabitants of the spice-growing regions in Southeast Asia, it was vital for the Companies to establish contacts with high-quality cotton-producing regions like Gujarat where such commodities could be obtained at relatively low prices.[20] For the English, Surat was the first foothold for the Company in India, and for nearly a century it was their most important factory and a crucial launch pad for future expansion. Both Companies sought a base specifically in Surat for two main reasons. First, it enabled them to bypass the Portuguese presence in Goa and other locations along the west coast. At the same time, a stronghold on the northwest coast of India could serve to challenge Portuguese supremacy in the Arabian Sea.[21] As a Mughal port from the late sixteenth century, Surat was neutral, and it was this status that kept it shielded, at least to some extent, from attack.[22] At the same time, the Mughal rulers encouraged Europeans because the primary revenue of the city was through customs duties.

Many exports passed through the busy port of Surat, including coir (coconut fibre), coral, iron and lead, but cotton was king. Whether raw or woven, cotton was the most significant export because it could be traded for spices in Southeast Asia.[23] Without cotton, products much in demand in Europe including spices and tea would have required bullion (and often still did), a significant drain on profitability. Thus, for the Dutch, and especially for the English, the northwest coast was an essential site for expansion. The VOC was drawn to Surat because a higher return on spices could be obtained, especially for cloves, than in Coromandel, another textile source. Sales of spices in Mocha generally covered any shortfall.[24] This dynamic

19   It did, nevertheless, retain prominence in the early seventeenth century and remained a secondary location for ivory into the eighteenth century. See e.g. British Library India Office Records (hereafter referred to as IOR) IOR G/36/11 1724 ff 20 for records of elephants' teeth brought to Khambat.

20   See Andaya, 'The Cloth Trade in Jambi'.

21   Cavaliero, *Strangers in the Land,* p. 8.

22   It was plundered early on by the Portuguese in 1512, 1530 and 1531, at the height of Portuguese aggression in the immediate area. Randar, Daman and Diu were greater prizes.

23   Even in 2015, Gujarat was the top cotton-producing state in India. Ahmed, 'Gujarat top cotton producing state, harvests 108 lakh bale'. In some periods, China was also important.

24   Israel, *Dutch Primacy in World Trade,* p. 178.

made Surat the lynchpin for VOC trade in the region and a port city second in importance only to Batavia.

In the seventeenth century, the VOC enjoyed more success in Surat than its English rival, in large part because the Dutch had better-developed trading networks. The VOC could supply the market more effectively and as a consequence the organisation had better relations with local middlemen and Mughal officials. By the time the EIC offered any serious competition, the VOC was firmly entrenched. This dynamic fluctuated, but Dutch dominance continued until the last two decades of the existence of the VOC when Coromandel began drawing some of the textile trade.[25] The Dutch factory was ultimately ceded to the EIC in 1796 after the Netherlands fell to Napoleon. Although it was returned in 1815, by the time Dutch commerce rebounded, Bombay was well established. Declining Dutch economic and political power in Surat had less to do with greater English effectiveness than the breakdown of the VOC through a decline of intra-Asian trade and supplies of Japanese copper.

In contrast, the EIC in Surat had to contend not just with VOC competition but with the various layers of Mughal bureaucracy as well as local commercial powers. Even in the early eighteenth century when Mughal power was in decline, these frictions caused problems for the EIC.[26] With a less reliable supply of products desired in Surat, the EIC was more reliant on imports of bullion. As a result, the EIC competed with other Europeans, which included at times the French, Danish, and Swedish Companies, and legal and illegal private trade, but especially the Dutch. It took almost a century for the British to firmly establish a foothold. By the time this had been accomplished, there were already official efforts to shift British trade to Bombay.

It took decades for Bombay to rival Surat. The English took over the seven islands that comprised Bombay from the Portuguese in 1668, when they were presented to Charles II as part of the dowry of Catherine of Braganza. Difficulties beset the site from the start, as the Portuguese initially refused even to hand over the territory. It was nevertheless officially made the EIC headquarters in 1687. Even though the English had good reason to shift operations from Surat, the move to Bombay did not make it an important commercial or political centre. Bombay was known for its noxious climate, rife with malarial mosquitos, and a territory comprised of islands was not conducive to growth. Despite serious efforts to move trade there as early as

25   Shimada, *The Intra-Asian Trade in Copper by the Dutch East India Company*, p. 107.
26   IOR G/36/10, 26 February 1719.

1718, growth required an expensive land reclamation project, only begun in the mid-eighteenth century, to connect the islands.[27] Thus, even in the 1730s, when according to some scholars Surat had already slipped from its position of dominance, Sir Robert Cowan (d. 1737), president and governor of Bombay from 1729 to 1734, complained he could not make inroads into the Surat trade because of fierce local competition.[28]

Perhaps even more importantly, a wide range of political conditions impeded growth in Bombay. Maratha admiral Kanhoji Angre (1669-1729) and his sons caused considerable disruption to shipping after he took office in 1698 or 1699 and well into the 1730s. On both land and sea, the Marathas continued to be a problem for the EIC for much of the eighteenth century. Mysore, to the south, also caused problems for the English, blocking connections further down the coast. Even in the late eighteenth century, the EIC was not able to bypass the Gujarati weaver contract system and make direct contracts to control production.[29] The Portuguese still controlled much of the Indian Ocean until the mid-eighteenth century. Once Bombay was viable, the English became more aggressive. By the time the Dutch Company folded, the English were well placed in Bombay. Lack of control over ivory, however, prevented Bombay from becoming the most important trading centre.

Ivory in western India

As an import *into* India, ivory has received little attention, but it was vital to trading networks in the early modern period. Moreover, as art historian Ananda Coomeraswamy has commented, 'no other craft would throw more light on the history and migrations of designs in India than this'.[30] It was key to the development and ongoing prosperity of both Surat and Bombay, and its history provides us with a better picture of the complex interaction of European and indigenous networks in western India. Nevertheless, the study of ivory is difficult because, although it appears regularly in Company trade documents, the entries are fragmented and scattered. In the early modern period, Europeans could not control points of supply, as ivory was sourced from many different outlets, including European trading companies,

27   IOR G/36/10, 10 August 1718.
28   Marshall, 'Private British Trade in the Indian Ocean before 1800', p. 115.
29   Nightingale, *Trade and Empire in Western India* , p. 150.
30   Coomaraswamy, *The Arts and Crafts of India and Ceylon*, p. 182.

Asian maritime traders and caravans. Nor were Europeans involved in its production because nearly all ivory was shipped as tusks rather than finished goods. Thus, although scholars have recognised that ivory flowed into Surat, they saw little consequence in it beyond the fact that it was one of a series of commodities brought to Gujarat.

The importance of ivory does not undercut the significance of cotton to Gujarat. Rather it was a function of it. Since the Companies did not want to pour their gold, silver and copper bullion into India, a trade commodity in demand in India was needed to exchange for raw cotton and cotton and silk textiles. It was not a direct exchange – the goods still needed to be sold on the market – but specie acquired locally was not a drain on money supplies in Europe. Ivory was in high demand in Gujarat, creating a sort of ouroboros, where cotton textiles were needed to obtain ivory, and ivory was needed to obtain cotton textiles. The symbiotic relationship formed through imports of ivory into India and exports of textiles to Africa is evidenced by a variety of external factors. For example, famines in Africa affected the amount of ivory available in Surat because the disruption to the East African economy denied local ivory middlemen the income to purchase Surati fabrics.[31] As long as this pattern of supply and demand was fairly constant, the exchange remained profitable for all parties. Even when the tusks were cracked, small or oddly shaped, they could still bring in profit.[32]

This connection between eastern Africa and northwestern India is a crucial piece of the story, but it can be swiftly summarised. The Gujarat–East Africa circuit of cotton and ivory was a vital part of Portuguese trade from the sixteenth century. Moreover, Gujarati cotton and textiles were important in other Portuguese trade sites, such as Brazil. It is for this reason that from the sixteenth to the eighteenth centuries, when Portuguese power in East Africa was at its apex, mentions of ivory outstrip even those of slaves in Portuguese records. Indeed, ivory trafficking exceeded human trafficking in export value from East Africa during this period.[33] Portuguese trade to India was primarily through Goa, which had its own ivory industry (albeit one of a very different sort) and secondarily through Diu. However, to obtain the Gujarati textiles in demand in Africa and later Brazil, Portuguese ships offloaded some ivory in Surat. Although the difficulty of obtaining supplies hindered English commerce in ivory until the mid-seventeenth

31   Sheriff, *Slaves, Spices & Ivory in Zanzibar*, pp. 84-85.
32   Maharashtra State Archives (hereafter referred to as MSA) Public Diary No. 8 (1734-35), ff. 238.
33   Beachy, 'The East African Ivory Trade in the Nineteenth Century,' p. 269.

century, the EIC worked actively to expand its trade of ivory in Asia in the seventeenth century in order to challenge Portuguese supremacy.[34] The English company's increasing success at finding supplies was a concern for VOC officials, who wanted to know where they were getting it.[35] For the Dutch and English Companies, Surat became the locus for ivory trade, whether it was to be worked locally or transshipped within India or other destinations further east like Java, China or Japan. The shift of South Asian trade to the Gulf caused by VOC spice monopolies also worked toward increasing this trade.

Ivory concentered in Surat from a range of sources. All European trading companies offloaded significant amounts of ivory in the port while Indian traders likewise purchased ivory from Africa or Muscat to bring to Surat, which was also the endpoint for caravans from Persia, Russia, central Asia and points south and west. Ivory was a significant reason that Surat remained a vital commercial centre long after British political and military power had shifted to Bombay, and even after the VOC had collapsed completely. Thus, even after Mughal control ceded in Surat, traders preferred to discharge their cargo there rather than in Bombay as that was where the market was.[36] Until the early nineteenth century, about 80 percent of ivory imports into Surat and Bombay remained in India, the remainder going to China and Southeast Asia, with small proportions going to Europe.[37] Surat was not only home to ivory traders; it was also where the craftsmen were located. This pattern continued until late in the nineteenth century, when European demand escalated considerably while it remained stagnant in India. Thereafter, as British power increased, the proportion (rather than the amount) that remained in India decreased. Thus, Bombay as an ivory centre expanded because of demands for ivory in England, rather than as a result of the usurpation of the historical networks of Surat.[38]

---

34   Bal, *Commercial Relations between India and England*, p. 115; Chaudhuri, *The Trading World of Asia and the English East India Company*, p. 216.

35   In the seventeenth and early eighteenth centuries, it was primarily Guinea and privateering. See e.g. VOC archives, Nationaal Archief in The Hague (hereafter referred to as VOC) 11326, September 1743, abstracts of correspondence expressing concern that the English were obtaining ivory from Africa.

36   Chaudhuri, *The Trading World*, p. 106.

37   Sheriff, *Slaves, Spices & Ivory in Zanzibar*, pp. 85-86.

38   Ibid.

Bangles before boxes

Why was there such consistent demand for ivory in Surat? Gujarat and Maharasthra (where the provinces Surat and Bombay, respectively, are located) rarely appear in histories of Indian ivory, even though humans have used and worked ivory in the region since at least the Indus Valley civilisations circa 3000 BCE. The ancient peoples of the region even traded ivory to Sumer and Mesopotamia. This trade disappeared in the seventh century for indeterminate reasons. Thereafter there is no record of significant ivory exports from anywhere in India, much less Gujarat, until the nineteenth century, when elephants were systematically exploited by the British. Moreover, Gujarat and Maharasthra have not been home to large populations of elephants in the last millennium. Elephants maintained in that region were used primarily by Mughal officials for ceremonial purposes. Animals like horses, bullocks and camels were used for draft and transportation. Additionally, while Surat is relatively close to the coast, it is not close enough to be a natural location for Indian Ocean trade, an inconvenience only partially offset by the fact that the Tapti River by which the city is located is one of the few Indian rivers that run east to west, providing access to weavers and interior markets. Therefore, geographically, Surat might seem an odd place to become the ivory emporium of India.

The answer to this conundrum lies in local custom, which mandated ivory as an important material of cultural expression. It was not driven by elite patronage as is often the stimulus for art and craft production, but rather by ivory bangles. These bracelets, made of every possible material, are the most widely worn item of jewellery in India, an essential part of any woman's wardrobe. As an animal product, wearing ivory was eschewed by Hindus in some regions, but in Gujarat, as well as surrounding areas like Rajasthan and Sindh, ivory bangles were commonly tied to wedding and marriage rituals, not just by Hindus, but Muslims and Parsees as well. The number, size and decoration of the bracelets varied by region, caste or ethnicity, and by income, as did the customs surrounding them. In the recent past, in Rajasthan and Gujarat, a full set consisted of 52 bangles, 26 on each arm. In general, it was believed that ivory bangles would keep the bride healthy and assure easy childbirth.[39] They were often coloured red, an auspicious colour, with madder dye or lac. As a symbol of marriage, wedding bangles had to be new rather than second-hand.[40] Thus, these

---

39   Untracht, *Traditional Jewelry of India*, p. 70.
40   Martin with Vigne, 'The Decline and Fall of India's Ivory Industry', p. 8.

Figure 8   Woman wearing ivory-like   Figure 9   Modern Punjabi-style wedding
           bangles, Rajasthan, c. 2011.   *chura*. Resin to look like ivory
                                                           with lac, 2017.

Photograph by Christopher Michel.   Photograph by the author.

bangles were often destroyed with the cremation of the body upon death, or smashed on becoming a widow, creating a continuous demand that was not subject to the vagaries of fashion.[41] It was this demand that brought ivory to Surat. Thus, ivory was not a coincidental import into Gujarat that developed as supplies appeared, but rather increased supplies merely allowed use to extend to greater numbers of women.[42] Western-language sources take scant notice of what must have been a significant industry because it was one that Europeans did not control or directly profit from. Yet bangles were clearly the driving force behind the ivory trade to Surat.

Contemporary reports vary as to the construction method of traditional ivory bangles. Ivory tusks are partially hollow from the root to accommodate tooth pulp and nerve, and solid toward the tip. According to William Milburn, the hollow part of the tusk was used, while nearly a century later Cecil Burns, artist and principal of the Bombay School of Art from 1899 to 1918, describes a lathe method used in Sindh in which graduated bangles are cut from a solid section.[43] What methods were used in which regions at what times is a matter for further research, but the method Burns describes appears to have been less common and probably used for more expensive, carved sets. Milburn further noted that the solid pieces could be obtained at

41   See Chaiklin, 'Surat: City of Ivory', pp. 226-231.
42   Chaudhuri, *The Trading World*, p. 222.
43   Milburn, *Oriental Commerce*, p. 62. Burns, *Monograph on Ivory Carving*, p. 3. Additionally, according to the *Universal History* of 1749, 'Their artisans show great genius [...] in turning and working in ivory, a staple commodity among them, which they polish with infinite beauty and dexterity'.

bargain prices because the value was in the hollow pieces for bangles.[44] In either case, a larger tusk is required to produce rings with a diameter large enough to fit over the hand, and in some regions the upper arms or ankles as well. On the average, Asian elephant tusks are smaller and narrower than those of either species of African elephant. Thus, the demand in Surat was not just for ivory, but specifically African ivory. Smaller tusks had little value in this market.[45] Tusks of appropriate size were actually called 'bangle tusks', while hollow sections from the upper two thirds were called 'bangle ivory' or 'bangle pieces'.[46] The most desirable tusks fetching the highest prices were medium-sized, not too pointy and relatively straight – over 60 bangles could be cut from these.[47] However, if we assume that Milburn was correct, there were significant portions of the tusk available for other uses. Moreover, Dutch sources make clear that the demand was not exclusively for African ivory.[48] Thus, Surat also became known for producing ivory combs, spinning tops, chess pieces, carvings of vegetables, and from perhaps the eighteenth century if not earlier, Bombay boxwork.[49]

Artisans of ivory were almost always located in urban areas, because the materials were too expensive for village craftsmen to purchase. Craftsmen received materials from merchants on spec, and were then paid for labour. While this relationship has not been documented in Western sources, it was the process followed for gold jewellery and similarly luxurious crafts in India, and many other parts of the world too. Ivory craftsmen did not belong to any particular caste or religion.[50] It was the prosperity of Surat in the late sixteenth and seventeenth centuries that brought ivory artisans

44   Milburn, *Oriental Commerce*, p. 62.

45   See e.g. the report from Laus Deo in Surat in 1609, 'The Prices of Goods in India', 30 August 1609 in Frederic Danvers, Vol. 1, p. 33. 'Elephants teeth that are large and sound (the small being worth nothing)'.

46   The earliest instance I have found for 'bangle tusk' is in *The British Trade and Export World*, Vol. 23. But it was probably in use much earlier than that. 'Bangle ivory' is found in Milburn from 1813 and later. It is specifically defined as the hollow part in Consul Webster, 'The Sheffield Cutlery Industry', in *Commercial Relations of the United States – Reports from the Consuls of the United States on the Commerce, Manufacture, etc. of their Consular Districts*, No. 25, pp. 46-49, at p. 49. Some sources call this 'cutch ivory'. See e.g. M'Culloch, *A Dictionary, Practical, Theoretical, and Historical of Commerce and Commercial Navigation*, p. 792.

47   Burton, *The Lake Regions of Central Africa*, p. 540; Untracht, *Traditional Jewelry*, p. 170.

48   E.g. VOC 11326 No. 186. A letter complaining that no elephant's teeth were available in Surat because the ships had not arrived in Batavia on time. These ships would most likely have had Siamese or Burmese ivory.

49   Burns, *Monograph*, p. 10.

50   Coomaraswamy, *The Indian Craftsman*, p. 8. Coomaraswamy did not specifically reference ivory craftsmen but wrote generally of urban craftsmen.

to the port.[51] Although some interpretations have Surat in decline by the early eighteenth century as Mughal control deteriorated, the number of craftsmen actually surged in Surat after the fall of Ahmedabad, where many Mughal elites resided, to Maratha forces in 1757.[52] A quarter century later this contingent was swelled by Sindhi craftsmen escaping chaos there. This influx of skilled craftsmen may well have contributed to the spread of Bombay boxwork. This merchant–craftsman relationship drew ivory to Surat, underpinning its continued centrality. Well into the nineteenth century, even if English ships offloaded in Bombay, the ivory still had to be brought to Surat, because that is where the craftsmen resided.[53]

The shifting of the market

The importance of ivory to shipping patterns on the northwestern coast of India thus lay in part in the locality of craft networks, but it was also connected to supply. Surat was an open market for much of the early modern period. Indigenous ship owners and merchants, caravan traders, private merchants and even Company servants conducting private trade on their own account all brought ivory to Surat. From there, they exchanged their goods for ivory and returned. Unlike textiles, nutmeg, cloves or coffee, for which production could be controlled to some extent, ivory supply was reliant on what came to market. Supplies were erratic, often obtained through transshipment, and were frequently part of poorly documented private trade.

In the early seventeenth century, the Dutch were much better placed to source ivory as the EIC had few strongholds anywhere, much less on ivory trade routes, where the Portuguese and Dutch had preceded them. Thus, despite the shifting of political power to Bombay, very little ivory was offloaded there. This is evident in the *Europa* incident of 1728 which involved the governor of Bombay, Sir Robert Cowan. He allowed the *Europa*, a Portuguese vessel, to offload cargo, including ivory, in Bombay. Although Cowan called the allegations that he had a personal financial interest in the private trade of this cargo 'false and malicious aspersions', he was nevertheless dismissed from Company service for so conspicuously violating EIC rules against

51   See e.g. *The Modern Part of a Universal History,* Vol. 10, p. 224.
52   Forbes, *Oriental Letters,* p. 258.
53   MSA Committee Custom Revision Diary 1/187 1817, ff. 3.

direct competition with the products it traded.[54] Cowan denied receiving
anything off the ship except a present of 'six hams, eight dozen of French
& Oporto wine & a pound of snuff' from the commander.[55] Nevertheless,
Cowan's very decision to offload ivory in Bombay was suspicious given the
market was in Surat, and was most likely made in an unsuccessful attempt
to avoid drawing attention to his illicit private trading activities.

Trade patterns set in place in the sixteenth century were not easily
disrupted. The merchants knew the system in Surat and early attempts to
change the balance of power were not successful. This is evident in the case of
English agent Bhimji Parekh (1610-1686). In 1669, he persuaded a large group of
merchants (8,000 according to some sources) to leave Surat for Bombay, where
he had been on English business, because of heavier taxation of non-Muslims
in Surat as compared to Bombay. It was a premature move for Bombay and
even the English did not support this migration because they feared Mughal
repercussions, so they returned to Surat.[56] Similar episodes occurred well into
the eighteenth century. For example, the EIC tried to lure Surati goldsmiths to
Bombay to mint coins in 1749 and they refused because they thought it might
damage their reputation as elite craftsmen if they went to the newer port.[57]
Thus, plans to shift trade to Bombay were not easily accomplished despite the
best efforts of the English company. Even in the 1760s, EIC Company servant
John Henry Grose described Surat as 'the centre of the Indian trade'.[58]

It was not until Mughal power declined that Bombay finally emerged as a
viable alternative.[59] The breakdown of the Mughal system caused some merchants to seek greener pastures in Bombay.[60] One significant shift involved the
migration of shipbuilders that began in the mid-eighteenth century. However,
this remained a slow process. Certainly, many factors worked against Surat,
including the further silting of the river and several disastrous fires, yet even
these difficulties proved not enough to alter trade patterns. The British were
ultimately unable to change trade patterns on their own. The government art
school established in Bombay in 1857 with the idea of adapting Indian crafts
for commercial markets was not successful for this reason. The art school in

---

54   Prakash, 'English Private Trade in the Western Indian Ocean'; Forrest, *Selections from
the Letters, Dispatches and Other State Papers Preserved in the Bombay Secretariat* (Bombay:
Government Central Press, 1887), p. xl.

55   MSA Public Diary 7 ff 234.

56   Gokhale, *Surat*, pp. 119-122.

57   Barendse, *Arabian Seas 1700-1763*, 1: 888.

58   Grose, *A Voyage to the East Indies*, p. 71.

59   White, *Competition and Collaboration*, p. 23.

60   VOC 11326 Letter 19 ff 186 for an example.

Bombay and similar schools in Madras and Calcutta were in European centres of government and commerce but they were not where the craftsmen were.[61]

For Bombay to emerge ahead of its rivals it was necessary to create a new circuit of cotton and ivory, but the city did not become a significant source for cotton thread until Bombay Spinning and Weaving was founded 1854, and industrial-scale weaving did not commence until about 1860.[62] Only when the American civil war cut off supplies of American cotton and machine-woven textiles did Bombay begin to create its own ivory and textile ouroboros.[63] As textile production moved there and transportation costs declined, Bombay became an industrial centre that drew more and more people into its orbit. This created a new market for a small coterie of bangle craftsmen who shifted there to supply bangles to Gujarati and Rajasthani migrants.[64]

As this account suggests, Surat remained important commercially even as it lost political power. It was the main destination for ivory from Zanzibar well into the nineteenth century.[65] Even a reduction of customs in Bombay about 1817, from 5 percent in Surat, to 3½ percent in Bombay, was not sufficient to bring about change.[66] However, sourcing from Zanzibar shifted the balance of power. When Portuguese Mozambique was the main source, this ivory was brought to Surat by Indian traders who acquired it in Africa or Muscat, or caravans which brought it overland. As the English took control of Zanzibar over the course of the nineteenth century, they gradually routed supply into Bombay.[67] Other ivory procurement sources such as Melinde (Kenya) also fell under English control. However, rival Portuguese trade continued as before to Surat as there was no benefit for them to move into the English stronghold.[68]

Surat down but not out

Craftsmen follow their patrons. The population of Bombay grew with migrants and Westerners, and the number of craftsmen grew along with

61   Rarapor, 'John Lockwood Kipling & the Arts and Crafts Movement in India', p. 14.
62   Goody, *The East in the West*, p. 133.
63   Presholdt, *Domesticating the World*, p. 79.
64   Martin with Vigne, 'India's Ivory Industry', p. 17. They wrote of five craftsmen in 1978 but one can assume that this is the tail end of a trend rather than the beginning.
65   See Smee, 'Proceedings at Zanzibar'; Bird, 'Commercial and Geographical View of Eastern Africa', p. 114.
66   MSA Committee Custom Revision Diary 1/187 1817, ff. 3.
67   Sheriff, *Slaves, Spices and Ivory*, p. 84.
68   Bauss, 'Textiles, Bullion and other Trades of Goa', p. 281.

it. As Victorian travel writer Mrs Eliot Montauban noted, 'For beautiful specimens of ivory, inlaid with silver mosaic, made into the most
captivating work boxes, elegant baskets and seducing little nicknacks
[sic] of all shapes and sizes and for every variety of purpose, the fame
of Bombay has spread far and wide.'[69] However, her observation should
not be taken as a denial of the importance of Surati ivory. She was not
making comparisons, nor does she note the production of bangles or combs
or other non-Westernised objects. Although these things were almost
certainly produced there, Bombay does not appear to have ever become
the significant production centre that Surat was at its peak. Bombay
was better known in the West because many of its craftsmen catered to
European markets or Westerners in India.[70] It was a colonial centre rather
than a commercial hub underpinned by indigenous demand or royal
patronage. The objects that were produced there tended to be for export
or for resident Westerners. This meant that something decorative like
Bombay boxwork could flourish, but high-quality art production, which
required patronage, or bulk production like bangles did not completely
shift because the main markets for those items were in Gujarat and other
regions north.

Other forces worked in combination to undermine Surat's role as an ivory
entrepôt. The abolition of the slave trade reduced the need for Gujarati
textiles. At the same time, European demand for cotton from Gujarat fell
because the quality of English textiles improved.[71] The ouroboros was
further eroded in the second half of the nineteenth century due to a surge
in ivory demand in Europe and America, in part because mass production
techniques had been developed for ivory. The functionality of ivory was
put to wide use in everything from knife handles to billiard balls and piano
keys. It is around this time that the phrase 'Bombay ivory' came into use
in the West. The term evolved from the practice of ships' papers listing
commodities by the port from which the vessel cleared.[72] Within India,
the same phrase referred to imported ivory.[73] These shifting patterns of
ivory demand led to a direct competition for ivory supplies, to the extent
that an American consular report from Zanzibar claimed, 'Bombay ivory

69   Montauban, *A Year and a Day in the East*, p. 50.

70   Roy, *Traditional Industry in the Economy of Colonial India*, p. 25.

71   *Imperial Gazetteer*, p. 176.

72   Holtzappfel, *Turning and Mechanical Manipulation*, p. 142.

73   Palit, *Sketches of Indian Economics*, p. 294. According to the author, this referred to hard
ivory, which would have excluded East African ivory. However, the demand for East African
ivory was largely on the west coast of India.

[...] comprises everything that is not suitable for other markets'.[74] In other words, better quality tusks were being redirected to other markets. Declining demand for Indian cotton and increased global demand for ivory altered the kinds of ivory going to India.

This displacement of early modern trading patterns is apparent in the observations of Charles Frederick Holder, a curator at the American Museum of Natural History and author of *The Ivory King*, that in the 1880s in the warehouses of F. Grote & Company of New York one could 'find numbers of rings of ivory that [were] awaiting shipment back to Bombay, where they will be sold as bangles or bracelets to Hindoo [sic] women'.[75] In other words, the solid portions of tusk, valued higher in the West, were retained, while only the hollow portions were sent back to India. American incursion into this market was most likely the result of increased American (and French) trade directly to Zanzibar.[76] Transport costs had dropped enough to make these new routes viable. Thus, from the 1870s until about 1915, Bombay was the third largest ivory market in the world .[77]

Yet even as British power pulled ivory to Bombay, it remained fundamentally a place of transshipment until perhaps 1850 or 1860. Private traders continued to bring ivory to Surat, either directly or after it had been offloaded in Bombay, throughout the tenure of the EIC. As the nineteenth century progressed, ivory was still brought to Surat, but less and less by European traders. In the end, Surat never entirely disappeared as an important link in a wider trading network until sometime in the twentieth century, because it remained a producer of textiles and bangle manufacturing centre. Cecil L. Burns noted in 1900 that Surat was still trading bangles and other small items to Bombay.[78] By 1913, all ivory carving was in decay in the region, supporting only some 554 people in the whole of the Bombay Presidency.[79] Changing lifestyles and declining

---

74   *Letter of the Secretary of State transmitting a report on the Commercial Relations of the United States with Foreign Nations for the Year Ended September 30, 1865*, p. 506. This report also says that ivory for bangles is called 'cutch ivory'.

75   Holder, *The Ivory King*, p. 221. This company was established in 1847. They were located at 114 E. 14th Street and lasted at least until 1899.

76   Bird, 'Commercial and Geographical View of Eastern Africa', p. 117; Postans, 'Some account of the present state of the trade', p. 170.

77   Martin with Vigne, 'India's Ivory Industry', p. 6. The other major markets were in London and Antwerp.

78   Burns, *Monograph*, p. 9.

79   *A Review of the Administration of the Presidency*, p. 151. Only 120 remained in Gujarat in 1978 and 3000 in Kerala. Martin with Vigne, 'Indian Ivory', pp. 16, 20.

supplies led to greater attrition. Women stopped destroying their bangles, or began to replace them with cheaper celluloid imitations from Germany or Japan. A government-sponsored survey conducted by G.P. Fernandes in 1926, a date significantly later than the period under examination here, is one of the earliest detailed examinations in the region. Noting ivory production in a variety of areas and its decay, he lists Ahmedabad and Surat as the only places of significance for ivory carving in the Bombay Presidency.[80] Fernandes found a mere 25 to 50 ivory artisans in Surat (and about an equal number in Ahmedabad), of whom only half knew the art of Bombay boxwork, which was inaccurately described as inlay.[81] He maintained that 'This art is now dying out, and something must be done to preserve it.' Fernandes further stated that the market was in Bombay and that the value was 200-300 percent above the intrinsic cost of materials. They did better than the artists making things such as bangles, buttons, rings, combs and stick handles, ear ornaments and chains. The output of the latter was estimated at only 5 percent above cost because competition with London for raw materials had driven the cost of materials up. Fernandes makes it evident that ivory only went to Surat via Bombay.[82]

Conclusion

Ivory was much more than just another profitable import into western India. It underpinned both early modern European and indigenous trading patterns and was driven by specific local demand for bangles. Ivory was not always profitable (although losses were usually insignificant) but it was a means through which Europeans could gain access to regional trading networks.[83] More important, ivory shows us that an overemphasis on European – especially Dutch and English East India Companies – documents and perspectives can cause us to miss important clues to wider trading patterns. Looking at the history of this commodity shows us that Surat

80   Ahmedabad is not discussed in this chapter because the artisans there had direct patronage from elites.

81   He lists twenty-five artisans who did Bombay boxwork under sandalwood carving, and fifty artisans of 'ivory and tortoiseshell', so it is difficult to know exactly how and what he was counting.

82   Martin with Vigne 'India's Ivory Industry', p. 8; Burns, *Monograph*, pp. 9-10.

83   VOC 11328 ff. 49-52 for a breakdown of profits and losses for the eighteenth century through 1759.

Figure 10   Boxmakers of Bombay, c. 1873.

© The British Library Board.

remained important as a commercial and production centre into the
nineteenth century, well after its presumed demise, because it was linked
to indigenous trading patterns and cultural traditions. Bombay only sup-
planted Surat when technology and imperialism altered the composition
of these networks.

Bombay boxwork is no longer produced in Surat or Bombay. Ivory
has been restricted in India since 1972, and the passage of CITES, the
Convention on International Trade in Endangered Species of Wild Fauna
and Flora, in 1989 ended all exports. These measures marked the end of
a declining market, which had been undercut by global demand and the
spread of plastics. The custom of wedding bangles continues even today
with ivory-coloured plastics, encased in red to look like the traditional
bangles that spread through all social classes in the region. Like Bombay
boxwork, the trade in ivory travelled with its craftsmen and consumers
from Surat to Bombay and into oblivion. Bombay boxwork may be a
dead term, but its existence as a term, rather than as Gujarati, Sindhi or
Shirazi boxwork, is not just because ivory was traded to these regions
but because it represented the successful imposition of new networks
onto old ones.

Works cited

Primary sources

A Review of the Administration of the Presidency (Bombay: Government Central Press, 1913).

General Report on the Administration of the Bombay Presidency (Bombay: Government Press, 1874).

International Exhibition St. Louis, 1904: Catalogue of a Selection of the Jubilee Presents of Queen Victoria (London: The Royal Commission, 1904).

Letter of the Secretary of State transmitting a report on the Commercial Relations of the United States with Foreign Nations for the Year Ended September 30, 1865 (Washington: 1866).

Report on the Administration of the Bombay Presidency (Bombay: Central Government Press, 1903).

Review of some of the Principal Acquisitions during the year 1931 (London: Victoria and Albert Museum, 1931).

The British Trade and Export World Vol. 23 (1885).

The Imperial Gazetteer of India. The Indian Empire Vol. III, new ed. (London: Oxford at the Clarendon Press, 1907).

The Modern Part of a Universal History, Vol. 10 (London, 1749).

Secondary sources

Ahmed, Syed Kalique, 'Gujarat top cotton producing state, harvests 108 lakh bales', *The Indian Express*, 3 April 2015 http://indianexpress.com/article/cities/ahmedabad/gujarat-top-cotton-producing-state-harvests-108-lakh-bales/

Andaya, Barbara Watson, 'The Cloth Trade in Jambi and Palembang Society during the Seventeenth and Eighteenth Centuries', *Indonesia* No. 48 (Oct. 1989).

Bal, Krishna, *Commercial Relations between India and England* (London: George Routledge & Sons, 1924).

Balfour, Edward, *The Cyclopaedia of Indian and Eastern and Southern Asia 1* (Madras: Scottish and Adelphi Presses, 1871).

Barendse, Rene, *Arabian Seas 1700-1763* (Leiden and Boston: Brill, 2009).

Bauss, Rudy, 'Textiles, Bullion and other Trades of Goa: Commerce with Surat, other areas of India, Luso-Brazilian ports, Macau and Mozambique, 1816-1819', *The Indian Economic and Social History Review*, Vol. 34 No. 3 (1997).

Beachy, R.W., 'The East African Ivory Trade in the Nineteenth Century', *Journal of African History*, Vol. VIII No. 2 (1967).

Bernier, François, *Travels in the Mogul Empire*, trans. Archibald Constable (Westminster: Archibald Constable and Co., 1891).

Bird, James, 'Commercial and Geographical View of Eastern Africa' *Transactions of the Bombay Geographical Society,* Vol. 3 (June 1839 – February 1840): 112-122.

Birdwood, George, *The Industrial Arts of India* (London: Chapman & Stuart, 1884).

Burns, Cecil, *Monograph on Ivory Carving* (Bombay: Bombay Art School, 1900).

Burton, Richard, *The Lake Regions of Central Africa* (New York: Harper and Brothers, 1860).

Cavaliero, Roderick, *Strangers in the Land: The Rise and Decline of the British Indian Empire* (London: I.B. Taurus, 2002).

Chaiklin, Martha, 'Surat: City of Ivory' in Edward A. Alpers & Chhaya Goswami, eds. *Transregional Trade and Traders: Situating Gujarat in the Indian Ocean from Early Times to 1900.* New Delhi: Oxford University Press, 2019: 218-238.

Coomaraswamy, Ananda, *The Indian Craftsman* (London: Probsthain & Co., 1909).

Coomaraswamy, Ananda, *The Arts and Crafts of India and Ceylon* (New York: Farrar, Straus and Company, 1964).

Chaudhuri, K.N., *The Trading World of Asia and the English East India Company* (Cambridge: Cambridge University Press, 1978).

Das Gupta, Ashin, *The World of the Indian Ocean Merchant, 1500-1800.* Oxford: Oxford University Press).

Forbes, James, *Oriental Letters, Selected from a Series of Familiar Letters* (London: White Cochrane and Co, 1813).

Forrest, George, *Selections from the Letters, Dispatches and Other State Papers Preserved in the Bombay Secretariat* (Bombay: Government Central Press, 1887).

Gokale, Balkrishna Govind, *Surat in the Seventeenth Century* (London and Malmo: Curzon Press, 1979).

Goody, Jack, *The East in the West* (Cambridge: Cambridge University Press, 1996).

Grose, John Henry, *A Voyage to the East Indies,* 2nd ed. (London: S. Hooper, 1766).

Holder, Charles Frederick, *The Ivory King* (New York: Scribner & Sons, 1886).

Holtzappfel, Charles, *Turning and Mechanical Manipulation* Vol. 1 (London: Holtzapffel & Co., 1843).

Israel, Jonathan I., *Dutch Primacy in World Trade, 1585-1740* (Oxford: Oxford University Press, 1989).

Jaffer, Amin, *Luxury Goods from India* (London: V&A Publications, 2002).

Kennedy, Richard Harley, *Narrative of the Campaign of the Army of the Indus in Sind and Kaubool in 1838-1839* (London: Richard Bentley, 1840).

Makrand, Metha, *Indian Merchants and Entrepreneurs in Historical Perspective* (Delhi: Academic Foundation, 1991).

Markovits, Claude, *The Global World of Indian Merchants, 1750-1947* (Cambridge: University of Cambridge, 2004).

Marshall, Peter, 'Private British Trade in the Indian Ocean before 1800', in Patrick Tuck, ed. *Trade Finance and Power* (London and New York: Routledge, 1998).

Mantauban, Mrs Eliot, *A Year and a Day in the East; or Wanderings over Land and Sea* (London: Longman, Brown, Green and Longmans, 1846).

Martin, Esmond Bradley, with Vigne, Lucy, 'The Decline and Fall of India's Ivory Industry', *Pachyderm* No. 12 (1989).

M'Culloch, J.R., *A Dictionary, Practical, Theoretical, and Historical of Commerce and Commercial Navigation* (London: Longman, Green, & Co., 1871).

Milburn, *Oriental Commerce* (London: Black, Parry and Company, 1811).

Moses, Henry, *Sketches of India* (London: Simpkin Marshall & Co. 1750).

Nadri, Ghulam, 'Exploring the Gulf of Kachh: Regional Economy and Trade in the Eighteenth Century', *Journal of the Economic and Social History of the Orient*, Vol. 51 No. 3 (2003).

Nadri, Ghulam A., 'Revisiting the "Decline of Surat": Maritime Trade and the Port Complex of Gujarat in the Late Eighteenth and Early Nineteenth Centuries', in Ulbe Bosma and Anthony Webster, eds. *Commodities, Ports and Asian Maritime Trade Since 1750* (Basingstoke: Palgrave Macmillan, 2015).

Nightingale, Pamela, *Trade and Empire in Western India* (Cambridge: Cambridge University Press, 1970).

Palit, R., *Sketches of Indian Economics* (Madras: Ganesh & Co. 1910).

Pope, Arthur and Ackerman, Phillis, *A Survey of Persian Art from Prehistoric Times to the Present,* Vol. 6 (Oxford University Press, 1964).

Postans, Lieut. T., 'Some account of the present state of the trade, between the Port of Mandavie in Cutch, and the Eastern Coast of Africa', *The Bombay Geographical Society* Vol. 3 (June 1839 – February 1840).

Postans, Mrs., 'Western India in 1838', *The Metropolitan Magazine* Vol. 8 No. 103 (November 1839).

Prakash, Om, 'English Private Trade in the Western Indian Ocean, 1720-1740', *Journal of the Economic and Social History of the Orient* (Vol. 50, nos. 2-3, 2007): 215-34.

Presholdt, Jeremy, *Domesticating the World* (Berkeley: University of California Press, 2008).

Rarapor, Mahrukh, 'John Lockwood Kipling & the Arts and Crafts Movement in India', *AA Files* No. 3 (January 1983).

Rodrigues, Louiza, 'Art Furniture and Household Decoration in Nineteenth Century Bombay: Trading Art Across the Globe' (unpublished article submitted to the K.R. Cama Oriental Institute, Mumbai, 2015).

Rothermund, Dieter, *Asian Trade and European Expansion in the Age of Mercantilism* (New Delhi: Manohar, 1981).

Roy, Thirthankar, *Traditional Industry in the Economy of Colonial India* (Cambridge: Cambridge University Press, 1999).

Sheriff, Abdul, *Slaves, Spices & Ivory in Zanzibar* (Athens, OH: Ohio University Press, 1987).

Shimada, Ryūto, *The Intra-Asian Trade In Copper by the Dutch East India Company during the Eighteenth Century* (Leiden and Boston: Brill, 2006).

Smee, Thomas, 'Proceedings at Zanzibar, from the 25th February to the 9th April, 1811, with Some account of the Island' *Transactions of the Bombay Geographical Society,* Vol. 3 (June 1839 – February 1840): 41-60.

Untracht, Oppi, *Traditional Jewelry of India* (London: Thames and Hudson, 1997).

Wales, Richard and Susan, *Souvenirs from the Diamond Jubilee of Queen Victoria* (Bloomington, IN: Author House, 2012).

Watt, Sir George, *Indian Art at Delhi, 1903* (Delhi: Motitlal Barnarsidasl, 1987).

Webster, Alex. G., 'The Sheffield Cutlery Industry', in Commercial Relations of the United States – Reports from the Consuls of the United States on the Commerce, Manufacture, etc. of their Consular Districts, No. 25, pp. 46-49

White, David, *Competition and Collaboration* (New Delhi: Munshiram Manoharlal Publishers, 1995).

Yule, Henry and Burnell, A.C., *Hobson-Jobson*, 2nd ed., ed. William Crooke (London: John Murray, 1903).

Contact details

chaiklin@pitt.edu

5 The English and Dutch East India Companies and Indian merchants in Surat in the seventeenth and eighteenth centuries

Interdependence, competition and contestation

Ghulam A. Nadri

Abstract

This chapter explores the dynamics of the commercial relationships between the European East India Companies and Indian merchants, and examines the local and global forces that shaped this relationship. In carrying out their large-scale trade in India, the EIC and the VOC depended heavily on Indian merchants, who extended a variety of professional commercial services to the companies. Indian merchants too benefited from this and sought affiliation with the companies as it presented lucrative commercial opportunities as well as social and political advantages. The relationship that developed between the two was one of interdependence and complementarity. It was also competitive and, at times, contestable. Through a comparative analysis of the EIC's and VOC's relationship with Indian merchants, this chapter seeks to understand the significance of this strategic alliance for European commercial enterprise in India in the early modern period.

Keywords: Portugal, Indian merchants, Banias, Parsis, Surat, Bombay, maritime trade, broker, Virji Vora

Clulow, Adam and Tristan Mostert (eds.), *The Dutch and English East India Companies: Diplomacy, trade and violence in early modern Asia*. Amsterdam: Amsterdam University Press, 2018
DOI: 10.5117/9789462983298/CH05

This chapter investigates the dynamics of the commercial relationship between the European East India companies and Indian merchants in the seventeenth and eighteenth centuries.[1] It explores the local and global forces that shaped this relationship. In carrying out large-scale trade in India, the English East India Company (EIC) and the Dutch Verenigde Oost-Indische Compagnie (VOC) came to depend heavily on Indian merchants, who offered a variety of professional commercial services to the companies. As bankers, brokers, large-scale suppliers and buyers of commodities, Indian merchants played a crucial role in the relative success of European commercial enterprise in the western Indian Ocean. The focus of this chapter is Surat, a port in Gujarat, where the companies had established their factories in the early seventeenth century and which served as their main trading post in the western Indian Ocean for the next two centuries. Surat was home as well to a large number of Indian and Asian merchants prominent in the region's maritime trade with West, East, and Southeast Asia throughout this period. Thus, any interaction between the European companies and Surat merchants, each with their own commercial ambitions, was bound to be dynamic and constantly changing. The relationship that developed between the two can best be characterised as one underpinned by interdependence and reciprocity. Affiliation with the companies presented lucrative commercial opportunities as well as social and political advantages. Many prominent merchant families in Surat therefore sought association with the companies. Both sides benefitted, but this was a relationship that was highly competitive and at times sharply contested.

While the role of brokers in servicing the European trade is generally recognised, the complexities of the relationship between the European companies and Indian merchants/brokers and its significance in the commercial success of both have not been fully explored. Moreover, past studies have examined the role and activities of brokers in a limited time frame, usually a century or sometimes just a decade.[2] There has been no attempt to study this group across a longer trajectory and to track the evolution of the relationship and the changes that took place over time, especially in the eighteenth century. This chapter is an attempt to address these issues and hence to shed light on the crucial role of brokers in European trading empire. Through a comparative analysis of the EIC's and VOC's relationship with

1   In this chapter, I use the term 'Indian merchants' to refer to indigenous or local Gujarati Bania, Muslim, and Parsi merchants, and 'Asian merchants' to denote Armenian, Jewish, Turkish and other merchants who lived in Surat or other Gujarat ports on a permanent or quasi-permanent basis and were engaged in the maritime trade of the region.
2   Qaisar, 'The Role of Brokers in Medieval India'; Pearson, 'Brokers in Western Indian Port Cities'; Gupta, 'The Broker in Mughal Surat'.

Indian merchants in the seventeenth and eighteenth centuries, the chapter seeks to understand the significance of this strategic alliance for European commercial enterprises in India but also for Indian merchants. By examining the activities of those merchants with whom the companies conducted business and by detailing the genealogy of brokers, I aim to illuminate the complexities of this alliance and show how both sides attempted to assert their position and maximise commercial benefits from their connections. It underlines long-term continuities as well as changes in the relationship during one of the most dynamic phases of European interaction with India.

Older understandings of the European presence in the Indian Ocean and its implications for Indian merchants emphasised European domination and Indian subordination.[3] Since the 1970s, this view has been contested by a number of scholars who have identified partnership and reciprocity in their relationship.[4] By showing the companies' dependence on Indian merchants and brokers and their inability to exert the desired level of authority over brokers across a longer timeline, this chapter contributes to our understanding of the European expansion in India in the early modern period. The following section outlines the historical context within which a relationship of trust and reliance was forged between the companies and Indian merchants.

European companies and Indian merchants in Surat: the beginning of a relationship

The arrival of the EIC and the VOC in India in the early seventeenth century marked the beginning of a new era of the European–Indian commercial exchange. The companies displayed a different approach to trade and trading from their predecessors, the Portuguese, whose relationship with Indian maritime merchants frequently ended in conflict.[5] Unlike the Portuguese, the English and the Dutch had a strong mercantile tradition and tended to be more pragmatic in their dealings with Indian and other Asian merchants. They forged a close commercial relationship with Indian

---

3   Moreland, *India at the Death of Akbar*, pp. 200-203; Panikkar, *Asia and Western Dominance*.

4   Kling and Pearson, *The Age of Partnership*; Gupta, 'Indian Merchants in the Age of Partnership'; Prakash, *European Commercial Enterprise in Pre-Colonial India*.

5   This was mainly because of the Portuguese assertion of monopoly of maritime trade in Asia, the Cartaz system, which required Asian ships to buy from the Portuguese a license to sail in the Indian Ocean, and violent reprisal against vessels without a license. Prakash, *European Commercial Enterprise in Pre-Colonial India*; Gupta and Pearson, *India and the Indian Ocean, 1500-1800*; Pearson, *The Indian Ocean*.

merchants and secured permission from Indian rulers to establish trading stations or factories in port cities and in the interior.[6] In part because of this, the volume and value of India–Europe trade substantially increased and there was also a significant shift in the commodities that were transported. Indigo and a variety of cotton and silk textiles came to constitute the largest proportion of exports from India to Europe and other parts of Asia. The companies' large-scale trading enterprise and the kind of commodities that they exported from India required a close interaction with Indian merchants, brokers, and bankers.[7] There was a well-developed market structure in place with a hierarchy of merchants and intermediaries as well as banking and brokering services.[8] These merchants and intermediaries were willing to extend their commercial services to the EIC and VOC and to take the business opportunities that the companies presented to them. The outcome was the beginning of a long-term relationship between the two groups based on interdependence and mutual benefit.

The EIC began its trade relations with Surat in the 1600s while the Dutch company followed in the 1610s. Both companies were interested in buying merchandise such as indigo and textiles from Gujarat for European markets. Since the VOC carried out an extensive intra-Asian trade, the company also purchased textiles and other commodities for markets within Asia while importing a variety of European and Asian merchandise into Surat. The companies' imports into Surat from Europe consisted mainly of gold and silver and some woollen and silk textiles as well as some non-precious metals and minerals like iron, lead, and vermillion. The EIC's trade with India was primarily an exchange of precious metals for Indian textiles, indigo, pepper, and other commodities. Intra-Asian trade enabled the VOC to import into Surat large quantities of fine spices (cloves, nutmeg, and mace), cinnamon, Japanese gold, silver, and copper, and Java sugar, ivory, sappanwood, and many other commodities.[9] Since the sale value of its

6   Prakash, *European Commercial Enterprise in Pre-Colonial India*, pp. 81-82; van Santen, 'De Verenigde Oost-Indische Compagnie in Gujarat en Hindustan'.

7   As Gupta has rightly noted, '[T]he shipowner-merchant and others dealing strictly in imports and exports relied on merchants and brokers who specialised in supplying a port with specific commodities. The bigger the business, the larger was such reliance upon the intermediaries.' Gupta, 'Indian Merchants and the Trade in the Indian Ocean', p. 420.

8   See for details, Qaisar, 'The Role of Brokers in Medieval India'; Pearson, 'Brokers in Western Indian Port Cities'; Gupta, 'The Broker in Mughal Surat'; Prakash, 'Sarrafs, Financial Intermediation, and Credit Network'; Prakash, *Bullion for Goods*.

9   For a detailed analysis of the Dutch intra-Asian trade in the eighteenth century, see Jacobs, *Merchants in Asia*; Prakash, *European Commercial Enterprise*; Shimada, *The Intra-Asian Trade in Japanese Copper*; Nadri, 'The Dutch Intra-Asian Trade in Sugar'.

imports often exceeded the purchase value of goods for Asian and European markets in much of the period after 1650, the VOC remitted the surpluses to its other establishments in India and occasionally to Batavia. Between 1672 and 1792, the average annual purchase value of VOC's exports from Surat varied between 340,000 and 1.08 million guilders and the sale value of imports varied between 390,000 and 1.16 million guilders during 1711–1793.

To carry out a large-scale trading enterprise, access to the interior, where export commodities were produced, was vital. Soon after their arrival in Surat, the EIC and the VOC established subordinate factories at a number of major production or exchange centres in Gujarat, including Ahmadabad, Baroda, Broach, and Cambay, as well as in Agra, which was a major market for textiles and indigo. From these places, they could reach out to the surrounding villages where indigo and textiles were produced. For operations in these centres, the services of Indian merchants, bankers, and brokers were indispensable. Equally crucial was the support of Mughal imperial government and local governors and officials, who were also cognisant of the significance of the companies as importers of gold and silver and a source of revenue in the form of customs or import/export duties. As a result, the EIC worked to secure imperial permission to trade and other commercial privileges (including remission of customs duties and exemption from inland transit duties) via Emperor Jahangir's *farman* (imperial order) which granted such permissions and privileges to the company.[10] Its main rival, the VOC, obtained similar privileges from the Mughals. It is clear from several *farmans* issued by Emperor Shahjahan in the 1630s to the Dutch that the Mughals recognised the economic benefits that imperial ports and their inhabitants derived from European trade and ensured that the company was able to carry out its trade without undue hindrance and extortion.[11] Sometimes, the companies used their naval power and violence against Surat merchants to secure trade privileges from the Mughal authorities or to force the latter not to hinder their trade or harm their commercial interests.[12] However, given their large-scale commercial transactions in inland territories from Gujarat to Agra, which was the site of Mughal imperial headquarters, the companies were generally reluctant to use

10   The efforts began with Thomas Roe who visited the Mughal court and sought trade privileges and concessions in the empire. Foster, *The Embassy of Sir Thomas Roe*.

11   See the copies of Mughal *farmans* among the Geleynssen de Jongh papers. Nationaal Archief, The Hague, Collectie Geleynssen de Jongh, 100, Briefboek van verscheyde soo becoomen als versonde brieven als formannen int Persiaens geschreven ende int Nederlants getranslateert begonnen anno 1639 in Agra [Letter-book of various letters received and sent as well as farmans written in Persian and translated into Dutch beginning in 1639 in Agra], not foliated.

12   Clulow, 'European Maritime Violence and Territorial States'.

violence. Their first responses were almost always petition and negotiation and only when such strategies failed to produce the desired result did they move to make use of their naval superiority.

Many Mughal governors and high officials also carried out trade from Surat to the Red Sea and Persian Gulf ports. They viewed the companies as competitors and, at times, used their political influence to restrict or stop the Dutch or the English from participating in this trade. Dealing with such competitors posed a considerable challenge to the companies, and it was here that the relationship with local authorities was fraught with clashing interests and fierce contests. As early as 1619, the governor of Surat ordered EIC's brokers in Surat, Broach, and Baroda not to purchase any merchandise for the company for Mocha and Aceh.[13] In the 1620s and 1630s, the indigo market in northern India was an arena in which local Mughal governors and nobles exerted their political influence by seeking to monopolise the indigo trade, generating resistance from the companies, which resisted any attempt to block their access to the indigo trade.[14] Under such circumstances, the companies' Indian brokers played a significant role in negotiating with the local administration and in obtaining permission to trade. In 1622, when the EIC was not allowed to trade in Baroda, its broker, Tapidas, offered to obtain permission from the Mughal authorities for the company to continue trade and also promised that if he failed to obtain the permission he would secretly supply the company with any merchandise that it wanted.[15]

Surat's shipowners, especially those trading with Red Sea and the Gulf ports, were the main victims of maritime violence. As direct competitors of the companies in the marketplace in West Asia and elsewhere, they were highly vulnerable to European violence in the western Indian Ocean. On many occasions in the early seventeenth century, Surat vessels were captured and plundered by the companies. In 1612, an EIC fleet commanded by Henry Middleton plundered some fifteen vessels mostly belonging to Surat merchants.[16] Similarly, in the early 1620s, the VOC and then the EIC captured several merchant vessels returning from the Red Sea to Surat and other ports of the Gujarat coast.[17] The companies claimed that these were retaliatory measures and a pressure

---

13   Prakash, *The Dutch Factories in India*, pp. 95-96.

14   For a discussion of this clash of interest in the indigo market and trade, see Nadri, *The Political Economy of Indigo in India*, pp. 155-164.

15   EFI 1622-23, Broach to Surat, 20 January 1622, p. 20.

16   Clulow, 'European Maritime Violence and Territorial States', pp. 74-75.

17   In 1623, the EIC despatched a fleet to capture Chaul and Dabhol ships returning from Mocha. EFI 1622-23, Consultations, Surat, 18 February 1623, p. 200; Ibid., Consultations, Surat, 3 March 1623, pp. 204-06; Ibid., Instructions from the President and Council at Surat to Captain John

tactic to make up for the losses and extortion they had suffered at the hands of the Mughal officials and governors as well as to secure trade concessions and privileges. They succeeded to a degree in forcing their terms of trade upon the local administration. The relationship became increasingly bitter at the end of the seventeenth century when some Surat ships were captured and plundered by European pirates in the Gulf of Aden. The merchants and the Mughal authorities held the companies (the English, Dutch, and French East India companies) responsible for this and demanded compensation from them. The companies were also forced to provide convoy protection to Surat ships in the western Indian Ocean.[18] Again in the second half of the eighteenth century, a prolonged conflict took place between the two when the EIC attempted to monopolise the freight trade from Surat to West Asia.[19]

The early seventeenth century was also the period when commercial relationships between the companies and Indian merchants, especially brokers and bankers, were forged and consolidated. From the very beginning, the companies depended on local merchants, brokers, and bankers to procure merchandise and dispose of their imports. Due to the shortage of funds for the timely purchase of merchandise, the companies often had to borrow money from local merchants and brokers. Many prominent merchants in Surat and elsewhere in Gujarat readily lent money on interest to the companies. By the mid-seventeenth century, as the EIC and VOC consolidated their trade, each employed a leading merchant of Surat as its broker, who then looked after its imports and exports. The families of some merchants who served the European companies as brokers during this period retained the position for several generations.[20] The meanings and functions attached to the office of the broker also changed over the period. Brokering, originally a purely commercial intermediation aimed at bringing buyers and sellers together and facilitating a smooth transaction in return for a commission from both sides, had by the mid-seventeenth century acquired social and political significance.[21] It had become a privileged

Hall and his Council for the Voyage of Mocha, 15 March 1623, pp. 207-208; Clulow, 'European Maritime Violence and Territorial States', pp. 75-76.

18   For a detailed description of these incidents, see Gupta, *Indian Merchants and the Decline of Surat* , pp. 94-133.

19   Torri, 'Surat during the Second Half of the Eighteenth Century'; Nadri, *Eighteenth-Century Gujarat*, p. 81.

20   Nadri, 'The Maritime Merchants of Surat'.

21   This was more so the case in the eighteenth century. Ashin Das Gupta has rightly pointed out that the position gave the holder 'enormous prestige' and 'the power to manage all official trade in the city'. Gupta, 'The Broker in Mughal Surat', p. 401.

position, with the result that some merchant families competed to obtain these roles, sometimes leading to a protracted struggle, as happened between the families of Tapidas Parekh and a Parsi merchant, Rustamji Manikji, in the early eighteenth century. The companies too, it seems, preferred to employ different generations of the same family as their brokers because it ensured stability and longevity for a relationship that was considered crucial to their success in Asia.

During this developmental phase, the European companies traded with a number of prominent merchants of Surat, possibly with the help of their brokers. Virji Vora was one such merchant with whom the companies, especially the EIC, transacted business on a large scale. By lending money to the companies, buying goods that the latter imported into Surat, and supplying key export commodities such as pepper, indigo, and textiles, he played a vital role in the EIC's and VOC's trade. A close look at the commercial transactions between Vora and the companies shows how much European commerce depended on Indian merchants and their capital and how Virji Vora drew commercial benefits from this association and almost always succeeded in dominating the terms of the relationship.

European companies and Virji Vora: a relationship of interdependence

Early seventeenth-century EIC records present Virji Vora as a prominent merchant, who often lent money to the company while also buying merchandise that the latter imported into Surat.[22] He was not formally a broker of either of the companies but he was often the principal buyer of merchandise that the English and Dutch companies imported into Surat. He held a sort of monopsony by keeping his competitors out of his way and buying the companies' imports almost entirely by himself. Being an

---

22   The EIC and VOC often borrowed money from the Bania merchant, Virji Vora. In 1622, the VOC borrowed 36,000 mahmudis from him. *Pieter van den Broecke in Azië*, vol. 2, p. 275; DFI 1617-1623, Surat to Batavia, 25 December 1623, p. 286. In 1628, EIC merchants in Agra received a letter of credit from Virji Vora for 20,000 rupees. EFI 1624-29, Agra to Surat, 1 February 1628, p. 234; Ibid., Agra to Surat, 17 March 1628, p. 271. In the same year, Virji Vora bought the company's coral. Ibid., Surat to London, 21 December 1628, p. 310. In 1629, the EIC bought 20,000 maunds of pepper from Virji Vora. Ibid., Surat to London, April 11-13, 1629, p. 327. In 1630, the EIC received a letter of credit from Virji Vora for 25,000 rupees. EFI 1630-33, Surat to Agra, 30 September 1630, p. 56. In 1634, the EIC borrowed 30,000 rupees from him. EFI 1634-36, Surat to London, 2 January 1635, p. 147. Mehta, *Indian Merchants and Entrepreneurs*, pp. 53-57.

influential merchant, he exerted monopolistic control over Surat's trade in major commodities like pepper and coral. A statement made at the EIC council meeting in Surat in 1625 describes the nature of Virji's commercial transactions with the company and other merchants in Surat.

> The President has accordingly been in treaty with 'Vergee Vora', 'a prime marchant of this towne', for 10,000L. worth [of pepper] at 16 mahmudis the maund; but the latter demands 16 ¼ mahmudis, and requires as part of the bargain the sale to him of 25 chests of their best coral at a price which would seriously diminish the expected profit. Meanwhile he has engrossed all the pepper brought in by 'the Decannee marchants', who are not permitted to sell it to any other.[23]

When the company sent its brokers to the Deccan to buy pepper, Virji Vora frustrated them by offering a higher price than the English could afford and forced the company to accept the deal that he had earlier proposed.[24] In 1634, similarly, EIC authorities noted:

> The potency of Virgee Vorah (who hath bene the usuall merchant, and is now become the sole monopolist of all Europian commodities) is observed to beare such sway amongst the inferiour merchants of this towne that when they would oftentymes buy (and give greater prices) they are still restrayned, not dareing to betray their intents to his knowledge and their owne sufferance, insomuch that the tyme and price is still in his will and at his owne disposure.[25]

Virji Vora also used the company's indebtedness to his own advantage or that of Surat merchants more generally. On many occasions, he forced the companies to provide Surat merchants with freight services to Mocha, Jeddah, Gombroon, and Basra. Company officials in Surat were forced to comply with his demands even if they had to defer the dispatch of their vessels to Batavia or England.[26] Both the EIC and VOC had extensive

23   EFI 1624-29, Consultations, Surat, 10 July 1625, p. 90.
24   Ibid., Consultations, Surat, 24 September 1625, p. 94.
25   EFI 1634-36, Consultations, Surat, 8 April 1634, p. 24. Similar sentiments were expressed in Surat's letter to London in 1636. Ibid., Surat to London, 28 April 1636, p. 218.
26   In 1628, he forced the Dutch to offload the merchandise on a VOC ship in Surat and take freight goods to Persia and also forced the EIC to defer the despatch of the *Hart* to England and sail instead to Persia with merchandise belonging to Surat merchants. EFI 1624-29, Consultations, Surat, 8 December 1628, p. 300; ibid., Surat to London, 21 December 1628, p. 306.

commercial dealings with Virji Vora. The EIC purchased large quantities of pepper from him and Virji often bought corals, amber, quicksilver, silver, and gold from the company. For Virji, the companies presented excellent business opportunities and he maintained cordial relations through the use of customary presents.[27] The companies too depended on him for the supply of money that was so crucial to the timely procurement of pepper and other merchandise. They were so dependent that the EIC was hesitant to take any commercial measure that would have displeased him. An EIC official, Edward Knipe, expressed the following sentiment when he wrote to London in 1643:

> I understood that Virge Vora yearly sends downe his people hither to Callicutt with cotten and opium, by which hee doth not [gain?] less then double his mony to those people hee buyeth his pepper off, [and] afterwards disposeth of his pepper to us for double what it cost him; for I finde pepper to bee worth here but 15 ½ and 16 fannams the maund, which is not halfe the rate hee usually valleweth it to our people in Suratt. It would obviously be cheaper to deal direct;' but indeed Virge Vora, by reason of our continuall mighty ingagements, must not bee displeased in any case......... Hee knoweth that wee (in regard of our extreame ingagement) must sell, and so beats us downe till wee come to his owne rates; and thus hath bynn his proceedings this many yeares. And I conclude that, so long as Virge Vora is so much our credittor, little or no proffitt [is] to bee made uppon any goods wee can bring to Surratt.[28]

Virji Vora kept his position as the richest merchant of Surat well up to the early 1660s and the EIC remained indebted to him. His commercial fortunes began to decline around the midpoint of the seventeenth century when he got into trouble with the governor of Surat and the local administration. The plunder of Surat in 1663 by the Marathas was catastrophic for Virji Vora and many of the city's other affluent merchants.[29] He was not, however, completely ruined. Soon he was back in business and once again the richest merchant. By the mid-seventeenth century, many other Bania merchant families of Surat rose to prominence and began to vie with each other to

27   In 1634, Virji Vora presented nine pieces of white cloth to the EIC as gift. EFI 1634-36, Surat to London, 19 January 1635, p. 97. In 1661, Virji Vora presented some calico pieces to the company. EFI 1661-64, Surat Presidency, 1661, p. 21.

28   EFI 1642-46, Edward Knipe to the Company in London, 18 July 1643, p. 108.

29   According to an estimate, Virji Vora lost about half a million rupees. EFI 1661-64, Shivaji's attack upon Surat, 1664, p. 310.

serve the companies as brokers, bankers, and suppliers of merchandise as well as to keep the position and its associated privileges within the family. One such family was that of the Parekhs, whose members served the EIC as brokers for much of the seventeenth and eighteenth centuries.[30]

The EIC and the Parekh family of brokers

In the early seventeenth century, the merchant family of Tapidas and Tulsidas Parekh consolidated its hold as the company's broker and shroff (Persian *sarraf*; money changer or banker) in Surat. For just over five decades from 1609 to 1660, Tapidas served as a broker and was engaged in diverse activities, from lending money to taking care of the logistics for the EIC in Surat.[31] In the records of the EIC, he is referred to as the house shroff, signifying the crucial role he played in the company's maritime trade.[32] In recognition of his services, the company paid him an annual allowance of 500 *mahmudis* in addition to his usual brokerage.[33] He had an extensive commercial network that reached into the interior. Disposing of merchandise that he bought in large quantities from the company was possible only through a chain of reliable sub-brokers and agents spread all over the region. Bania ingenuity in building such networks was famous among their contemporaries and because of this they came to dominate the profession of brokering and banking in Gujarat. Tapidas traded extensively in commodities like coral and silver, which he purchased from the company. As a maritime merchant, he also had trade relations with West Asian ports like Basra. He did not own ships but freighted merchandise to his partners at other ports and sometimes sent them on a hired ship.[34] His brother, Tulsidas Parekh, also served the company as its main shroff for several years between 1636

30   Somji Chitta and Chota Thakur served as EIC's brokers on several occasions in the seventeenth century. In 1652, Benidas replaced Tulsidas Parekh as the Company's shroff. Gokhale, *Surat in the Seventeenth Century*, pp. 122-23.

31   Qaisar, 'The Role of Brokers in Medieval India', p. 230; Gokhale, Surat in the Seventeenth Century, p. 119; Nadri, 'The Maritime Merchants of Surat'.

32   In 1636, he issued a bill of exchange for 50,000 rupees to the EIC. EFI 1634-36, Surat to Ahmadabad, 12 February 1636, p. 169; Qaisar, 'The Role of Brokers in Medieval India', p. 235; *EFI 1642-45*, Swally Marine to London, 27 January 1642, p. 21.

33   Gokhale, *Surat in the Seventeenth Century*, p. 119. Mahmudi was a silver coin of smaller denomination current in Gujarat, whose exchange value with the Mughal rupee varied between 2/5 and 4/9 of a rupee in the seventeenth century.

34   In 1642, he hired an English vessel, the *Prosperous*, for 5,000 mahmudis to send his goods to Basra. *EFI 1642-45*, Surat to London, 27 January 1642, p. 21.

and 1667. Tulsidas was a rich merchant in his own right and had extensive commercial dealings with the company and private English merchants. Both brothers received an annual allowance from the company.[35]

Their family fortunes improved still further in the second half of the seventeenth century when Tulsidas's son, Bhimji Parekh, entered the service of the EIC as a broker along with his three brothers, Kalyandas, Kisso and Vithaldas.[36] Bhimji Parekh was the most dynamic of all, and apart from being a leading merchant he also exercised great influence over the Bania community of Surat.[37] Under him the family fortune, as reported in a letter of 5 July 1682 from the Court of Directors to Surat, exceeded one million pounds sterling (approximately 8 million rupees).[38] Until his death in 1686, he was at the helm of affairs in Surat and as a key broker was influential in the management of the company's imports and exports. What is also remarkable is that he held this position jointly with his brothers, each having a fixed share in the joint undertaking with the EIC. After Bhimji, his brothers Vithaldas Parekh and Kisso served the company in much of the 1680s and 1690s. The Parekh family played a vital role in the EIC's commercial enterprise. The company depended heavily on the financial services and commercial mediation of the Parekh merchants. For the latter, too, affiliation with the company was equally vital for their extensive trade as well as for their reputation and prestige in Surat.

In the early eighteenth century, the family lost this office to a Parsi family, that of Rustamji Manikji. It was only after Manikji's death in 1719 that Laldas Parekh, son of the former broker Vithaldas Parekh, regained the position. Laldas was also instrumental in the private commercial undertakings of Robert Cowan, governor of Bombay, and Henry Lowther, the EIC chief at Surat, in the 1720s and 1730s.[39] With the support of people in the upper echelon of the company at Bombay and Surat he restored the position and respectability of the family. After his death in 1732, the feud between the families of Laldas Parekh and Naoroji Rustamji flared once again. Jagannath,

---

35   Tapidas received 500 mahmudis while Tulsidas got 25 English pounds and later 500 mahmudis. Gokhale, *Surat in the Seventeenth Century*, pp. 119-20.

36   Qaisar, 'The Role of Brokers in Medieval India', p. 226; Gupta, *The World of the Indian Ocean Merchant*.

37   In 1669, Bhimji Parekh protested against the local Qazi who had forcibly converted a member of his family to Islam. He mobilised his community and withdrew from Surat together with about 8,000 Bania merchants. Mehta, 'Some Aspects of Surat', p. 258; Chaudhury 'The Gujarat Mahajans'.

38   Chaudhury 'The Gujarat Mahajans', p. 360.

39   Prakash, 'English Private Trade in the Western Indian Ocean'.

son of Laldas Parekh, lost the position and was imprisoned in 1736. With much difficulty, he managed to escape to the Marathas in 1738 but the family fortune was greatly damaged.[40] This was mainly because, with the departure of Robert Cowan and Henry Lowther, the family lost its company patronage and it took some time to cultivate cordial relations with Cowan and Lowther's successors, who were not so favourably inclined towards the Parekhs initially.

Jagannath Laldas Parekh made a comeback in the 1740s and regained his commercial prominence. He took up the role of *marfatia* (agent or go-between) for the EIC and continued in that position until his death in 1761. He played an important role in the politics of Surat in the 1750s and was active in the struggle for political control of Surat which culminated in the English takeover of the castle in 1759.[41] Since the EIC had already, by 1740, curtailed the authority of the broker by changing the designation from broker to *marfatia*, Jagannath Laldas and later his son, Naraindas Jagannath, played a limited role in the commerce of the company.[42] But against all odds, the family's commercial enterprise was still considerable and the Parekhs certainly benefited from their association with the EIC. As the *marfatia* of the company, they were involved in the company's sales in Surat and were, often, the principal buyers of the imports.[43]

The VOC and the family of Kishandas, the broker

Like the EIC, the VOC was also dependent on brokers. In the first half of the seventeenth century, Mohandas Naan, a leading Bania merchant and shipowner of Surat, served as a broker to the VOC. In 1659, another Bania merchant, Kishandas, was appointed as a broker and the role remained in his family until 1795 when the VOC was dissolved.[44] Kishandas served the

---

40 Gupta, *The World of the Indian Ocean Merchant*, p. 326.

41 Subramanian, 'Capital and Crowd', p. 212; Subramanian, 'The Eighteenth Century Social Order in Surat'; Torri, 'Surat during the Second Half'.

42 Gupta, *The World of the Indian Ocean Merchant*. As the *marfatia*, Naraindas Jagannath was no longer involved in the procurement of merchandise.

43 In 1762, he bought 5,000 maunds of copper from the company, and the Bombay Presidency advised Surat authorities to assist him in disposing of copper either through minting coins or by other means. Maharashtra State Archives, Mumbai, Surat Factory Diary, 1761-63, No. 16 part 1, Surat to Bombay, 10 November 1761, p. 55; ibid., Bombay to Surat, 5 February 1762, p. 119. In 1764, his name appears among other buyers of tin from the company. Surat Factory Diary, 1763-65, No. 17 part 1, p. 187.

44 Nadri, 'The Maritime Merchants of Surat', pp. 241-43.

company in that capacity from 1659 until his death in 1686. He was a rich merchant who was primarily engaged in buying merchandise and selling it to others in Surat and in the interior through his network of sub-brokers and agents. Throughout his service tenure, he was the principal buyer of most of the Dutch imports into Surat.[45] He owned ships and his trading enterprise extended to several overseas destinations.[46] After him his grandsons, Risikdas and Bhagwandas, served as brokers and as such played an important role in the VOC's trade in Gujarat. They usually exercised their monopoly and bought all merchandise that the company imported into Surat. They did their best to prevent other merchants from buying goods from the company. In the late 1680s and 1690s, the VOC attempted to sell its imports in small quantities to other merchants who were offering higher prices instead of selling everything to the brokers, but the strategy proved a failure.[47]

In the eighteenth century, the descendants of Kishandas served the VOC as brokers but there were times when they had to share this office with other Bania or Parsi merchants. Between 1715 and 1727, for example, Risikdas and a Bania merchant, Wanmalidas served as co-brokers.[48] From 1749 to the mid-1780s, Rurdraram Raidas and his son Govindram Rudraram shared an office with a Parsi merchant, Mancherji Khurshedji. In partnership with their co-broker, Mancherji Khurshedji, they conducted large-scale trade and jointly bought the merchandise imported into Surat by the VOC. Rudraram Raidas and his son Govindram Rudraram were not shipowners but conducted overseas trade by sending merchandise on their co-broker's ships, as well as that of another Parsi merchant, Manik Dada, the company's *modi* (supplier of provisions to the company at Surat and caretaker of its logistics). After the fourth Anglo-Dutch War (1781-83), which caused the suspension of all commercial activities of the VOC in Surat and elsewhere in India, Govindram's son Prem Shankar was instated as a broker. But he had to share the office with two other merchants as his co-brokers, Ram Narain Shiv Narain and Tarachand Nagardas. Unlike their predecessors, however, these brokers were not the principal buyers of the company's merchandise. Other merchants of Surat generally purchased the company's imports.

45   *Generale Missiven van Gouverneurs-Generaal en Raden aan Heren XVII der Verenigde Oostindische Compagnie* [General letters of the governors-general and council to the Gentlemen XVII of the Dutch East India Company], vol. IV, pp. 355, 357, 739, 825.
46   Van Dam, *Beschrijving van de Oost-Indische Compagnie*, pp. 368, 374.
47   Nationaal Archief, The Hague, Hoge Regering te Batavia, 844, Memorie van Overgave, Louis Taillefert, 1758.
48   Nationaal Archief, Hoge Regering te Batavia, Memorie van Overgave, J. Jesua Ketelaar, 1716, pp. 257-259; VOC 3238, Resoluties, Surat, 1758, 29 October 1768, ff. 378r-379r.

European companies and their Parsi brokers

By the end of the seventeenth century, the Parsis (Zoroastrians who had immigrated from Persia to western India during the preceding centuries) emerged as a prominent merchant community in Surat. They were not simply another addition to the already ethnically diverse merchant community; rather, the rising fortunes of the Parsis contributed to the dynamism of the trading world of Gujarat and the western Indian Ocean. In the 1700s, Rustamji Manikji was one of the richest merchants of Surat. It was around this time that the Parsis began to challenge Bania domination of brokering in Gujarat. Rustamji Manikji made his debut in the early years of the eighteenth century, when he became a broker for the New English East India Company. After the merger of the new and the old companies, he managed to overthrow Banwalidas Parekh and replaced him as the United East India Company's broker in 1712.[49] After Rustamji's death in 1719, his three sons Framji, Bahmanji, and Naoroji Rustamji assumed the office of the broker. Soon after, they were removed from the office, however, and were replaced by Laldas, son of the former broker, Vithaldas Parekh. After the family's removal from the position of broker, Naoroji Rustamji travelled to London to plead his case before the Court of Directors, the EIC's apex governing body. He not only secured from the directors a compensation for the family, but also succeeded in reviving an old EIC claim of 150,000 rupees against the Parekhs.[50] However, Laldas Parekh managed to survive the counteroffensives from the Rustamji family and brought the office of broker for the company back to the family. The tussle between the two families over the office of company broker continued up to the early 1740s, during which period the office swung back and forth between these families. In 1736, Naoroji Rustamji once again assumed the office of the company's broker, albeit for a short period. In the early 1740s, he forever lost the office to his rival, Jagannath Laldas.

In the second half of the eighteenth century, several other Parsi families rose to prominence and served as brokers and contractors or suppliers to the companies. Mancherji Khurshedji was one of the richest merchants of Surat, owning about half a dozen ocean-going ships that carried out large-scale

---

49   In 1698, the New East India Company was established, which rivalled the old company in the trade of the East. The two, however, merged officially in 1709 as the United East India Company. Rustamji as the chief broker of the united company worked in such a way that the Parekhs lost the credibility and trust of the company. Gupta, 'The Merchants of Surat, c. 1700-1750', pp. 324-327.
50   Ibid., p. 325.

maritime trade with West and East Asia.[51] From 1750 to the early 1780s, he was the broker of the VOC, a position which he held together with Bania merchant Rudraram Raidas and after him his son, Govindram Rudraram. Like other brokers before him, Mancherji Khurshedji and his co-broker looked after the company's sale of imports and usually bought most of its merchandise. Throughout his tenure as broker, he exerted a monopsonistic control over merchandise that the VOC imported into Surat.[52] He kept other merchants from competing with him and purchased the company's most important imports including spices, sugar, copper, tin, tusk, lead, and alum. VOC authorities tried to reduce their dependence on brokers by selling goods through public auctions and requiring the brokers through written contracts to pay the company in a timely manner. Mancherji Khurshedji, however, frustrated them by disregarding the terms of contract. He did not pay in time for merchandise he bought, which resulted in him amassing a huge debt to the company. Notwithstanding these inconveniences, Mancherji Khurshedji was indispensable for the company because of his important role in the sale and purchase of merchandise. Several factors including large-scale imports of merchandise into Surat and purchase of export goods from the sale proceeds and the political ascendancy of its commercial rival in Surat seem to have hampered the VOC in its assertion of control over its brokers.[53]

Another prominent Parsi merchant, Dhanjishah Manjishah, was also a shipowner and a maritime trader. He was for some time a broker for the EIC and therefore came under the protection of the company. Sorabji and Ratanji and their sons similarly served as contractors and suppliers of merchandise to the VOC throughout the eighteenth century. Other Parsi merchants, such as Dadabhai Manikji and Edul Dada, were contractors and suppliers of textiles to the EIC. Both the companies depended heavily on these merchants for their annual purchase of textiles and other commodities. The merchants also generally kept the terms of the contract and supplied the specified quantity and variety of textiles at the prices stipulated.

The above data underlines the role and significance of the commercial relationship for the companies as well as for brokers and merchants in the seventeenth and eighteenth centuries. The relationship was dynamic and was shaped by several economic and political forces, like availability of funds to finance trade, merchant networks and structure of the market, political power, and the degree of control over production and market. These

51   Nadri, 'Commercial World of Mancherji Khurshedji'.
52   Ibid., pp. 334-340.
53   Ibid., pp. 334-341.

forces were transient and changed rapidly across the eighteenth century. What were the implications of the economic and political changes for the companies' relationship with their brokers and other Indian merchants? How and why did the role and position of brokers change over the period? The rest of the chapter addresses these questions by first outlining the change and long-term continuity in the relationship and then explaining what caused the change.

Companies' relationship with Indian merchants: continuity and change

In the seventeenth century, the companies and Indian merchants were highly dependent on each other in the marketplace, but it was often the latter who were better positioned to benefit from European trade. Indian merchants were well placed to take advantage of the standing constraints on the companies' trade. These were, first, a shortage of funds, which required the companies to borrow from local merchants, and second, the urgent need to sell their imports and purchase export goods in order to ensure a timely dispatch of ships from Surat. Having a broker and forging a trustworthy commercial relationship with Surat merchants were responses to this specific situation, and the arrangement seems to have worked reasonably well for the two companies. This was a relationship of interdependence and shared benefits, but each side was also always eager to take advantage of the other's situation and to maximise its share. The companies attempted, sometimes through the use of violence, to turn the balance to their favour, but could not succeed. The nature of this relationship finally changed in the eighteenth century, although even then it continued to be based on interdependence and mutual benefit. The companies managed to assert their position and curtail the authority of brokers.

In the eighteenth century, the role of the company's broker was more or less confined to the disposal of merchandise, although the brokers could outmanoeuvre the sales at the auction to make transactions in their favour. A division of tasks seems to have occurred between brokers and suppliers of merchandise. Both the EIC and the VOC had access to merchants other than their brokers as suppliers of merchandise. The VOC, for instance, distinguished its brokers (*makelaars*) from its suppliers (*leveranciers*). The former generally bought the company's imports and the latter supplied the export merchandise. The VOC and the EIC in Surat employed two merchants jointly serving as brokers and two others jointly working as suppliers.[54] This was the companies' strategy to diversify risk and avoid too much dependence on a single merchant family. The relationship, however, was still essentially based on interdependence, with brokers being more dependent on the companies than their seventeenth-century predecessors. Most brokers in the eighteenth century were merchants with several portfolios in their hands. They diversified their risk and invested their human and capital resources in multiple businesses such as banking, brokering, large-scale overseas trading, and shipping. Brokering became an additional source of wealth and it gave them respectability in the community as well as in political circles.[55] Association with the company also ensured protection for their person and wealth from threats and actual losses. As stakes were high, the latter came to depend more on the companies. The promise of protection made an impact on the relationship between the companies and their brokers and suppliers and hence requires further analysis.

Protection: its impact on the relationship

Why did brokers and suppliers work closely with the companies? One obvious reason was because it was profitable, but they also relied on the companies for protection. Protection did not necessarily imply patronage or an unequal relationship; it was rather contractual and based on mutual trust and cooperation. It seems that the merchants promised not to harm the commercial interests of the companies and, in return, the companies ensured protection and extended other privileges such as low customs duties at the ports, which the EIC and VOC controlled. This may have circumscribed the brokers in the exercise of power that came with the office. The companies too, in view of growing competition and the problems of logistics, vied with each other to secure this commitment from the leading merchants of the city. Merchants and the companies both benefited from this complementarity.[56]

---

54   In much of the eighteenth century, two Parsi merchants, Sorabji and Ratanji, and after them their sons, Bahramji Sorabji and Hormusji Ratanji, managed the VOC's purchase of textiles and other goods in Surat. Similarly, Parsi merchants, Dadabhai Manikji and Edul Dada, were the principal contractors of the EIC's investment in textiles in the late eighteenth century. Nadri, *Eighteenth-Century Gujarat*, pp. 75-76.

55   Gupta, 'The Broker in Mughal Surat', p. 401.

56   Nadri, 'Commercial World of Mancherji Khurshedji', p. 318.

On many occasions in the late eighteenth century, the companies intervened and protected their brokers. In 1768, the VOC protected Mancherji
Khurshedji when he was threatened by the Parsi merchant (and commercial
rival) Dhanjishah Manjishah.[57] Three years later, the EIC and the Portuguese
entered into a prolonged conflict over the latter's capture of a ship belonging
to Dhanjishah Manjishah, a former broker of the EIC who sailed under the
company's protection. This remarkable episode illustrates the significance
of protection and the alliance that existed between the companies and their
Indian allies. It shows how beneficial it was for Indian shipowners to be
under the companies' protection, especially under the EIC's protection. It
also reveals what protection actually meant for the EIC and what else that
entailed. The capture by the Portuguese of Dhanjishah's ship returning to
Surat from the East African coast and its taking over to Daman in September
1771 initiated a protracted fight over the legality of the capture, its recovery,
and reprisals. It soon turned into a contest between two sovereign nations,
each claiming and defending its authority in the Indian Ocean.[58]

The Portuguese cruisers in Daman captured the ship because it did not
have a Portuguese pass and the captain also failed to produce a pass issued
by the EIC. When the matter was reported in Surat, the EIC demanded the
ship's return by claiming that its owner was the company's *marfatia* and
therefore a company subject under its protection.[59] EIC authorities in Bombay
wrote letters to the Portuguese governor of Goa demanding the return of
the captured ship to Surat and informing him that, if he failed to comply,
reprisals would be made to the amount of the value of the ship and its cargo.
The governor of Goa persisted in his refusal to return the ship, insisting that
the Portuguese cruisers were within their rights to capture the ship as it
did not have a valid EIC pass to sail. The English blamed the Portuguese
for violating the company's rights to issue passes and protect its subjects,
while the Portuguese invoked their 'ancient' and exclusive jurisdiction over
Indian waters and the rights to issue passes to Asian ships. In a letter to the
EIC President in Bombay, the governor of Goa wrote:

> I very well know the conditions by which the nuptial treaties of Senhora
> Donna Catherina were made and by which the Island of Bombay was given
> to the British nation, and the said nation did thereby promise and bind

---

57   Ibid., pp. 315-316.
58   British Library, Home Miscellaneous 108, Extract of Bombay General Consultations, pp. 83-
123, 159-183.
59   Ibid., Extract of Bombay General Consultations, 17 December 1771, p. 159.

themselves not to prejudice in any manner the ancient rights which the Crown of Portugal had acquired in Asia; These treaties alone would have been sufficient; wherefore the Hon'ble Company could not grant the abovementioned pass without infringing and prejudicing the rights of the Crown of Portugal.[60]

In the same letter, the governor also warned the EIC's Bombay government that if reprisals were taken against the Portuguese in Surat, they would do whatever was 'necessary for due recompence and satisfaction'. He wrote, 'I will acquaint his most faithful Majesty therewith that he may make an end of recompencing in the interests which England now has in Portugal; and it is certain that his British Majesty and all the English nation will make you responsible for all that may happen on this account.' The dispute also involved the question of jurisdiction. Because the EIC claimed that the owner of the ship was its subject, it was not acceptable to the company that he should seek justice at the Portuguese court in Goa. In reply to Portuguese claims, EIC authorities at Bombay wrote that 'though we pay a due regard to the rights of other nations, we shall not permit our own to be infringed; on this account our broker cannot be permitted to apply to your tribunal for justice'.[61] In another letter, the Bombay authorities justified reprisals and wrote to the Portuguese that we 'hereby declare that you are answerable for every bad consequence which may ensue therefrom as you may be assured that we shall not suffer the rights and privileges of our Nation to be infringed under any pretence or by any power whatever.'[62] An exchange of letters, claims, and counter-claims continued between Bombay and Goa for months. The matter was reported to the authorities in London and Lisbon. In November 1772, the EIC persuaded the *nawab* (governor) of Surat to detain the property of Portuguese merchants equal to the value of the captured ship and its cargo (amounting to 48,808 rupees).[63]

We do not know if the ship and cargo were restored to the owners or whether the Portuguese were able to get back their merchandise detained

---

60   Ibid., Extract of Bombay General Consultations, 27 March 1772 (English translation of a Portuguese letter from Goa, 20 February 1772), p. 168. Similar sentiments were expressed in another letter from Goa to the EIC president at Bombay. Ibid., Extract of Bombay General Consultations, 10 November 1772 (English translation of the Portuguese letter from Goa, 15 October 1772), pp. 174-183.

61   Ibid., Extract of Bombay General Consultations, 9 April 1772, p. 172.

62   Ibid., Bombay to Goa, 16 December 1772, p. 110.

63   Ibid., Extracts of the East India Company's Advices received by the ship *Speaker*, 10 September 1773, pp. 83-97. In early 1773, the governor of Surat detained goods belonging to the Portuguese merchants to the value of 61,517 rupees. Ibid., List of articles belonging to the Portuguese detained by the Nabob, 2 February 1773, p. 107.

in Surat. What is remarkable about this incident is that it opened up a discourse on their respective jurisdictions in the Indian Ocean and within it the position of Indian merchants and shipowners. It tells us something about the meaning and implications of issuing passes for sea voyages and protection that the company granted to its brokers, bankers, suppliers, and other merchants. The persistence with which the EIC undertook to retrieve the ship and its cargo for their owners in a period when Britain and Portugal were in a relationship of peace and amity reveals the significance of Indian merchants for the company's successful commercial enterprise. This also shows how beneficial such a strategic alliance could be for Indian merchants and their commercial world during this period. Instances like this point to the persistent value that a company association held for Indian merchants.

Conclusions

As is clear from the discussion above, the relationship between the European East India companies and their Indian brokers, bankers, and other merchants evolved over a period of time and was based on interdependence and complementarity. In transacting business in the seventeenth century, the companies were heavily dependent on Indian bankers and brokers and the latter often exercised monopsonistic and monopolistic control over the companies' sales and purchases of merchandise in Surat. A qualitative change in this relationship, however, occurred in the eighteenth century. Instead of dealing with one broker, the EIC and VOC split the broker's portfolio of responsibilities and employed several merchants, each with a particular assignment. One merchant, designated as a broker, mainly looked after the sale of the company's imports. Another merchant was responsible for supplying export goods, and yet another was employed to handle daily affairs relating to local administration. By doing so, the companies were able to curtail the authority of their broker. Several factors seem to have created the circumstances in which these changes took place.

First, the character of Surat's mercantile community changed in the eighteenth century. It was no longer dominated by a few merchant princes possessing enormous wealth and commanding influence in political circles and local administration.[64] Mercantile wealth was not concentrated in a few hands, instead several wealthy merchants came to represent the merchant

---

64   Abdul Ghafur (d. 1718), who owned about 17 ocean-going ships and whose total wealth at the time of his death exceeded 8 million rupees, was perhaps the last of this generation of merchant

community of eighteenth-century Surat. These merchants were not able to assert their monopoly or monopsony in the marketplace to the same degree as their seventeenth-century predecessors, like Virji Vora. Second, these merchants lost their political patronage due to the decline of the Mughal central authority and the ensuing political instability in Gujarat in the early eighteenth century. Third, the EIC's takeover of Surat castle in 1759 and its political ascendancy in the region certainly had an impact on the relationship. This enabled the company to assert itself and maximise commercial benefits. For many years, the company monopolised freight trade between Surat and West Asia and attempted to control the textile market of Surat.[65] Fourth, the potential and real threat of piracy and vulnerability of Asian shipping to maritime violence forced many to turn to the European companies for protection. Finally, the rise of the Parsi merchant community in Surat as competitor of the Banias in brokering and, to some extent, in banking sectors enlarged the pool of resourceful merchants with whom the European companies could transact business and thereby reduced the latter's dependence on a particular Bania family of bankers and brokers.

The companies succeeded to a degree in limiting the role of their brokers. The EIC did this more successfully than the VOC because the balance of political and economic power had shifted in favour of the former, both in Europe and India. Neither, however, could dominate the relationship. The companies and the Indian merchants continued to play complementary roles and their relationship remained mutually beneficial. Even the EIC's 1759 takeover of the Surat castle and its control over the city's revenue resources did not free the company from its dependence on brokers/merchants. This reflects the limited power of the European companies in Surat and their need to rely on indigenous allies. The commercial profiles of Mancherji Khurshedji and Dhanjishah Manjishah are illustrative of this. Their relationship with the VOC and the EIC was dynamic, interdependent, and endowed with extensive complementarity.

princes in Surat. For more details on his trading activities, see Gupta, *Indian Merchants and the Decline of Surat*, pp. 94-133.

65   The monopoly implied that only ships chartered by the English chief were first allowed to take in freight goods and proceed to the Red Sea and the Persian Gulf. For more details on and merchants' response to the monopoly, see Torri, 'In the Deep Blue Sea'; Nadri, 'Sailing in Hazardous Waters'. For an analysis of the EIC's attempt to control Surat's textile market, see Nadri, *Eighteenth-Century Gujarat*, pp. 145-146.

Works cited

Broecke, Pieter van den, *Pieter van den Broecke in Azië*, vol. 2, ed., W.Ph. Coolhaas (The Hague: Martinus Nijhoff, 1963).

Chaudhury, Sushil, 'The Gujarat Mahajans: An Analysis of their Functional Role in the Surat Crisis of 1669', *Proceedings of the Indian History Congress* (New Delhi, 1980).

Clulow, Adam, 'European Maritime Violence and Territorial States in Early Modern Asia, 1600-1650', *Itinerario: International Journal on the History of European Expansion and Global Interaction,* 33, no. 3 (2009): 72–94.

Dam, Pieter van, *Beschrijving van de Oost-Indische Compagnie,* ed. F.W. Stapel, vol. 2, part 3 (The Hague: Martinus Nijhoff, 1939).

Foster, William, *The Embassy of Sir Thomas Roe to the Court of the Great Mogul, 1615-1619,* 2 vols. (London: Hakluyt Society, 1899).

Gokhale, B.G., *Surat in the Seventeenth Century: A Study in Urban History of Pre-modern India* (Bombay: Popular Prakashan, 1978).

Gupta, Ashin Das, 'Indian Merchants in the Age of Partnership, 1500-1800', in *Business Communities of India: A Historical Perspective,* ed. Dwijendra Tripathi (Delhi: Manohar, 1984), pp. 27–39.

Gupta, Ashin Das, 'Indian Merchants and the Trade in the Indian Ocean', in *The Cambridge Economic History of India,* vol. 1, ed. Tapan Raychaudhuri and Irfan Habib (New Delhi: Orient Longman, 1984).

Gupta, Ashin Das, *Indian Merchants and the Decline of Surat, c. 1700-1750* (New Delhi: Manohar, 1984).

Gupta, Ashin Das and M.N. Pearson (eds.), *India and the Indian Ocean, 1500-1800* (Oxford: Oxford University Press, 1987).

Gupta, Ashin Das, 'The Broker in Mughal Surat, c. 1740', in *The World of the Indian Ocean Merchant, 1500-1800: Collected Essays of Ashin Das Gupta*, ed. Uma Das Gupta (New Delhi: Oxford University Press, 2001).

Jacobs, Els, *Merchants in Asia: The Trade of the Dutch East India Company during the Eighteenth Century* (Leiden: Leiden University Press, 2006).

Kling, Blair B., and M.N. Pearson, *The Age of Partnership: Europeans in Asia before Domination* (Honolulu: University of Hawai'i Press, 1979).

Mehta, Makrand J., *Indian Merchants and Entrepreneurs in Historical Perspectives: With Special Reference to Shroffs of Gujarat: 17th to 19th Centuries* (Delhi: Academic Foundation, 1991).

Mehta, Makrand J., 'Some Aspects of Surat as a Trading Centre in the 17th Century', *Indian Historical Review* 1, no. 2 (1974): 247–61.

Moreland, W.H., *India at the Death of Akbar: An Economic Study* (Delhi: Macmillan & Company, 1920).

Nadri, Ghulam A., 'The Maritime Merchants of Surat: A Long-term Perspective', *Journal of the Economic and Social History of the Orient* 50, no. 2/3 (2007): 235–58.

Nadri, Ghulam A., 'Commercial World of Mancherji Khurshedji and the Dutch East India Company: A Study of Mutual Relationships', *Modern Asian Studies* 41, no. 2 (2007): 315–42.

Nadri, Ghulam A., 'The Dutch Intra-Asian Trade in Sugar in the Eighteenth Century', *International Journal of Maritime History* 20, no. 1 (2008): 63–96.

Nadri, Ghulam A., *Eighteenth-Century Gujarat: The Dynamics of Its Political Economy, 1750-1800* (Leiden: Brill, 2009).

Nadri, Ghulam A., 'Sailing in Hazardous Waters: Maritime Merchants of Gujarat in the Second Half of the Eighteenth Century', in *The Trading World of the Indian Ocean 1500-1800*, ed. Om Prakash (New Delhi: Pearson, 2012: 255-84.

Nadri, Ghulam A., *The Political Economy of Indigo in India, 1580-1930: A Global Perspective* (Leiden: Brill, 2016).

Panikkar, K.M., *Asia and Western Dominance: A Survey of the Vasco Da Gama Epoch of Asian History, 1498-1945* (George Allen and Unwin, 1961).

Pearson, M.N., 'Brokers in Western Indian Port Cities: Their Role in Servicing Foreign Merchants', *Modern Asian Studies* 22, no. 3 (1988): 455–72.

Pearson, M.N., *The Indian Ocean* (Oxford: Routledge, 2003).

Prakash, Om, *The Dutch Factories in India, 1617-1623* (New Delhi: Munshiram Manoharlal, 1984).

Prakash, Om, *European Commercial Enterprise in Pre-Colonial India* (New Delhi: Cambridge University Press, 1998).

Prakash, Om, 'Sarrafs, Financial Intermediation, and Credit Network in Mughal India', in *Bullion for Goods: European and Indian Merchants in the Indian Ocean Trade, 1500-1800*, ed. Om Prakash (New Delhi: Manohar, 2004).

Prakash, Om, 'English Private Trade in the Western Indian Ocean, 1720-1740', *Journal of the Economic and Social History of the Orient* 50, nos. 2/3 (2007): 215–34.

Qaisar, A. Jan, 'The Role of Brokers in Medieval India', *Indian Historical Review* 1, part 2 (1974): 220–46.

Santen, Hans Walther van, 'De Verenigde Oost-Indische Compagnie in Gujarat en Hindustan, 1620-1660' (PhD dissertation, Leiden University, 1982).

Shimada, Ryuto, *The Intra-Asian Trade in Japanese Copper by the Dutch East India Company during the Eighteenth Century* (Leiden: Brill, 2006).

Subramanian, Lakshmi, 'Capital and Crowd in a Declining Asian Port City: The Anglo-Bania Order and the Surat Riots of 1795', *Modern Asian Studies* 19, no. 2 (1985): 205–37.

Subramanian, Lakshmi, 'The Eighteenth Century Social Order in Surat: A Reply and an Excursus on the Riots of 1788 and 1795', *Modern Asian Studies* 25, no. 2 (1991): 338–42.

Torri, Michelguglielmo, 'In the Deep Blue Sea: Surat and its Merchant Class during the Dyarchic Era, 1759-1800', *Indian Economic and Social History Review* 19, nos. 3-4 (1982): 267–99.

Torri, Michelguglielmo, 'Surat during the Second Half of the Eighteenth Century: What Kind of Social Order? A Rejoinder to Lakshmi Subramanian', *Modern Asian Studies* 21, no. 4 (1987): 679–710.

Contact details

Ghulam A. Nadri, Georgia State University

Part 3

Violence

6 Empire by Treaty?

The role of written documents in European overseas
expansion, 1500-1800

Martine van Ittersum

Abstract

Treaty-making was integral to European imperialism and colonialism
in the early modern period. Europeans did not seek to enter into equal
treaties with indigenous rulers or peoples, but to conclude agreements that
advanced their own claims to trade and/or territory. Two case studies – the
Banda Islands and the Hudson Valley in the seventeenth century – serve
to illustrate this point. Of course, the extent to which Europeans achieved
their aims depended on local power constellations in Africa, Asia or the
Americas, and the diplomatic fallout back in Europe. Still, in a world of
endemic violence, treaty and alliance making were essential preparations
for the next round of warfare and, thus, empire-building.

Keywords: treaty making, claims making, Banda Islands, Hudson Valley,
Dutch West India Company (WIC), international law

In August 1999, nine members of Gerakan Aceh Merdeka (GAM) entered
the grounds of the Dutch embassy in Jakarta, demanding that the Kingdom
of the Netherlands support Aceh's independence at the UN and retract its
1873 declaration of war against the Sultanate of Aceh. As the GAM members
were well aware, the Sultanate had been incorporated into the Dutch East
Indies in 1904, after a decades-long guerrilla war in the jungle of Sumatra.
A retraction of the 1873 declaration of war would, GAM members imagined,
be the first step in restoring Acehnese sovereignty and independence. Yet
it was not so easy to turn back the clock. In 1948, the Dutch government
had recognised the Republic of Indonesia as the sole successor state to
the Dutch East Indies. Since then, it has carefully refrained from offering

Clulow, Adam and Tristan Mostert (eds.), *The Dutch and English East India Companies: Diplomacy,
trade and violence in early modern Asia*. Amsterdam: Amsterdam University Press, 2018
DOI: 10.5117/9789462983298/CH06

any kind of support for independence movements active in Sumatra, the Spice Islands and Timor. In the end, Indonesian police removed the GAM protesters from the embassy compound after three days, but, at the Dutch government's request, did not place them under arrest.[1]

What makes these protests especially interesting is that GAM justified its actions with reference to modern international law, particularly the role played by written documents in orchestrating transfers of sovereignty. This was not an isolated episode, rather it forms part of a broader interest by indigenous groups and their supporters in mobilising the language of earlier treaties and agreements. One place this can be seen is in the writings of James Tully, who served on the Canadian Royal Commission on Aboriginal Peoples from 1991 until 1995. Tully assigns an important role to treaty-making in the process of reconciliation between the aboriginal and non-aboriginal peoples of Canada. He suggests a return to an idealised past of early modern treaty-making, a period of time when Europeans and indigenous groups were evenly matched and treated each other as equals. While recognising the presence of abuses, he places considerable value on what he considers to be the original intentions behind treaties from the early modern period, namely to settle differences between natives and Europeans 'by means of discussion and consent, without interfering in the internal government of either society'.[2]

A similar desire to look again at early modern treaties animates a number of recent publications by historians who have increasingly entered the debate about treaty-making past and present. Two important contributions are *Native Claims: Indigenous Law against Empire, 1500-1920* (2012) and *Empire by Treaty: Negotiating European Expansion, 1600-1900* (2015), both edited by Saliha Belmessous. These volumes raise the important question whether treaties between Europeans and indigenous populations around the world can be read as alternatives to conquest and war and, possibly, as the means by which indigenous peoples have sought to turn the tide of Western imperialism and colonialism. Belmessous notes in her introduction to *Empire*

---

1   'Actie Atjeërs bij ambassade', *Trouw*, 5 August 1999; A. Jansen, 'Aceh kan prima overweg met Nederland', *Reformatorisch Dagblad*, 5 August 1999; 'De prijs van het zwijgen', *De Groene Amsterdammer*, 8 September 1999; Wim van den Doel, 'Het Hoge Woord', *Historisch Nieuwsblad* (2003) nr. 5; Esther Pan, 'Indonesia: The Aceh Peace Agreement', Council on Foreign Relations, 15 September 2005, www.cfr.org/indonesia/indonesia-aceh-peace-agreement/p8789. It was only after the 2004 Indian Ocean tsunami, which destroyed large swathes of Bandar Aceh, that Dutch government representatives started to visit the area on a regular basis – primarily to check on rebuilding activities, to which the Netherlands contributed $100 million. The Dutch government was not involved in the 2005 peace negotiations between GAM and the Indonesian government, not officially at least.

2   Tully, *Public Philosophy in a New Key*, p. 226.

by Treaty that treaty-making plays an important role in 'the resolution of conflicts over indigenous rights in postcolonial settler societies'. Similarly, Paul Patton, one of the contributors, argues that the treaty relationship reflects a desire 'on all sides' to legitimise settler sovereignty 'by reference to the consent, however belated or hypothetical, of [...] indigenous peoples'.[3]

But is this more positive view justified? Not all the contributors to *Empire by Treaty* are as sanguine as Belmessous and Patton appear to be about the capacity of indigenous groups to negotiate or resist empire via treaties. In her chapter on territorial conflict and alliance-making in pre-1800 South America, Tamar Herzog convincingly shows that treaties were 'instruments of containment' aimed at realising 'to the degree that this was possible – the subjection of all things indigenous'.[4] Similarly, in a review of *Empire by Treaty*, Dane Kennedy suggests that the history of treaty-making raises serious concerns about the legitimacy of settler sovereignty, since 'indigenous consent was often coerced'.[5]

This chapter argues that treaty-making should not be seen as an alternative to conquest and war, but was, in fact, integral to the process of European possession and indigenous dispossession. Europeans who ventured overseas in the early modern era did not aim to enter into equal treaties with indigenous rulers or peoples, but to conclude agreements that advanced their own claims to trade and/or territory. In a world of endemic conflict, treaty- and alliance-making were essential preparations for the next armed conflict.

If treaties were an instrument of European expansion, their deployment depended on the nature of the states that opposed them. When Europeans encountered regional powers like Ming or Qing China and Tokugawa Japan, their advantages disappeared.[6] Significantly, the polities capable of withstanding the onslaught of European company-states such as the English and Dutch East India Companies were those that possessed sizable armed forces and bureaucracies of their own or that could successfully play off European competitors against each other.

But in places where Europeans did not face entrenched powers, the treaty became a document that was closely linked to expansion. To illustrate this, I examine two cases studies from opposite ends of the world, Dutch trade and settlement in the Banda Islands in Asia and in the Hudson Valley

3   Belmessous, *Native Claims Against Empire*; Belmessous, *Empire by Treaty*; Belmessous, 'The Paradox of An Empire By Treaty', p. 15; Patton, 'The "Lessons of History"', p. 269.

4   Herzog, 'Struggling over Indians', pp. 78–79.

5   Kennedy, 'Review of Saliha Belmessous (ed.), Empire by Treaty'.

6   Clulow, 'The Art of Claiming'; Clulow, *The Company and the Shogun*; Clulow, 'European Maritime Violence'.

in the Americas.[7] Neither area was under the direct rule of the federal government of the Dutch Republic. Instead, the Dutch States General had established two corporate bodies with sweeping powers: the Dutch East and West India Companies (VOC and WIC), founded in 1602 and 1621, respectively. Both companies operated simultaneously as associations of private merchants and, in their charter areas, as full-fledged sovereign states. They had no qualms about initiating armed conflicts with European or native competitors. The outsourcing of overseas expansion to Dutch and English merchant corporations explains why imperial powers in northwestern Europe tended to thrive on the toxic combination of warfare and treaty-making – to the detriment of indigenous rulers and peoples.[8] Looking at these examples reveals the ways in which trade, treaty-making and the use of armed force were inextricably intertwined.

Treaty-making and armed conflict in the Banda Islands[9]

Located 2,000 kilometres east of Java, the Banda Islands – a group of seven small islands, including one volcano, the Gunung Api – are now a forgotten backwater in the Republic of Indonesia. It used to be very different. For centuries, the Spice Islands – meaning the Northern Moluccas, Ambon, and the Banda Islands – were part of an Asian trading network connecting the island of Java with the Philippines and the South China Sea. Merchants from ports on Java's north coast frequented the Banda Islands on a regular basis, exchanging rice from Java and textiles from the Indian subcontinent for nutmeg and mace. They brought Islam as well. As elsewhere in Southeast Asia, state development was slow in the Banda Islands. Confederations of villages, most prominently *ulilima* (a group of five villages) and *ulisiva* (a group of nine villages), competed with each other. *Orangkayas* (aristocrats, generally with wealth from trade) met on the island of Nera in order to reduce conflict between villages and negotiate trade deals. Although the

7   This is not the first attempt to compare Dutch trade and settlement in Asia and the Americas. Almost 30 years ago, an article analysing Dutch-native relations in Formosa (now Taiwan) and the Hudson Valley was published in the *Proceedings of the American Philosophical Society*. The authors, Hauptman and Knapp, concluded that the differences outweighed the similarities. Hauptman and Knapp, 'Dutch-Aboriginal Interaction'. I thank Tonio Andrade and Leonard Blussé for bringing this article to my attention.
8   Borschberg, *Hugo Grotius, the Portuguese, and Free Trade*; van Ittersum, *Profit and Principle*; Stern, *The Company-State*; Weststeijn, 'The VOC as a Company-State'; Wilson, *The Savage Republic*.
9   For a much more extensive treatment, see van Ittersum, 'Debating Natural Law in the Banda Islands'.

Bandanese successfully played Javanese merchants off against each other, they had become dependent on the spice trade for their livelihoods. Not much was left of the islands' original subsistence economy by the time the first Europeans arrived in the sixteenth century.[10]

Nutmeg, mace, and cloves had reached Europe via ports in the Middle East during the Middle Ages. One of the aims of European expansion into Asia was to cut out Muslim middlemen and establish direct trade links with the Spice Islands. The Portuguese were the first to reach the Banda Islands. However, they were not able to establish a military presence there, in sharp contrast with the Northern Moluccas and Ambon, where they built and garrisoned fortresses. Nor did the Portuguese obtain any special privileges in the Banda Islands, but traded on the same footing as Javanese merchants.[11]

The situation in the Banda Islands changed dramatically when the VOC appeared on the scene. A swift Dutch penetration into Southeast Asia went hand-in-hand with naked aggression against both Portuguese and indigenous shipping. The voyage of Pieter Willemszoon Verhoef (1573-1609), the VOC's so-called Fourth Voyage (1607-1612), was crucial in tipping the balance of power in the Banda Islands. With an eye to the Twelve Years' Truce (1609-1621) – then being negotiated between the Dutch Republic and the King of Spain and Portugal – the VOC directors authorised Verhoef in April 1608 to create a monopoly of trade in the Spice Islands. He received orders to sign contracts with 'all the villages in the Moluccas and Banda', and to build fortresses in strategic places, 'with the consent of the Indians'. The directors' logic was impeccable: as they noted in their letter, 'neither the King of Spain, nor any of his subjects may visit, or trade in, those places in Asia or Africa where we have possession or exclusive contracts'. Verhoef did as he was told. For the first time, the Bandanese had to accept a European military presence in their country. Dutch fortresses were established on Nera in 1609, on Pulo Way in 1616, and on Great Banda (also known as Lonthor) in 1621. Despite this, Banda's indigenous inhabitants had no intention of surrendering without a fight, and took up arms against the VOC. An already complex situation was complicated even further by the presence of merchants and mariners employed by the English East India Company (EIC), eager to secure their own trading interests.[12]

10   Reid, *Southeast Asia in the Age of Commerce*, Vol. 1: *The Lands Below the Wind*, pp. 11–31, pp. 90–96; Vol. 2: *Expansion and Crisis*, pp. 1–61, pp. 114–173; Gupta, 'The Maritime Trade of Indonesia'; Knaap, *Kruidnagelen en Christenen*.

11   Villiers, 'Trade and society in the Banda Islands'; Vlekke, *Nusantara*, pp. 68-90.

12   Nationaal Archief (Dutch National Archives), The Hague, VOC 478 f. 1v, 2 v (the directors' instructions for VOC commanders and officers in the East Indies, 10/11 April 1608); Locher-Scholten

By establishing fortresses in Asia during the Twelve Years' Truce and signing new, exclusive contracts with local allies, the VOC sought to tighten up the protection/tribute exchange and strengthen its position as a co-ruler in these territories. In the directors' view, the VOC protected indigenous peoples against the 'tyranny' of the King of Spain and Portugal and had to be rewarded by means of exclusive spice deliveries. The Bandanese saw things differently, of course. As Adam Clulow notes, the *orangkayas* 'had long been accustomed to finding security by playing off foreign powers'.[13] Until Verhoef's arrival in the archipelago, they had treated the VOC as simply one more merchant bidding for their produce. If and when the VOC failed to supply the trade goods they required, such as textiles and rice, they had been at liberty to sell their nutmeg and mace to somebody else, and frequently did. Verhoef was determined to change that. His murder in May 1609 suggests that many Bandanese objected to establishing closer ties with the VOC through a new treaty, and were desperate to avoid the construction of a Dutch fortress. They may well have suspected that, ultimately, it would result in a complete loss of indigenous sovereignty.[14]

Thanks to the presence of William Keeling (1577/8-1620) in the Banda Islands in spring 1609, followed by visits from other EIC merchants and commanders, local opponents of the VOC were confident that they could play off the English against the Dutch and thus regain control of the situation. The Bandanese suffered from internal divisions, however. According to Governor-General Laurens Reael (1583-1637), they governed themselves 'entirely in a democratic fashion (*populariter*), like a republic', meaning in this case a high level of internal disunity. It may explain why they dismissed Keeling's suggestion to surrender their sovereignty to the King of England. Only in April 1616, when VOC commander Jan Dirckszoon Lam (d. 1626) was about to launch an all-out assault, did inhabitants of Pulo Way enact a ceremony formally acknowledging James I of England as their protector. It failed to stop Lam's conquest of the island. But it did create a very useful precedent for the EIC. Eight months later, Nathaniel Courthope had little

and Rietbergen, *Hof en Handel*; Knaap and Teitler, *De Verenigde Oost-Indische Compagnie*; Milton, *Nathaniel's Nutmeg*; Loth, 'Armed Incidents and Unpaid Bills'; Keay, *The Honourable Company*; Masselman, *The Cradle of Colonialism*; Chaudhuri, *The English East India Company*; Foster, *England's Quest of Eastern Trade*.

13   Clulow, 'The Art of Claiming', p. 30.

14   Opstall, *De Reis van de Vloot van Pieter Willemsz*, pp. 94–105, 267–69; Purchas, *Hakluytus Posthumus*, pp. 534–39; Heeres and Stapel, *Corpus diplomaticum Neerlando-Indicum*, 1907-1955, Vol. I, pp. 11–12, 23–26, 36–41, 66–69 (contracts with the Bandanese of 18 March 1599, 23 May and 17 June 1602, 13 July 1605, 10 August 1609).

difficulty persuading inhabitants of Pulu Run – many of whom were refugees from Pulo Way – to repeat the ceremony and sign a treaty with him.[15]

Meanwhile, VOC officials continued to sign contracts with the Bandanese as well, primarily with inhabitants of Rosengain and Great Banda. From the VOC perspective, the military conquests of Nera and Pulo Way in 1609 and 1616, respectively, had turned local populations into Company subjects. By concluding treaties with inhabitants of Rosengain and Great Banda in May 1616, April 1617, and June 1618, both Lam and Reael sought to obtain native recognition of the changed status of Nera and Pulo Way, secure a steady supply of nutmeg and mace for the VOC, and completely isolate Pulo Run and its inhabitants, who had sided with the English. Although Reael failed to launch a successful invasion of Pulo Run in the spring of 1617 and 1618, he used all the other means at his disposal to make life difficult for Courthope and his indigenous allies. Citing the contracts already signed with the Dutch, he forbade any contact between Bandanese allies of the VOC and inhabitants of Pulo Run, for example. The wavering loyalties of the Bandanese proved to be the Achilles' heel of his strategy. In summer 1618, Reael signed a truce treaty with the '*orangkayas* and magistrates' of Selamon only, not with any other villages on Great Banda. Those villages had effectively sided with the inhabitants of Pulo Run.[16]

From the Dutch perspective, the next logical step was to conquer and pacify Great Banda. More nutmeg trees grew on Great Banda than on all the other islands of the archipelago combined. The inhabitants of Pulo Run were crucially dependent for their survival on foodstuffs and water reaching them from Great Banda. In other words, a Dutch conquest of the island would make it impossible for the English to continue in actual possession of Pulo Run. The strategy proved effective. Inhabitants of Great Banda repulsed Lam's expeditionary force in June 1618, but were soundly defeated by Governor-General Jan Pieterszoon Coen (1587-1629) three years later. Coen commanded a formidable naval and military force of sixteen warships and nearly a thousand soldiers. The Treaty of Defence concluded by the VOC and EIC in London in

---

15   Opstall, 'Laurens Reael in de Staten-Generaal', p. 197; Foster, *England's Quest of Eastern Trade*, pp. 261–67; Foster, *The Journal of John Jourdain*, pp. 328–29; Stapel, *Geschiedenis van Nederlands Indië*, p. 99; Loth, 'Armed Incidents and Unpaid Bills', pp. 713–14; van Goor, *Jan Pieterszoon Coen*, p. 281.

16   *Corpus diplomaticum Neerlando-Indicum* Vol. I: *1596-1650* pp. 66–69 (treaty with the Bandanese of 10 August 1609), pp. 122–24 (treaty with the Bandanese of 3 May 1616), pp. 127–30 (treaty with the Bandanese of 30 April 1617), pp. 133–35 (treaty with the Bandanese of 25 June 1618), pp. 160–61 (treaty with the Bandanese, March 1621?), pp. 162–70 (treaty with the Bandanese of 9 May 1621); Stapel, *Geschiedenis van Nederlands Indië*, Vol. III pp. 102–04; Foster, *England's Quest of Eastern Trade*, pp. 261–70.

June 1619 proved an unexpected benefit in pacifying the archipelago. Since the companies were now officially allied, neither the EIC merchants in Bantam and Jakarta, nor the few Englishmen left at Pulo Run, dared to interfere with Coen's invasion plans or offer any support to the Bandanese.[17]

Coen's brutal conquest of Great Banda presents an inconvenient truth for many global historians writing today who are eager to ascribe agency to indigenous peoples through various forms of 'negotiating' and 'resisting' empire. Yet the power differential between Europeans and certain native groups in Asia and the Americas is something that we ignore at our peril. At the time, many Bandanese clearly underestimated the VOC's determination to secure a monopoly of the spice trade and the enormous resources which it could marshal against a weak, isolated polity. Of course, there were plenty of areas in the pre-modern world where Europeans struggled to get a foot in the door, but the Banda Islands were not one of these.[18]

Coen's punitive expedition resulted in the near-total destruction of Bandanese society. Forty-eight *orangkayas* were captured, tried, and executed at his order and approximately 789 old men, women, and children were shipped off to Batavia (modern-day Jakarta), the VOC headquarters in Asia, where they were put to work as slaves. In the end, there were only about a thousand of an estimated 15,000 original inhabitants left in the Banda Islands. The arable land on Great Banda was divided into plots called *perken*, and distributed among European tenants. Many of these so-called *perkeniers* were former VOC soldiers. Together with Company officials, they would form the elite level of the new colonial society for centuries to come. In their cultivation and harvesting of the valuable spices they could dispose of a large labour force of slaves, imported by the VOC from all parts of Asia. The Dutch conquest, then, marked a fundamental break with the past.[19]

---

17   Van Goor, *Jan Pieterszoon Coen*, pp. 433–65; Loth, 'Armed Incidents and Unpaid Bills', pp. 724–27.
18   On indigenous peoples 'negotiating' and 'resisting' empire, see e.g. Belmessous, *Empire by Treaty*; Belmessous, *Native Claims*; Meuwese, *Brothers in Arms*; Clulow, 'The Art of Claiming'. Clulow emphasises Bandanese legal resistance against the Dutch. He shows how, through both treaty texts and indigenous ceremonies, certain Bandanese groups successfully manipulated the English into supporting them against the VOC. Clulow recognises, however, that the English put their own spin on the treaty texts, and tended to overstate their case in negotiations with the VOC. The VOC repaid the compliment, of course: it routinely over-interpreted its treaties with indigenous rulers and peoples, if doing so served its own interest.
19   Van Goor, *Jan Pieterszoon Coen*, pp. 433–66; Winn, 'Slavery and Cultural Creativity in the Banda Islands'; Loth, 'Pioneers and Perkeniers'; Niemeijer, '"Als eene Lelye onder de doornen'; Hanna, *Indonesian Banda*. In 1638, slaves constituted approximately two-thirds of the population of the Banda Islands. Inevitably, a degree of racial mixing occurred, with *perkeniers* routinely

In this way, the Bandanese were the victims of Anglo-Dutch imperial competition in Asia. Caught in a downward spiral of increasingly brutal violence, their room for manoeuvre diminished rapidly. Appeals for help to EIC servants and indigenous leaders elsewhere (the rulers of Ternate, Makassar, and Bantam, among others) went unheeded or did not have the desired effect, in large part due to internal divisions among the Bandanese. If there was a 'middle ground' in the Banda Islands (i.e. an equilibrium of native and European power), it can only have existed for a fleeting moment in the 1610s. A toxic combination of warfare and treaty-making stripped the Bandanese of their sovereignty. From a European perspective, treaties with indigenous peoples were never meant to be agreements between equals. Even English assistance against Dutch aggression came at a high price for the Bandanese: according to the treaty concluded with Nathaniel Courthope in December 1616, they did not just promise the EIC all spices harvested on Pulo Run in perpetuity, but also surrendered the island to James I of England and put themselves under the latter's protection as his subjects. It was all to no avail. Lacking sufficient EIC support, the game was up for the inhabitants of Pulo Run by the time Coen arrived in February 1621.[20]

It is instructive to compare and contrast the Dutch imperial projects in the Hudson Valley and Banda Islands in the seventeenth century. Although these areas are usually treated separately, there are clear parallels in terms of Dutch claims-making and ensuing conflicts with indigenous peoples and European competitors. Thanks to the sovereign powers delegated by the Dutch States General, the VOC and WIC were able to conclude treaties of alliance with native peoples, impose protection/tribute exchanges on them, and insert themselves as co-rulers in far-flung areas of the world. Fortresses – even if these just consisted of blockhouses – functioned as nuclei of Dutch sovereignty, radiating influence outward. Both companies employed soldiers to enforce their own interpretations of treaties concluded with indigenous peoples. Warfare and treaty-making went hand in hand in these imperial projects.

marrying slave women. Although a steady trickle of slaves escaped to other nearby archi-pelagos, *marronage* never threatened colonial society in the Banda Islands. At the end of the eighteenth century, slave numbers had increased to 4,112, constituting three-quarters of the islands' population.

20   Purchas, *Hakluytus Posthumus* Vol. V, pp. 181–83; Masselman, *The Cradle of Colonialism*, pp. 417–22; van Goor, *Jan Pieterszoon Coen*, pp. 433–66.

Treaty-making and armed conflict in New Netherland

In September 1609, Henry Hudson – then employed by the VOC – sailed up the river that would later be named after him. He explored it as far as present-day Albany in New York State. The journal of Robert Juet of Limehouse, an officer aboard the *Halve Maen*, reveals that Hudson engaged in both trade and armed conflict with the various Munsee bands that lived along the river's shores. Juet recorded that the local people offered food and tobacco to their uninvited guests, while also exchanging furs for European trade goods. Yet Hudson and his men lived in constant fear of a surprise attack by the far more numerous locals – as Juet noted, we 'durst not trust them'. In the space of two months, a number of the local inhabitants were captured and killed for supposedly posing a threat to the *Halve Maen* and its crew. It was a harbinger of things to come.[21] In the wake of Hudson's voyage, Dutch merchants visited the river in increasing numbers during the 1610s and 1620s.

This period has given rise to a number of controversies over agreements supposedly concluded between the Dutch and local groups, which must be considered in any analysis. One such controversy centres on the Tawagonshi Document, which the Onandaga Nation in New York State considers a genuine 1613 treaty between 'the chiefs of the Long House' and two Dutch merchants, Jacob Eelckens and Hendrick Christiaenssen.[22] Allegedly, it guaranteed each of the signatory parties the right to self-determination and non-interference. If true, it would show a considerable degree of local agency in the face of European incursion. Yet there is good reason to question the validity of this document, as historians and linguists recently did in a special issue of the *Journal of Early American History* (2013).

Jaap Jacobs notes in his contribution to this special issue that there were no Dutch plans for settlement in the Hudson Valley prior to the WIC's founding. Dutch merchants simply sailed up the river for the summer trading season. The companies that employed them were relatively short-lived enterprises, and lacked the sovereign powers that the Dutch States General would bestow on the WIC in 1621. By virtue of its charter, the New Netherland Company (1614-1618) enjoyed a monopoly over all Dutch trade

---

21   Jameson, *Narratives of New Netherland*, pp. 18–20, p. 26; Otto, *The Dutch-Munsee Encounter in America*, pp. 37–47. As Paul Otto notes, archaeological evidence suggests that indigenous peoples in the Northeast first obtained European trade goods from French merchants on the St. Lawrence River in the mid-sixteenth century.

22   *Journal of Early American History* Vol. 3 issue 1 (2013), available in open access at http://booksandjournals.brillonline.com/content/18770703/3/1.

Figure 11   *Novi Belgii Novae que Angliae Nec Non Partis Virginae Tabula multis in
              locis emendata / Nieuw Amsterdam op t Eylant Manhattans*, **map of New
              Netherland and New England published by Nicolaas Visscher II (1649-
              1702). This map is based on a map produced by Johannes Janssonius in
              Amsterdam in 1651. Visscher added the view of New Amsterdam in the
              cartouche at the bottom centre.**

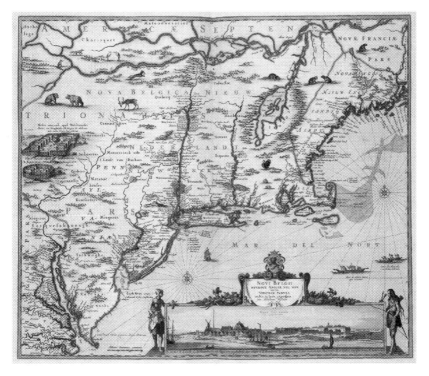

Collection Koninklijke Bibliotheek, The Hague, inv. nr. 1049 B 13, 74.

and shipping with the Hudson Valley, but it could not represent or act on
behalf of the Dutch States General. Only the WIC was entitled to 'make
contracts, agreements and alliances with the princes and natives of the
land'. Prior to 1621, any 'treaties' or alliances concluded by Dutch merchants
and native groups in the Hudson Valley would have been, from the Dutch
perspective at least, purely private agreements.[23]

---

23   Jacobs, 'Early Dutch Explorations in North America'. An English translation of the WIC
charter is available in *Van Rensselaer Bowier Manuscripts*, pp. 86–125. Article II of the WIC
charter (3 June 1621) reads as follows: "sal mogen maecken Contracten, Verbintenissen ende
Alliancien met de Princen ende Naturelen vande Landen."

At the same time, linguistic evidence suggests that the Tawagonshi Document cannot be a seventeenth-century Dutch text. The document – which is only available to scholars as a 1959 photocopy – contains a number of spelling and grammatical mistakes, along with Anglicisms and various other word forms and meanings unknown to seventeenth-century Dutch. It was, in all likelihood, the handiwork of the American physician Lawrence G. van Loon (1902-1982), who was notorious for his forgeries of historical documents relating to the history of Dutch New York.[24]

Similar concerns apply to the Two Row Wampum Belt, another controversial artifact supposedly from this period of initial contact. For the Onandaga Nation and other indigenous groups in the United States and Canada, it symbolises the treaty allegedly concluded with the Dutch four hundred years ago.[25] Crafted from marine shell, the Two Row Wampum Belt consists of two rows of purple beads set against a background of white beads. As Otto notes, indigenous peoples of the Hudson Valley did not start to produce purple beads until the 1630s or later. The purple beads are made from the dark purple section of the Quahog clam shells (*Mercenaria mercinaria*), the outer surface of which is so hard as to require the use of European-supplied metal drills. These were in short supply in the Hudson Valley in 1613. Although seventeenth-century oral traditions may have associated the Two Row Wampum Belt with an agreement between natives and Dutch merchants concluded before the 1630s, it is far more likely a recent development.[26]

If we do not accept the Tawagonshi Document and Two Row Wampum Belt as reliable sources, are there other seventeenth and eighteenth-century documents which speak to European–indigenous relations in the Hudson Valley and reflect a wider consensus about non-interference? In his contribution to the special issue of the *Journal of Early American History*, the historian Jon Parmenter accepts that the so-called Tawagonshi Document is a fake, but argues that the Western documentary record still corroborates the Haudenosaunee tradition of *kaswentha*, which stresses 'the distinct

24   Hermkens, Noordegraaf and van der Sijs, 'The Tawagonshi Tale'. The article suggests that, in 1978, van Loon gave 'the original piece of hide' – which he identified as the original of the 'Tawagonshi Treaty' – to two Onondaga chiefs, Leon Shenandoah and Irving Powless, for safekeeping in the Syracuse, NY, headquarters of the People of the Longhouse. So far, scholars have been unable to examine this 'original piece of hide'.
25   'On the Electoral War-Path', *The Economist*, 19 September 2015 (available at www.economist.com/news/americas/21665035-after-years-abstaining-aboriginal-people-could-now-be-swing-voters-electoral-war-path).
26   Otto, 'Wampum, Tawagonshi, and the Two Row Belt'; Gehring and Starna, 'Revisiting the Fake Tawagonshi Treaty'; Gehring and Starna, 'The Tawagonshi Treaty of 1613'.

identity of the two peoples and a mutual engagement to coexist in peace
without interference in the affairs of the other'. According to Parmenter,
Haudenosaunee speakers explicitly mentioned or recited the *kaswentha*
tradition for Anglo-American and French colonial audiences on at least fifteen
different occasions between 1656 and 1744.[27] However, as Parmenter admits,
contemporary written records of negotiations between French and English
officials and the Five, later Six, Nations do not make any reference to the Two
Row Wampum Belt specifically. In his efforts to find continuity over time,
Parmenter tends to emphasise elements in the recitations that correspond with
the current concept of *kaswentha*, while ignoring contradictory elements.[28]

Parmenter is correct that the idea of a covenant chain can be found in
the Haudenosaunee recitations. But who were the European interlocutors
with whom Haudenosaunee speakers wished to affirm bonds of 'friendship'
and 'good understanding'? According to the *Jesuit Relations*, a Mohawk
chief handed a 'great collar of Porcelain beads' (i.e. wampum beads) to the
French governor at Trois-Rivières in April 1656, claiming that he would tie
the Dutch, the French, and the 'Agnieronnons' together by means of this 'iron
chain, much larger than the trees that grow in our forests'.[29] The Mohawk
chief did not wish for Europeans and native peoples to co-exist in isolation
from one another. If any misfortune should happen to the French and
'Agnieronnons', they would mingle their 'weeping' and 'tears'. He requested
that the French governor close the doors of 'his houses and his forts' to the
'Onnontageronnon', enemies of the speaker, who were hatching 'some plot
of war against me'.[30] The Mohawk chief, then, sought French assistance
and cooperation for the next round of warfare.

Such accounts show that indigenous groups sought to play off different
European groups against each other. When Onondaga chiefs appeared
before the New York Commissioners for Indian Affairs in Albany in 1678,
they did so to ally themselves with the English as successors of the Dutch.
An 'ancient covenant', allegedly dating back to the days of Jacob Eelckens
and Arent van Curler (two Dutch merchants who had traded in the Hudson
Valley in the 1610s and 1630s), was said to have 'continued to the Time of Old
Corlaer [Curler] and from Old Corlaer to His Present Excellency', meaning
Sir Edmund Andros, governor of New York.[31]

---

27   Parmenter, 'The Meaning of Kaswentha'.
28   Ibid., pp. 83, 90.
29   Ibid., p. 100; Thwaites, 'Travels and Explorations', pp. 107–09.
30   Ibid., pp. 108–09.
31   Parmenter, 'The Meaning of Kaswentha', p. 100; Richter, 'Rediscovered Links in the Covenant
Chain', p. 76. Richter is absolutely right to caution us against reading treaty minutes as unmediated

It is clear from other recitations at Albany in the years following that indigenous peoples did not interpret the covenant chain as signifying peaceful coexistence without interference in the affairs of the other. When the Oneidas, Onondagas, Cayugas, and Senecas affirmed their 'covenant of friendship' with 'Christians' in 1691, they took it to mean that 'whoever should hurt or prejudice, the one should be guilty of injuring all, all of us being comprehended in one common league'. In 1694, representatives of the Oneidas, Onondagas, Cayugas, Senecas, and Mohawks recounted that when 'Christians' first arrived in the Hudson Valley and were still 'but a Small People', they had not just extended a hand of friendship, but also entered into an alliance with the 'Christians' in order to protect the latter 'from all enemies whatsoever'.[32] This does not amount, as is claimed, to a policy of non-interference. As late as 1751, Archibald Kennedy of the New York Council echoed the Five Nations' understanding of the covenanting chain when he declared that 'we [the English] have assisted them in their wars and wants, and they have assisted us in our wars, and we have their Furs. This is the original Contract and Treaty of Commerce with the Five Nations.'[33] On balance, the evidence suggests that the modern concept of *kaswentha* was unknown to both European and indigenous inhabitants of the upper Hudson and St. Lawrence River valleys in the early modern period. As a result, we should be cautious of reading too much into such sources.

What can we say, then, about the situation on the ground? As Otto shows in *The Dutch-Munsee Encounter in America* (2006), Dutch trade and settlement in the lower Hudson Valley led to increasing conflict and war with local Munsee bands in the 1640s and 1650s, resulting in the latter's submission to Dutch sovereignty. European settlement, particularly land purchases, was key in this respect. Initially, indigenous views of land ownership and sovereignty differed radically from the Dutch perspective. When Indian leaders signed agreements 'selling' their land, they agreed to its joint use and occupancy by both themselves and the Dutch. They did not envision anything like a permanent transfer of land or sovereignty to

recordings of Indian speech. The treaty minutes require critical analysis just like any other historical document. Still, Richter believes that no other Euro-American source has preserved 'the memoir of Indian thoughts, concerns, and interpretation of events' with less distortion than the treaty minutes. It is, quite literally, as close as we are going to get to the words and thoughts of illiterate indigenous peoples in the Northeast in the pre-modern period.

32   Parmenter, 'The Meaning of Kaswentha', pp. 101–02; O'Callaghan and Fernow, *Documents Relative to the Colonial History of the State of New York*, Vol. 3, 1853-1883, p. 775.

33   Parmenter, 'The Meaning of Kaswentha', p. 108.

the Dutch. The Munsees who 'sold' Manhattan island in summer 1626 for European trade goods worth 60 Dutch guilders continued to live there, as did their counterparts on Staten Island, who ended up 'selling' the land several times over the years. As Otto notes, land transactions served to shore up social cohesion among the Munsees at a time when individualistic trade exchanges with European settlers tended to undermine traditional tribal leadership. Land transactions allowed Indian leaders to reassert their influence through the distribution of gifts among tribal members. Indian leaders may also have believed that land transactions would ensure continued access to European goods. By officially meeting Dutch magistrates to finalise land transactions, they gave the magistrates the impression, however, that permanent control over a territory had been ceded, along with sovereignty.[34]

The decline of the beaver trade in the lower Hudson Valley served to fuel land transactions as well. No longer able to supply valuable furs, the Munsees could offer instead food for subsistence, wampum for trade, information about the continent's interior, and, of course, land for habitation. By 1645, the Dutch population in the Hudson Valley had reached approximately 2,500. Many colonists settled in the outlying areas around Manhattan in order to be able to trade with nearby Munsee villages.[35]

Increased contact between settlers and the local people resulted in greater tension and conflict. Settlers sought to employ Indians as domestic servants, for example, only to find that they were not accustomed to Dutch concepts of wage labour, and disappeared as soon as they became weary of the work. The Indians' unfenced gardens, essential for their cultivation of corns and beans, proved vulnerable to European livestock foraging freely in the woods. To protect their crops, Indians frequently killed the animals. This did nothing to improve native–European relations.[36]

Growing Indian dependence on European trade goods had a number of dismal effects, which ranged from alcoholism among aboriginal peoples to yet more land transactions, resulting in the loss of indigenous political power and sovereignty. In January 1639, a group of Indians that lived on Long Island sold one-third of the island to the Dutch West India Company. They explicitly renounced all 'authority over it' and placed themselves under WIC protection, but, crucially, reserved for themselves the right 'to remain upon the aforesaid land, plant corn, fish, hunt and make a living there as

---

34   Otto, *The Dutch-Munsee Encounter in America*, pp. 97–98.
35   Ibid., pp. 99, 107–08.
36   Ibid., pp. 107–09.

well as they can'.[37] As Otto notes, this group of Indians were undoubtedly wampum producers who had been fully integrated into the European market economy. They required sufficient land for the year-round production of wampum, but little else. By the 1640s, wampum had become the currency of choice for European settlers in the Dutch and English colonies in the Northeast (while retaining important spiritual meanings for aboriginal peoples). Other Munsee bands that lived close to the Dutch population centres on Manhattan faced a catastrophic situation. With little access to beaver pelts and wampum, the Hackensacks, Tappans, and Wiechquaeskecks found themselves surrounded by settlers and more powerful Indian groups.[38]

The tipping point was reached in September 1639 when Director Willem Kieft decided to impose a protection/tribute exchange on all Munsee bands living near Fort Amsterdam. Indians whom 'we have protected against their enemies' were told to pay a levy of beaver pelts, sweet corn, and wampum in order to defray the spiralling costs of Dutch garrisons and fortresses.[39] Kieft's proposals found little favour from the indigenous inhabitants of the lower Hudson Valley. One second-hand report in Dutch suggests that representatives of several Munsee bands travelled to Fort Amsterdam to offer a spirited rebuttal. If this report is to be believed, a Munsee spokesman explained to Kieft that Dutch soldiers would be totally useless to them 'in case of war with other nations'. It took far too long for news to reach Fort Amsterdam, 'which was at a great distance from them'. Moreover, they had allowed the Dutch to settle peaceably on their land, without imposing any charge, which meant that the Dutch were 'under obligation to them', not the other way around. They reminded Kieft that, for two winters in a row, Dutchmen marooned in the Hudson Valley had been cared for by the locals, who had supplied victuals and assisted in the repair of the ship. The Munsees had always traded on a quid-pro-quo basis with the Dutch and saw no reason to supply Kieft 'with maize for nothing'. Although the Dutch now inhabited some of their land, they were still 'masters' (*meesters*) of the land they yet possessed.[40]

---

37   Gehring, *New York Historical Manuscripts Dutch, Volumes GG, HH and II*, p. 9; The Indian leaders appeared before the Director and Council of New Netherland on 15 January 1639. A deposition testifying to the sale was signed at Fort Amsterdam by Cornelis van Tienhoven, secretary of the Council, and two Dutch witnesses, but not by the sachems involved.

38   Otto, *The Dutch-Munsee Encounter in America*, p. 113.

39   Ibid., p. 114; van Laer, *New York Historical Manuscripts Dutch*, Vol. 4, p. 60.

40   *Breeden Raedt Aen de Vereenighde Nederlandsche Provintien* (Antwerp, 1649) f. C1; O'Callaghan, *Documentary History of the State of New-York*, Vol. 4, 1851, pp. 101–02 ('extracts from a work called *Breeden Raedt Aen de Vereenighde Nederlandsche Provintien*, printed in Antwerp

As Otto notes, the underlying theme of these complaints is Munsee frustration with the Dutch failure of social reciprocity. 'Until this time, the Munsees had engaged in a range of exchanges with the Dutch – food, comfort, wampum, hospitality – which, from their perspective, kept their world in balance.'[41] Kieft's levy presented a significant challenge to the Indians' worldview. On this occasion, the giving of gifts would not be matched with reciprocal exchanges. David de Vries, a Dutch merchant trusted by the Munsees, witnessed their dissatisfaction first-hand in October 1639. Eager to exchange cloth for sweet corn, De Vries was told by his Tappan interlocutors to wait until the WIC sloop collecting the levy had left. Following its departure, they expressed their dismay that Kieft 'dare [...] exact it'. The Dutch Director-General had to be 'a very mean fellow', first to come to the Hudson Valley uninvited and then to command the locals 'to give him their corn for nothing'.[42]

In spring 1640, hostilities broke out with the native inhabitants of the Raritan Valley (currently in northern New Jersey). Other Munsee bands quickly became involved in the conflict as well. The First Dutch–Munsee War lasted until 1645, and was marked by carnage on both sides. Indians attacked isolated Dutch farmsteads, killing colonists and livestock, while burning down houses, barns, etc. WIC soldiers committed atrocities against Indian villages, with the most notorious campaign led by Captain John Underhill. Married to a Dutch woman, Underhill was a veteran of New England's Pequot War. He had been responsible for the massacre of an entire Pequot village at Mystic River in 1637. He reprised this feat in WIC employ in February 1644. At night, he arrayed his troops around a fortified Tankitekes village near modern Pound Ridge, New York, and ordered his men to open fire. When the Indians refused to fight, he ordered his men to torch the entire village, knowing full well that the inhabitants would prefer a fiery death to slaughter at the hands of WIC soldiers. Over five hundred Indians were killed on this occasion. According to Otto, the entire conflict cost the lives of 1,600 native people at least. On the Dutch side, many European settlers left the colony or retreated to Manhattan island and Long Island. In 1648, one settler made the dramatic claim that, apart from private traders and WIC personnel, there were just one hundred colonists left in New Netherland. Yet the conflict hit

in 1649, translated from the Dutch original by Mr. C.'); Jacobs, *New Netherland*, p. 134; Otto, *The Dutch-Munsee Encounter in America*, pp. 114–16; Meuwese, *Brothers in Arms*, pp. 241–49.

41   Otto, *The Dutch-Munsee Encounter in America*, p. 115.

42   Murphy, *David Peterson de Vries, Voyages from Holland to America, A.D. 1632 to 1644*, p. 144; Otto, *The Dutch-Munsee Encounter in America*, p. 115.

Figure 12   *Nieuw Amsterdam ofte Nieuw Iorx op't Eylant Man*, **a watercolour**
drawing of New Amsterdam by an anonymous artist, probably
produced in 1665, i.e. after the English takeover of New Amsterdam in
September 1664.

Rijksmuseum.

the Munsees hardest. Demographic catastrophe (caused by European disease)
went hand-in-hand with the collapse of indigenous political structures. For
many Munsees in the lower Hudson Valley, the overlordship that the WIC
claimed over New Netherland had become a reality.[43]

European migration to New Netherland recovered during Peter
Stuyvesant's tenure as Director-General. There were about 2,000 colonists
living in the Hudson Valley by the time of the English takeover in 1664. As
before, increasing population pressure resulted in conflicts with native
villages. Stuyvesant waged a Second Dutch–Munsee War in 1655-1657
and took on the Esopus Indians in 1659-1660. Significantly, many of
the Munsee bands on Long Island – wampum producers living close to
European population centres – pledged to keep the peace with Stuyvesant,
and assist him in his fight against Indian aggressors. As Otto notes, it
was symptomatic of 'decreasing Indian sovereignty radiating out from

43   Ibid., pp. 116–25; Meuwese, *Brothers in Arms*, pp. 242–49; Becker, 'The Raritan Valley Buffer
Zone'.

Figure 13   View of the *West-Indisch Pakhuis* in Amsterdam, as seen from the Kalkmarkt. This building —a warehouse— doubled as the headquarters of the Dutch West India Company from 1647 to 1674. The etching was made by Jan Veenhuysen in Amsterdam in 1665.

Rijksmuseum.

Manhattan Island'.[44] After 1656, the Munsees no longer occupied or visited Manhattan in significant numbers. In July 1657, Staten Island – 'by us called Eghquaons' – was sold to the Dutch as 'free hereditable property, now and forever, without any further claims to be made by us or our descendants'.[45] Significantly, the 20 Munsee leaders who signed the property deed promised to come to the aid of European settlers if the latter were under attack from other Indian groups. Treaties and property deeds now signified wholesale Munsee subjection to the Dutch. It was

44   Otto, *The Dutch-Munsee Encounter in America*, p. 147.
45   Gehring, *Correspondence*, pp. 141-142. (I thank Jaap Jacobs for this reference).
In selling Staten Island, the Munsees received the following trade goods in return: '10 boxes of shirts; 10 ells of red checked cloth; 30 pounds 30 pairs of Faroese stockings; 2 pieces of duffel; some awls; 10 muskets; 30 kettles, large and small; 25 adzes; 10 bars of lead; 50 axes, large and small; some knives'.

Figure 14   **The Amsterdam merchant Abraham de Visscher (1605-67) was a director**
of the Dutch West India Company. He had his portrait painted sometime
between 1650 and his death in 1667, probably by Abraham van den
Tempel. The WIC director is wearing a beaver felt hat in the painting.

Rijksmuseum.

understood as such by both sides. Meeting Stuyvesant at Fort Orange
(modern-day Albany) in July 1660, the Senecas did not just endorse his
peace treaty with the defeated Esopus Indians, but also recognised the
Dutch as 'masters of the country' (*ooversten vant heele landt*), 'to whom
we all look up'.[46]

Conclusion

Warfare and treaty-making were inextricably intertwined in European
imperial projects. In many cases, the result was the 'dispossession of the
native', either by incorporating individual Indians into colonial society, as
happened to the wampum-producing Munsees of Long Island, or by pushing
indigenous peoples out, as happened to the Esopus Indians in the Hudson
Valley, or by exterminating the local population, as happened in the Banda

---

46   Otto, *The Dutch-Munsee Encounter in America*, pp. 143–48; Meuwese, *Brothers in Arms*,
pp. 251–55; Gehring, *Fort Orange Court*, pp. 515–16 (I thank Jaap Jacobs for this reference).

Islands. Given this dismal record, was there such a thing as empire by treaty? The case studies discussed here suggest that treaties, trading contracts, and land deeds played an important role in European expansion overseas. Crucially however, written documents were not an alternative to conflict and war, but rather an essential part of it. These tools of empire served multiple purposes, which ranged from diplomatic negotiations between European powers to, as Herzog puts it, 'the subjection of all things indigenous'.[47] The modern notion of equal treaties was totally unknown to Europeans in the early modern period, and, arguably, to many local rulers and peoples in Asia and the Americas. It was simply a given that relations between human beings, whether as individuals or groups, were ordered hierarchically. High literacy rates in northwestern Europe in the early modern period ensured that English and Dutch colonial officials, merchants, and colonists sought to preserve these hierarchical relations in writing. Indigenous peoples past and present have sought to use legal systems originating in Europe to contest the meaning of written documents and offer their own readings. Yet the decks remain heavily stacked against them. In the early modern period, the ultimate aim of treaties concluded between Europeans and native rulers and peoples was the subjection of one or more groups of human beings by others. There is a great danger that the 'fetishism' of treaties will continue to reinscribe itself in contemporary international relations.

Works cited

Becker, Marshall Joseph, 'The Raritan Valley Buffer Zone: A Refuge Area for Some Wiechquaskeck and other Native Americans during the 17th Century', *Bulletin of the Archaeological Society of Connecticut*, 78 (2016): 55–92.

Belmessous, Saliha, ed., *Empire by Treaty: Negotiating European Expansion, 1600-1900* (Oxford: OUP, 2015).

Belmessous, Saliha, 'The Paradox of An Empire By Treaty', in *Empire by Treaty*, ed. Saliha Belmessous, pp. 1–15.

Belmessous, Saliha, ed., *Native Claims: Indigenous Law against Empire, 1500–1920* (Oxford: OUP, 2012).

Borschberg, Peter, *Hugo Grotius, the Portuguese, and Free Trade in the East Indies* (Singapore: NUS Press, 2011).

Chaudhuri, K.N., *The English East India Company: The Study of an Early Joint-Stock Company 1600-1640* (New York: Frank Cass & Co, 1965).

---

47   Herzog, 'Struggling over Indians', pp. 78–79.

Clulow, Adam, 'The Art of Claiming: Possession and Resistance in Early Modern Asia', *American Historical Review* 121, no. 1 (2016): 17–38.

Clulow, Adam, *The Company and the Shogun: The Dutch Encounter with Tokugawa Japan* (New York: Columbia University Press, 2014).

Clulow, Adam, 'European Maritime Violence and Territorial States in Early Modern Asia, 1600-1650', *Itinerario* 33, no. 3 (2009): 72–94.

Das Gupta, Arun, 'The Maritime Trade of Indonesia, 1500-1800', in *India and the Indian Ocean, 1500-1800*, ed. Ashin Das Gupta and M.N. Pearson (Calcutta: OUP, 1987), 240–75.

Foster, William, *England's Quest of Eastern Trade* (London: A. & C. Black, 1933).

Foster, William, ed., *The Journal of John Jourdain, 1608-1617, describing his experiences in Arabia, India, and the Malay Archipelago* (Cambridge: Hakluyt Society, 1905).

Gehring, Charles T., trans., ed., *Correspondence, 1654-1658*, New Netherland Documents Series, vol. XII (Syracuse, NY: Syracuse University Press, 2003).

Gehring, Charles T., trans., ed., *Fort Orange Court Minutes 1652-1660*, New Netherland Documents Series, vol. XVI, part two (Syracuse, NY: Syracuse University Press, 1990).

Gehring, Charles T., trans., ed., *New York Historical Manuscripts Dutch, Volumes GG, HH and II: Land Papers* (Baltimore MD: Genealogical Publishing Co., Inc. 1980).

Gehring, Charles T., and William A. Starna, 'Revisiting the Fake Tawagonshi Treaty of 1613', *New York History*, 90 (Winter 2012): 95–101.

Gehring, Charles T., and William A. Starna, 'The Tawagonshi Treaty of 1613: The Final Chapter', *New York History*, 60 (1987): 373–93.

Goor, Jurriën van, *Jan Pieterszoon Coen, 1587-1629: Koopman-Koning in Azië* (Amsterdam: Boom Publishers, 2015).

Hanna, Williard A., *Indonesian Banda: Colonialism and Its Aftermath in the Nutmeg Islands* (Philadelphia PA: Institute for the Study of Human Issues, 1978).

Hauptman, Laurence M., and Ronald G. Knapp, 'Dutch-Aboriginal Interaction in New Netherland and Formosa: An Historical Geography of Empire', *Proceedings of the American Philosophical Society* 121, no. 2 (1977): 166–82.

Heeres, J.E., and F.W. Stapel, eds., *Corpus diplomaticum Neerlando-Indicum: verzameling van politieke contracten en verdere verdragen door de Nederlanders in het Oosten gesloten*, 7 vols. (The Hague: Martinus Nijhoff, 1907-1955), vol. I (*1596-1650*).

Hermkens, Harrie, Jan Noordegraaf, and Nicoline van der Sijs, 'The Tawagonshi Tale: Can Linguistic Analysis Prove the Tawagonshi Treaty to be a Forgery?', *Journal of Early American History* 3, no. 1 (2013): 9–42.

Herzog, Tamar, 'Struggling over Indians: Territorial Conflict and Alliance Making in the Heartland of South America (Seventeenth to Eighteenth Centuries)', in *Empire by Treaty*, ed. Saliha Belmessous, 78–100.

Ittersum, Martine J. van, 'Debating Natural Law in the Banda Islands: A Case Study in Anglo-Dutch Imperial Competition in the East Indies, 1609-1621', *History of European Ideas* 42, no. 4 (2016): 459–501.

Jacobs, Jaap, 'Early Dutch Explorations in North America', *Journal of Early American History* 3, no. 1 (2013): 59–81.

Jacobs, Jaap, *New Netherland: A Dutch Colony in Seventeenth-Century America* (Leiden: Brill Academic Publishers, 2005).

Jameson, J. Franklin, ed., *Narratives of New Netherland, 1609-1664* (New York: Charles Scribner's Sons, 1909).

Keay, John, *The Honourable Company: A History of the English East India Company* (London: Harper Collins Publishers, 1993).

Kennedy, Dane, 'Review of Saliha Belmessous (ed), Empire by Treaty: Negotiating European Expansion, 1600–1900', H-Diplo, H-Net Reviews (May 2015), accessed 18 April 2017 at www.h-net.org/reviews/showrev.php?id=43387.

Knaap, Gerrit, *Kruidnagelen en Christenen: De VOC en de bevolking van Ambon, 1656-1696*, second edition (Leiden: KITLV Publishers, 2004).

Knaap, Gerrit, and Ger Teitler, eds., *De Verenigde Oost-Indische Compagnie tussen oorlog en diplomatie* (Leiden: KITLV Publishers, 2002).

Laer, Arnold J.F. van, et al., trans., eds., *New York Historical Manuscripts Dutch*, vol. 4 (Baltimore MD: Genealogical Publishing Company, 1974)

Locher-Scholten, Elsbeth, and Peter Rietbergen, eds., *Hof en Handel: Aziatische Vorsten en de VOC, 1620-1720* (Leiden: KITLV Publishers, 2004).

Loth, Vincent C., 'Armed Incidents and Unpaid Bills: Anglo-Dutch Rivalry in the Banda Islands in the Seventeenth Century', *Modern Asian Studies* 29, no. 4 (1995): 705–40.

Loth, Vincent C., 'Pioneers and Perkeniers: The Banda Islands in the 17th Century', *Cakalele* 6 (1995): 13–35.

Masselman, George, *The Cradle of Colonialism* (New Haven: Yale University Press, 1963).

Meuwese, Mark, *Brothers in Arms, Partners in Trade: Dutch-Indigenous Alliances in the Atlantic World, 1595-1674* (Leiden: Brill Academic Publishers, 2012).

Milton, Giles, *Nathaniel's Nutmeg: How One Man's Courage Changed the Course of History* (London: Sceptre, 1999).

Niemeijer, H.E., '"Als eene Lelye onder de doornen": Kerk, kolonisatie en christiani-sering op de Banda-eilanden 1616-1635', *Documentatieblad voor de Geschiedenis van de Nederlandse Zending en Overzeese Kerken* I, no. 1 (1994): 2–24.

O'Callaghan, E.B., ed., *Documentary History of the State of New-York*, vol. 4 (Albany: Charles van Benthuysen, 1851).

O'Callaghan, E.B. and B. Fernow, eds., trans., *Documents Relative to the Colonial History of the State of New York*, vol. 3 (Albany: Weed, Parsons and Company, 1853-1883).

'On the Electoral War-Path', *The Economist*, 19 September 2015 (available at www.economist.com/news/americas/21665035-after-years-abstaining-aboriginal-people-could-now-be-swing-voters-electoral-war-path).

Opstall, M.E. van, ed., *De Reis van de Vloot van Pieter Willemsz Verhoef naar Azie, 1607-1612* ed. 2 vols. (The Hague: Martinus Nijhoff, 1972).

Opstall, M.E. van, 'Laurens Reael in de Staten-Generaal, het verslag van Reael over de toestand in Oost-Indië', in *Nederlandse Historische Bronnen* (The Hague 1979): 175–213.

Otto, Paul, 'Wampum, Tawagonshi, and the Two Row Belt', *Journal of Early American History*, 3 (2013): 110–25.

Otto, Paul, *The Dutch-Munsee Encounter in America: The Struggle for Sovereignty in the Hudson Valley* (New York: Berghahn Books, 2006).

Parmenter, Jon, 'The Meaning of Kaswentha and the Two Row Wampum Belt in Haudenosaunee (Iroquois) History: Can Indigenous Oral Tradition be Reconciled with the Documentary Record?', *Journal of Early American History* 3, no. 1 (2013): 82–109.

Patton, Paul, 'The "Lessons of History": The Ideal of Treaty in Settler Colonial Societies', in *Empire by Treaty*, ed. Saliha Belmessous, pp. 243–69.

Purchas, Samuel, *Hakluytus Posthumus or Purchas his Pilgrimes, Contayning a History of the World in Sea Voyages and Lande Travells by Englishmen and Others*, Hakluyt Society extra series, 20 vols. (Glasgow: Maclehose, 1905-1907), vol. II.

Reid, Anthony, *Southeast Asia in the Age of Commerce, 1450-1680*, 2 vols. (New Haven: Yale University Press, 1988),

Richter, Daniel K., 'Rediscovered Links in the Covenant Chain: Previously Unpublished Transcripts of New York Indian Treaty Minutes, 1677-1691', *American Antiquarian Society Proceedings* 92, no. 1 (1982): 45–85.

Stapel, F.W., ed., *Geschiedenis van Nederlands Indië*, vol. 3 (Amsterdam, 1939).

Stern, Philip, *The Company-State: Corporate Sovereignty and the Early Modern Foundations of the British Empire in India* (Oxford: OUP, 2011).

Thwaites, Reuben Gold, ed., 'Travels and Explorations of the Jesuit Missionaries in New France, 1610-1791', *The Jesuit Relations and Allied Documents* (Cleveland: The Burrows Brothers Company, 1899), vol. XLIII: *Lower Canada, Iroquois, 1656-1657*.

Tully, James, *Public Philosophy in a New Key*, 2 vols., Ideas in Context 93 (Cambridge: Cambridge University Press, 2008).

Villiers, John, 'Trade and society in the Banda Islands in the sixteenth century', *Modern Asian Studies* 15, no. 4 (1981): 723–50.

Vlekke, Bernard H.M., *Nusantara: A History of the East Indian Archipelago* (Cambridge MA: Harvard University Press, 1944).

Vries, David Pietersz de, *David Peterson de Vries, Voyages from Holland to America, A.D. 1632 to 1644*, trans. Murphy, Henry C. (New York, 1853).

Weststeijn, Arthur, 'The VOC as a Company-State: Debating Seventeenth-Century Dutch Colonial Expansion', *Itinerario* 38, no. 1 (2014): 13–34.

Wilson, E., *The Savage Republic: De Indis of Hugo Grotius, Republicanism and Dutch Hegemony within the Early Modern World-System, c.1600-1619* (Leiden: Martinus Nijhoff Publishers, 2008).

Winn, Philip, 'Slavery and Cultural Creativity in the Banda Islands', *Journal of Southeast Asian Studies* 41, no. 3 (2010): 365–89.

Contact details

Dr. Martine J. van Ittersum, History Department, University of Dundee, Nethergate, Dundee, DD1 4HN, UK
Tel.: +44 (0) 1382 384522
ittersum@post.harvard.edu and m.j.vanittersum@dundee.ac.uk

7 'Great help from Japan'

The Dutch East India Company's experiment with Japanese soldiers

Adam Clulow

Abstract

This chapter examines a short-lived VOC experiment to recruit soldiers in Japan and dispatch them to fight on behalf of the organisation in Southeast Asia. As a number of historians have noted, the Japanese mercenary was not an unfamiliar figure in Southeast Asia in this period. In the early seventeenth century, Japanese fighters found employment in Siam, where successive kings deployed a large contingent of these troops; in the Philippines, where Japanese recruits engaged in the bloody suppression of Chinese revolts on behalf of their Spanish masters; and in Cambodia, where Japanese recruits bolstered local forces gathered to resist a potential invasion. But if there were parallels, the Company's recruits were also set apart. This chapter argues that a small group of VOC officials enthusiastically embraced Japanese soldiers as part of their drive to solve the perennial European problem of inadequate military manpower in Asia. In the process, they departed from past patterns by attempting to engineer the figure of the professional Japanese mercenary, constrained by draconian contracts and governed by Dutch officers. Not surprisingly, however, the vision put forward by high-ranking officials, most of whom had never visited Japan, clashed with the reality on the ground where Japanese recruits proved unruly soldiers who became embroiled in a series of disciplinary incidents.

Keywords: Mercenaries, non-state violence, Southeast Asia, Hirado. Amboyna Conspiracy Trial

In 1623, a contingent of Japanese soldiers in the employ of the Dutch East India Company was accused of plotting with a group of English merchants

Clulow, Adam and Tristan Mostert (eds.), *The Dutch and English East India Companies: Diplomacy, trade and violence in early modern Asia*. Amsterdam: Amsterdam University Press, 2018
DOI: 10.5117/9789462983298/CH07

to seize control of a fort on the remote island of Ambon in modern-day Indonesia.[1] Tortured, they confessed that they had agreed to deliver the fort into English hands in return for a significant payoff and a share of the plunder. The result was a swift trial that ended in the execution of 21 men, ten Japanese soldiers, ten English merchants and an Asian slave overseer caught up in the legal proceedings. When news of what had happened reached London in 1624, it sparked immediate controversy as English officials denounced the flawed nature of the judicial procedures while ridiculing the notion that a conspiracy had existed in the first place. As news of the trial spread, propelled by the publication of cheap broadsheet ballads and incendiary pamphlets, everyone seemed to be talking about Japanese soldiers and their particular capabilities. For Dutch writers determined to emphasise the potential strength of the Amboina plotters, the Japanese were fearsome warriors capable of swaying the outcome of any conflict.[2] A 'small number of Japonians were not slightly to be regarded', exclaimed one writer, as the 'valour & prowess of that Nation' made them far more potent than an equivalent contingent of European soldiers.[3] Not so, ridiculed their English opponents, the Japanese were no military 'Gyants' and the wondrous feats ascribed to them nothing more than 'Apochriphal Legends' with no basis in fact.[4]

Within a few years, this sudden rush of attention had faded as the Japanese soldiers caught up in the trial largely disappeared from view.[5] But if they

---

1   I would like to thank the participants of the Global Company Conference for their very valuable comments which greatly improved this piece. This chapter represents a return to a topic that I first published on in *Itinerario* in 2007 and I remain very grateful for the many suggestions I received from the editors and reviewers.

2   The VOC was based in the town of Kota Ambon on the island of Ambon in the wider VOC administrative area of Amboina (often spelled Amboyna in this period). The most widely read account of the Amboina trial is Giles Milton's popular history, *Nathaniel's Nutmeg*, which sold hundreds of thousands of copies. For a highly perceptive, scholarly examination of the trial and its background, see Coolhaas, 'Aanteekeningen en Opmerkingen over den zoogenaamdem Ambonschen Moord', pp. 49-93.

3   *A remonstrance of the directors of the Netherlands East India Company presented to the Lords States Generall of the united Provinces, in defence of the said Companie, touching the bloudy proceedings against the English merchants, executed at Amboyn* (London, 1632).

4   *A Reply to the Remonstrance of the Bewinthebbers or Directors of the Netherlands East India Companie lately exhibited to the Lords States-Generall in justification of the proceedings of their Officers at Amboyna against the English there* (London, 1632).

5   The VOC commonly referred to these troops as 'soldiers from Japan' (*soldaten van Japon*). Steven van der Haghen to the Amsterdam Chamber, 18 July 1616, VOC 1063: 53v. In this chapter, I use two terms, Japanese soldiers and Japanese mercenaries, to refer to them. The distinction between soldier and mercenary is frequently murky and this was especially the case when it

flashed only briefly into the global spotlight, these soldiers occupy an important position in the wider history of the two companies in Asia. Over time, both the Dutch and English companies came to rely heavily on Asian troops to provide vital military manpower that enabled the expansion of European influence away from port cities, where they could be backed up by formidable fleets, into the interior. Over the course of the companies' long existence, hundreds of thousands of Asian troops would serve in their armies as regular soldiers, mercenaries or allies, culminating in the establishment of institutions like the Presidency Armies in India.[6] Within this wider trajectory, Japanese soldiers were arguably the first Asian troops to serve either of the companies in significant numbers.[7] Certainly, the available evidence suggests they were the first soldiers from Asia to be systematically recruited and the first to be dispatched across great distances to wage war on behalf of their European masters. All of this means that although the VOC's experiment with Japanese soldiers may not have been successful, it did establish the outlines of a familiar template that would be deployed again and again as Europeans pushed further into Asia and where their success depended to a significant degree not on soldiers imported from distant homelands but on the mobilisation of large numbers of local allies and troops.

This chapter explores the forces that brought a group of Japanese soldiers thousands of miles from Kyushu to the walls of a remote VOC fortress in Southeast Asia. As a number of historians, including Iwao Seiichi who has authored a series of foundational studies on the Japanese in Southeast Asia, have noted, the Japanese mercenary was already a familiar figure in Southeast Asia in this period.[8] In the early seventeenth century, Japanese

came to VOC forces. The Dutch East India Company was a private, commercial company that waged war with a polyglot collection of soldiers drawn from Europe, including many from outside the United Provinces, and Asia. As a result, it is essentially impossible to draw a clear line between mercenaries and soldiers. Although I refer to these soldiers as Japanese throughout this chapter, I do not, as will be clear later, suggest that notions of Japanese identity were fixed or applied equally to all residents of the archipelago. Rather I use the term because this is what the VOC called these troops even as they recruited some soldiers who clearly had closer ties with other parts of Asia.

6   For a discussion, see Roy, *Military Manpower, Armies and Warfare in South Asia*.

7   For an excellent analysis of the importance of Asian troops including Japanese mercenaries to the VOC, see Raben, 'Het Aziatisch legioen'. There are occasional references to individual Asian troops in Company employment prior to this, but Japanese soldiers were the first employed in any significant number.

8   Iwao's groundbreaking examination of Japanese settlements across Southeast Asia remains a remarkable feat of scholarship. Tracing Japanese migrants, merchants and mercenaries across the region, it includes an extended discussion of Japanese soldiers employed by the VOC. Iwao,

fighters found employment in Siam, where successive kings deployed a large contingent of these troops, in the Philippines, where they engaged in the bloody suppression of a Chinese revolt on behalf of their Spanish masters, and in Cambodia, where Japanese recruits bolstered local forces gathered to resist a potential invasion. But if there were parallels, the Company's soldiers were also set apart. This chapter argues that a small group of VOC officials within the organisation, led by Jan Pieterszoon Coen, enthusiastically embraced Japanese recruits as part of a wider drive to solve the perennial European problem of inadequate military manpower in Asia. Believing that Japan's warlike energies could be harnessed, subjected to Dutch control and used to further the Company's goals, they pictured long columns of Japanese soldiers marching outwards in service of VOC aims. In the process, they departed from past patterns by attempting to engineer the figure of the professional Japanese mercenary constrained by draconian contracts and governed by Dutch officers. Not surprisingly, however, the vision put forward by high-ranking officials, most of whom had never visited Japan, clashed with the reality on the ground where Japanese recruits proved unruly soldiers who became embroiled in a series of disciplinary incidents.

Merchant and mercenary

The Dutch East India Company was neither the first nor the only employer of Japanese troops in Southeast Asia but it did introduce a series of innovations that set it apart. In the early seventeenth century, thousands of Japanese migrants, merchants and mercenaries arrived in ports across Southeast Asia. This wave of arrivals was made possible by an unprecedented surge in maritime links between Japan and Southeast Asia. In the second half of the sixteenth century, Chinese maritime entrepreneurs such as Wang Zhi had pioneered new routes between Southeast Asia and Japan, but the volume of traffic remained relatively limited.[9] The situation was transformed in the first decade of the seventeenth century with the creation of a stable

---

Zoku nanyō Nihon machi no kenkyū, pp. 61-66, pp. 231-36. For an excellent analysis of Japanese mercenaries across the region, including those hired by the VOC, see Turnbull, 'The Japanese "Wild Geese"'. See also: Clulow, 'Unjust, Cruel and Barbarous Proceedings'; Mulder, *Hollanders in Hirado*.

9   'Qinhuo Wang Zhi', in Zheng, *Chouhai tubian*. *Chouhai tubian* provides an account of Wang Zhi's role in opening up commercial ties between Japan and Southeast Asia. Although he started his career as a merchant, Wang Zhi later shifted to piracy and organised a series of destructive raids against the Chinese coast.

framework for international commerce within Japan. This took the form of the *shuinjō* or maritime pass system, which required all outgoing merchant vessels to obtain special trading licenses authorising the holder to undertake a single voyage from Japan to a stated destination.[10] As any merchant vessel carrying one of these documents was ensured a friendly welcome in ports across Southeast Asia, the passes became highly prized and drove a significant increase in long-distance commerce.

After 1604, the first year for which records exist, a total of 356 licenses were issued to Japan-based merchants. The overwhelming majority of these, just less than 300, were intended for ships travelling to Southeast Asia, with 85 licenses issued for Cochinchina, 44 for Cambodia, 52 for the Philippines, and 56 for Siam.[11] Although the size of these vessels varied considerably, the best estimate puts the average around 300 tonnes with the largest reaching 800.[12] As a result, these ships were able to transport large numbers of passengers, who paid for space for themselves and their goods, thereby defraying the costs of these voyages and ensuring at least a moderate rate of return for the shipowners even if trade was not successful. The largest recorded vessel to ply these routes, the 800-tonne behemoth referenced above, carried just 80 crew members and 317 passengers, but this was an outsized exception and most vessels probably transported around 200 passengers.[13] Nonetheless, if we multiply this figure by the almost three hundred ships that travelled to Southeast Asia during the lifespan of the system, the total of potential passengers moves very quickly past fifty thousand.[14]

Scholars have traditionally divided these passengers into three neat categories, merchants eager to trade, former samurai who intended to support themselves by selling the services of their sword arms, and Christians on the run from the increasingly fierce persecution of the Tokugawa state.[15]

---

10   The classic work on the *shuinsen* is also by Iwao, *Shuinsen bōekishi no kenkyū*. For a more recent study see Nagazumi, *Shuinsen*.

11   For these figures, see Iwao, *Shuinsen bōekishi no kenkyū*. The figure for Cochinchina includes fourteen ships sent to Annan.

12   Iwao, *Shuinsen bōekishi no kenkyū*, p. 5.

13   Iwao estimates the average number of passengers and crew at 236. Iwao, *Shuinsen bōekishi*, p. 273.

14   Ishizawa Yoshiaki has suggested that 71,200 men and women left aboard Japanese vessels and roughly another 30,000 on foreign shipping in this period. Ishizawa, 'Les quartiers japonais'.

15   William Wray divides them into merchants 'with commercial experience,' Christian refugees and 'mercenaries or political exiles from the unification wars'. Wray, 'The 17th-Century Japanese Diaspora', p. 77. Hung-Guk Cho suggests three categories: 'merchants [...] who went to Southeast Asia for trade', 'Christians who went to Southeast Asia to escape the oppression

This division may seem self-evident but it has the added effect of imposing overly narrow categories on a turbulent period. While some individuals surely fitted neatly into just one of these three groupings, they presuppose the existence of a rigid line between merchant, mercenary, and Christian refugee that has little place in the fluid world of early modern Asia, where individuals switched easily between occupations and identities depending on the exigencies of the moment. It is also based more on general assumptions about the kind of individuals who would have wanted to leave Japan than actual sources from the period.[16] While the existence of Tokugawa records related to the issuance of *shuinjō* makes it possible to construct tables listing the number of vessels that left Japan in this period, we have almost no travel accounts documenting individual voyages or materials produced on the Southeast Asian side describing what happened when these vessels actually dropped anchor at their intended destination.[17]

One way around this problem is to tap into a different kind of source, diplomatic letters. The decade and a half after the decisive battle of Sekiga-hara in 1600, which brought the Tokugawa family to power, saw a surge in such letters that was unmatched in any previous period of Japanese history. Between 1601 and 1614, Tokugawa Ieyasu dispatched 48 diplomatic missives while his advisers contributed a further 28 for a total of 76.[18] The bulk of this diplomatic correspondence, 41 of the 48 letters sent by the shogun, was directed towards Southeast Asia. Between 1601 and 1606, for example, Ieyasu dispatched one letter each year to Nguyễn Hoàng, the leader of the emerging state of Cochinchina in what is now Vietnam. Eleven missives were sent to Cambodia between 1603 and 1610 while eighteen letters were dispatched to the Philippines between 1601 and 1613.[19] The flow of letters out of Japan was matched by an equal influx of correspondence to the archipelago as rulers and officials engaged enthusiastically with the Tokugawa regime.

---

of the Edo shogunate', and a third group consisting of 'jobless Samurai, from Kyushu who were dispatched to Korea in two Japanese invasions in 1592 and 1597 and then returned'. Cho, 'The Trade between China, Japan, Korea and Southeast Asia', p. 79.

16   One source frequently cited is *Shamukoku Fudo Gunki*, which describes the adventures of Yamada Nagamasa, a prominent Japanese adventurer in Siam, but this was produced in the late seventeenth century and hence has limited value. For a complete copy of *Shamukoku Fudo Gunki*, see Yamada Nagamasa Kenshōkai.

17   One exception is accounts penned by European travellers, especially missionaries. Although clearly important, these tend to emphasise the transplantation of Christian communities from Japan. For a useful study, see Ribeiro, 'The Japanese Diaspora'.

18   Fujii, 'Jūnana seiki no Nihon'.

19   Ibid., p. 35.

The content of these letters varied. Some were essentially formulaic, little more than diplomatic boilerplate, but others addressed specific issues. By far the most frequent point of discussion concerned the violent conduct of Japanese merchants. A typical complaint penned in 1606 by the lord of Cochinchina addressed what had happened when Japanese vessels arrived in his territory the previous year. The writer explained that he had welcomed the arrival of these merchants and extended them all possible courtesies, but rather than engaging in trade they had run 'rampant in my lands stealing goods and money belonging to Fujianese merchants and abusing neighbouring residents and women'.[20] At the heart of this complaint, as with many others that followed, was a single charge: although Japanese merchants arrived seemingly intent on trade, they shifted swiftly and without warning or apparent provocation to violence. A 1610 letter from the king of Cambodia complained bitterly about the violent aftermath of the arrival of Japanese merchant vessels, lamenting that the 'people of your country are cruel and ferocious. They come to engage in commerce but quickly act contrary to this purpose and rampage along the coast.'[21] The result was to disrupt maritime traffic and undermine the prosperity of Cambodian ports.

In this way, the writers charged that Japanese merchants switched back and forth between peaceful commerce and violence. Arriving ostensibly to buy and sell goods, they opted instead to engage in 'violent plunder and harmful disruptions'.[22] The ruler who welcomed Japanese merchants into his ports could thus never be certain if he was receiving peaceful merchants or dangerous pirates, legitimate traders or opportunistic marauders. The complaints are all the more striking because they came from rulers who were eager to court Tokugawa favour in order to expand commercial ties with a rich trading partner. The Nguyễn lords of Cochinchina were, for example, heavily dependent on foreign trade, seeing it as 'key to their survival against the more powerful Trinh state, a source of revenues, weapons, and information'.[23] As a result, they had little reason to exaggerate the scale of Japanese depredations and in many cases almost certainly underplayed what was actually happening. This tendency is clear in a letter dispatched by one of Hoàng's successors in Cochinchina, which attempted to tiptoe around the issue in order to avoid giving offence. In 'recent years', the

---

20 Kondō, *Gaiban tsūsho*, p. 107.
21 Ibid., p. 184.
22 Ibid., p. 198.
23 Lockard, '"The Sea Common to All"', p. 234. Li Tana notes that while for some states 'the question of overseas trade may have been a matter of determining whether they were rich or poor. For early Cochinchina, it was a question of life and death'. Li, *Nguyễn Cochinchina*, p. 60.

writer explained, 'ignorant men [...] have increased their selfish actions and prevented merchants from sailing [freely]'.[24] Not surprisingly, these 'ignorant men' turned out to be Japanese merchants whose violent conduct had made it necessary to raise the issue directly with the Tokugawa regime. Other observers were far less diplomatic, among them Richard Cocks, an English merchant based in Japan, who described the 'burning [of] China junckes [...] whereof the King of Cochinchina advised themperour [shogun] of their vnrulynesse'.[25]

The letters exchanged between Japan and Southeast Asia make it clear that trade and violence mixed together to form a volatile compound. Given this fact, it did not require much prompting to make the leap from merchant to mercenary. In some cases, the shift seems to have originated with local officials who decided that the warlike talents of Japanese merchants could be put to better use. This was the situation in the Philippines where Japanese merchants were enlisted to put down a Chinese revolt in 1603 and in Cambodia where they were recruited to ward off a potential invasion in 1623.[26] In other instances, the shift seems to have been driven by enterprising merchants who realised that there was more money to be made by selling the services of their sword arms than their goods. In Siam, for example, Japanese merchants seem to have initiated this shift themselves by eagerly and aggressively claiming the role of palace guards.[27] There, the available sources, both royal chronicles and European diaries, suggest that Japanese merchants went so far as to kidnap the monarch, holding him to ransom until they had succeeded in extracting concessions including a promise that the king would employ them as 'soldiers and as bodyguards to the end

24   Kondō, *Gaiban tsūsho*, pp. 115-116.

25   Cocks, *Diary of Richard Cocks*, p. 385.

26   Information about Japanese recruits in Cambodia comes from a letter sent from Ayutthaya to Japan designed to find out how the shogun would react if his subjects were harmed during a potential campaign. Satow, 'Notes on the Intercourse between Japan and Siam', p. 178. For the Philippines, see Morga, *History of the Philippine Islands from the discovery by Magellan in 1521 to the beginning of the XVII Century,* 2, pp. 41-42.

27   There are four separate descriptions, two Dutch accounts, one English, and one Ayutthayan chronicle, detailing this particular episode. Most of the descriptions agree that the Japanese attacked the palace and held the king hostage and that they extracted some concessions before they released him. However, some accounts emphasise that the Japanese outmanoeuvred Ayutthayan officials, whiles others insist that it was Japanese merchants who found themselves outwitted. The four accounts are as follows: Cushman, trans., *The Royal Chronicles of Ayutthaya,* p. 208; Baker, et al., *Van Vliet's Siam,* p. 136; Floris, *His Voyage to the East Indies,* pp. 56-7; Council of the Vajiranāna National Library, *Records of the relations between Siam and foreign countries,* pp. 6-8.

of his life'.[28] The result was to entrench their place at court while boosting the influence of the Japanese community in Ayutthaya.[29]

Such descriptions make it clear that the twin roles of merchant and mercenary blurred into each other, and there is little evidence of any sort of rigid dividing line. Merchants became mercenaries and then shifted back again, often holding multiple identities at the same time and deploying them according to the circumstances. In Cambodia or the Philippines, recruitment was propelled by the eruption of crises that, once abated, allowed for a return to commerce; but even in Ayutthaya, where the Japanese claimed the semi-permanent role of palace guards, there is no evidence that military duties took precedence over commercial interests. This was certainly the case with the most famous of all Japanese mercenaries, Yamada Nagamasa (d.1630), who juggled his twin identities as a violent soldier of fortune and prosperous merchant with apparent ease, engaging in successful military campaigns while building a highly profitable commercial network that saw him compete with the VOC for control of the lucrative trade in deer skins.[30]

While few Japanese migrants were quite so successful, Yamada's template, which mixed commercial and military entrepreneurship, would have been familiar to many inhabitants of Southeast Asia's various *nihonmachi* (Japanese communities). The result is that even though there were plenty of Japanese fighters operating across the region, it is difficult to speak of a professional Japanese mercenary in this period. Rather, Japanese migrants seem to have existed along a shifting continuum, transforming into mercenaries when it suited them but equally swiftly reclaiming their role as merchants when opportunities for profit emerged. They were, in other words, military and commercial entrepreneurs rather than professional soldiers, and it was this template with its blurred lines and overlapping roles that became standard across Southeast Asia.

The Dutch East India Company aimed to do something different. In contrast to other employers, VOC officials attempted to straighten out these lines by establishing a structured programme to recruit soldiers in Japan exclusively for military service. In the process, they attempted to engineer the figure of the professional Japanese mercenary constrained and controlled by strict contracts.

28 Baker, et al. *Van Vliet's Siam*, p. 136.
29 Japanese mercenaries remained active in Siam for years. In the words of one observer, the king of Siam's 'power by water and land consists most of his own Vassals and Natives, he hath indeed some few Strangers, as Moors, Malayers and some five hundred Japanners, the most esteemed for their courage and fidelity'. Caron and Schouten, *A True Description*, pp. 133-134.
30 Nagazumi, 'Ayutthaya and Japan', p. 96.

'Bold men'

The first detailed mention of Japanese mercenaries in VOC sources occurs in a February 1613 letter sent by the head of the Japan trading outpost, Hendrik Brouwer, to the Governor-General, Pieter Both:

> We regard here the Japanese under good command to be bold men. Their monthly pay is also low and moreover they can be maintained with a small cost of rice and salted fish. With the oral instructions that you gave me last time, we wanted to send 300 men with these ships, but so as to bring more provisions, only 68 heads were shipped, including 9 carpenters, 3 smiths and 2 or 3 masons, the rest sailors and soldiers. If you value the service of these, there will always be enough people here [to recruit] as his majesty [the shogun] has given us his consent to take out as many as we desire.[31]

As he makes clear, Brouwer had not conceived of the idea himself. Rather he was responding to a verbal instruction delivered by his superior, Pieter Both, to recruit large numbers of Japanese soldiers. Although the documentary trail is limited, the Governor-General's plans were clearly ambitious. Three hundred men, the initial figure set for Brouwer to fill, may not seem like an especially large number at first, but the Company's total military force across its various colonies, castles and outposts numbered less than a thousand soldiers, both European and Asian.[32] In this way, if Both's initial quota was met, the very first shipment of Japanese troops would have constituted a significant share of the organisation's total fighting force. These were not in other words purely ancillary troops designed to make up numbers around the edges. Rather, Both clearly believed Japanese soldiers could become a crucial part of the Company's fighting force.

31   Hendrik Brouwer to Pieter Both, 29 January 1613, VOC 1056: 34v. The Company also shipped a Japanese bark that could be manned by the new recruits in the Banda islands. The reference to "sailors" is to the crew for this bark.

32   The fluid nature of the Company's operations in this period make it difficult to obtain a precise number but the figure cited above is supported by a number of sources. Coen to *Heeren* 17, 1 January 1614, Colenbrander, *Jan Pietersz. Coen,* 1:16. Van Dam, *Beschrijvinge van de Oostindishe Compagnie,* 1.2:525-6. Part of the reason for the Company's perennial problem with military manpower stemmed from the length of the voyage from Europe. Soldiers brought from ports in the Dutch Republic required eight months on average to reach Batavia. Scholars estimate that about 7 percent of those embarking at the Netherlands did not survive the first leg of the voyage to the Cape of Good Hope, and another 3 to 4 percent perished on the way from the Cape to Batavia.

To facilitate its plan to recruit large numbers of mercenaries in a short space of time, the Company introduced two key innovations, both of which appear in Brouwer's 1613 letter. Unlike other employers who did their hiring in the *nihonmachi* that had sprung up in key ports across Southeast Asia, the VOC opted to go straight to the source by recruiting directly in Japan. The advantages were clear. Recruiting in Japan removed any possible constraints brought about by the size of the *nihonmachi* communities or the limited number of vessels transiting between Japan and Southeast Asia each year. It also served to breathe new life into the Company's trading outpost in Hirado on the northwest coast of Kyushu, which had struggled since its establishment in 1609 to turn a profit. Now, VOC officials believed that their faltering commercial hub could be transformed into a booming recruitment centre from which shipments of experienced soldiers could be dispatched.[33]

The second innovation was tied to the first. The Company did not want to recruit in the shadows, discreetly hiring soldiers behind closed doors, but out in the open with the explicit permission of the Tokugawa shogun. Gaining Tokugawa consent would, it was hoped, smooth over any potential difficulties and open the floodgates for recruitment. And the Company appears to have done precisely this. Brouwer's boast that he had secured shogunal consent is supported by other sources that suggest that he had asked for and received permission to recruit mercenaries.[34] The reasons for *bakufu* consent are less clear. Certainly, the Company was in no position to demand concessions from Japanese authorities and in fact one purpose of Brouwer's embassy was to apologise for the lack of incoming goods and to assure the regime that the VOC would in future send more ships to trade with Japan. Instead the decision stems from the *bakufu*'s deliberate and systematic severing of links between the regime and the activities of its subjects abroad. While ships carrying a *shuinjō* were guaranteed shogunal protection, Tokugawa representatives made it clear in letter after letter dispatched to Southeast Asia that they had no interest in either regulating or protecting Japanese merchants or migrants once they were abroad. Rather, local officials across Southeast Asia were encouraged to 'punish them immediately according to the laws of your country' if they stepped out of line.[35]

33   Katō Eiichi has argued persuasively that the VOC used Hirado primarily as a strategic rather than a commercial outpost between 1609 and 1621. Katō, 'Rengō Oranda Higashi-Indo'.
34   Hendrik Brouwer to Pieter Both, 29 January 1613, VOC 1056: 34v. Copia da Carto do Bispo de Japao para el Rey, feita em Nangasaqui a 15 de Novembro de 1612. Ms Biblioteca de la Real Academica de la Historia, Jesuitas 9-2655 (Cortes, 566), pp. 174-7.
35   Kondō, *Gaiban tsūsho*, p. 185.

While Pieter Both was the first VOC official to issue instructions to recruit Japanese soldiers, the driving force behind the Company's experiment came from another source, Jan Pieterszoon Coen, who was rising in the organisation's ranks on his way to becoming Governor-General. One year after Brouwer's 1613 letter, Coen laid out a series of far-reaching plans involving the use of Japanese soldiers. These came in the form of an ambitious document, *Discoers aen de E. Heeren Bewinthebberen touscherende den Nederlandtsche Indischen staet* (Discourse to the Honourable Directors touching the Netherlands Indies State), submitted in 1614, that was intended as a blueprint for a VOC empire in Asia.[36] In it, Coen laid out the political and economic challenges faced by the Company across Asia before presenting a number of strategies through which the organisation could, he believed, seize control of key trade routes and hubs. Rather than being condemned to the defensive in its wider struggle against Portugal and Spain, which were both entrenched in Asia, the Company should, Coen wrote, attack by striking at the great Iberian centres of power in Asia: the bustling Portuguese entrepôt of Macao and the heavily fortified Spanish colony at Manila. The key to this multipronged assault lay in the participation of large numbers of Japanese mercenaries:

> [By conquering Manila] the Spaniards shall be forced from the Moluccas, and indeed out of the East Indies [...] and along with this we shall get the riches of China. In executing such an important assault we can expect no small support from the islands of Manila as the poor subjects are weary of the Spanish yoke. For the execution [of the assault] we can get great help from Japan, [...] because the Japanese soldiers are as good as ours and the Kaiser [shogun] has given us his promise that we can take out as many people as we can get hold of. We can get enough as they are ready and willing, as we have found from our experience. These same Japanese soldiers can be used to do great service in the expedition to Macao, and with whom this expedition can be effected. With these victories, we shall not only capture a great treasure but also the rich Chinese trade [...].[37]

36 'Discoers aen de E. *Heeren* Bewinthebberen touscherende den Nederlandtsche Indischen state', Colenbrander, *Jan Pietersz. Coen*, 5: 451-474. Masselman, *The Cradle of Colonialism*, p. 307. Masselman described this document as a 'Blueprint for Empire' and I take my formulation from him. For a brilliant new biography of Coen that includes a long discussion of this document, see Van Goor, *Jan Pieterszoon Coen*, pp. 151-184.

37 Colenbrander, *Jan Pietersz. Coen*, 5, p. 468.

In this way, the recruitment of Japanese troops promised to contribute to a remaking of the strategic map, helping the VOC to evict the Portuguese and the Spanish from vital chokepoints and ensuring Dutch dominion over key trade routes.

The *Discoers* lays bare the scale of Coen's ambitions when it came to Japanese soldiers. Rather than the occasional shipment, he conjured up a large-scale, systematic programme of recruitment that would bolster the Company's military presence in Asia. In sketching out such an aggressive vision, he introduced a distinctively martial twist on a much older idea. For decades, the Jesuits and other European religious orders had seen Japan as a zone of unrealised possibilities where dreams of mass conversions could be achieved. One senior Jesuit official wrote that this 'enterprise of Japan is without doubt the most important and beneficial of all being undertaken in these oriental parts and, indeed in all of discovery' and for these reasons 'a very great harvest may be expected here.'[38] For such writers, Japan represented uniquely fertile ground, a bountiful field waiting only to be harvested by Jesuit missionaries. With minimal expense and only a small number of personnel, the archipelago could yield an army of converts. In much the same way, Coen saw Japan as a zone of possibility where outsized ambitions could be realised. Just as the Jesuits confidently predicted 'a very great harvest' of souls, he anticipated a great harvest of willing bodies. But rather than an army of Christian converts able to carry the fight to the heathen, Coen saw the possibility of long columns of Japanese mercenaries with Dutch officers at their head marching through Southeast Asia in service of the Company's aims.

It is easy to understand why the image proved so appealing. The recruitment of these troops would, first, allow the Company to secure its already sprawling holdings. By 1614, when Coen penned the *Discoers*, the VOC had expanded rapidly, acquiring a string of colonies and trading posts across Asia, but these possessions were under constant threat, both from increasingly hostile local populations and also from the Portuguese and the Spanish, who had been entrenched in Asia for decades. They were also, as Coen constantly protested, chronically undermanned. By his estimate, the Company needed at least 2,500 to 3,000 additional soldiers to hold and strengthen its position.[39] The recruitment of Japanese mercenaries promised to help remedy this situation, providing a reliable buttress for Dutch power in Asia. In addition to filling the depleted ranks of garrisons, such soldiers

38   Quoted in de Bary, Gluck, and Tiedemann, ed. *Sources of Japanese Tradition: Volume 2*, p. 156
39   Coen to *Heeren* 17, 1 January 1614, Colenbrander, *Jan Pietersz. Coen*, 1:16.

could play a role, VOC officials believed, in pacifying local populations. In the Banda islands, for example, where local residents had persistently defied the Company's attempt to establish a monopoly over the trade in nutmeg, Japanese mercenaries could compel obedience simply via the 'reputation alone they have in the Indian nations'.[40] Crucially, this could all be done without requiring additional troops from Europe or diverting 'the might of the Netherlanders'.[41]

Recruitment in Japan

The task of recruiting these soldiers fell to Jacques Specx, the VOC's long-serving chief merchant in Japan who had taken over from Brouwer. Specx set about binding Japanese recruits to draconian contracts that subordinated them to Company demands while stipulating harsh punishments if these were violated. Writing to his superiors, he explained that the first contingent had been placed 'under an appropriate oath and articles that I put together and translated in the Japanese language and writing'.[42] Such contracts were designed to convert unruly recruits into dependable soldiers who could be relied upon to defend isolated garrisons to the last man or to carry the fight to the enemy's walls. They were also intended to focus their actions: the Company was clear that it had no intention of recruiting part-time military entrepreneurs who toggled back and forth between trade and violence. It wanted professional soldiers who would be docile in the barracks and ready for deployment wherever their service was needed.

Rather than fitting neatly into such expectations, Japanese mercenaries proved, however, difficult to control. One VOC official complained that 'of the Japanese we have the bellyful already; it is an excitable and difficult race'.[43] Another exclaimed that the 'soldiers from Japan are of no service to us, because they are very dangerous and difficult to govern'.[44] It would, he declared, be far 'better to leave these people in their own lands'. The result was a constant jostling between expansive plans engineered by high-ranking

40   Coen to Specx, 14 May 1616, Ibid., 2:106.
41   Extract uijt verscheijden resolutiën ghenomen op 't comptoir Firando in Jappan in datis 12 en 16 Augustus, 3 September 1614, VOC 1058: 112.
42   Originele missive door Jacques Specx, geschreven ten ancker liggende voor het veroverde Portugese fort op 't eijlant Tijdoor aen d'Ed. *Heeren* bewinthebberen tot Amsterdam in dato 2 Augustus 1613, VOC 1056: 89.
43   Laurens Reael to the Amsterdam Chamber, 18 July 1616, VOC 1063: 19.
44   Steven van der Haghen to the Amsterdam Chamber, 18 July 1616, VOC 1063: 53.

VOC officials like Coen and the reality on the ground. This is evident in the career of one group of these soldiers, the contingent dispatched aboard the *Fortuijn*, which sailed from Hirado in 1616. Although the sources are far from complete, this is the best documented of the Company's mercenary cohorts and it provides some sense of the wider experience of VOC service.

In late 1615, Specx, the head of the Japan factory in Hirado, began to assemble a new contingent of mercenaries, the first to be shipped out after the 68 soldiers that Brouwer had discussed in his 1613 letter.[45] They were to travel aboard two ships, the *Enckhuijsen* and the *Fortuijn*, which were anchored in the narrow confines of Hirado harbour. Although both were blessed with good Dutch names, these were very different vessels. The *Enckhuijsen* was a typical VOC workhorse, a cargo vessel built in the United Provinces and estimated at some 300 *last* or roughly 600 tonnes, that had made the long voyage from Europe to Asia in May 1614.[46] By contrast, the *Fortuijn* was a local junk that had been purchased by the Company in order to make up for its shortage of available vessels and then outfitted with a new rigging.[47] It was far smaller than its sister vessel, just 140 *last* or roughly 280 tonnes, making it less suitable for a long ocean-going voyage.[48]

By November, Specx had finished recruiting and he recorded the names of 59 men alongside their salaries in a long document. As was standard practice, he moved quickly to bind them to the Company with a contract dated the 'year and age named Iewa guannien [first year of Genna] in the 11th month and 11th day' or 31 December 1615. This document is the only extant example of an agreement signed between Japanese mercenaries and the VOC.[49] The contract itself was to last for three years, but crucially this was three years

45   We know of at least four shipments of Japanese troops dispatched from Hirado although there were probably more. The *Roode Leeuw met Pijlen* sailed in 1613 with the initial shipment of 68 men recruited by Brouwer; the *Enckhuijsen* and *Fortuijne* transported 67 recruits in 1615; the *Nieuw Bantam* and *Galiasse* carried 90 troops in 1619, and in 1620 another shipment of roughly 100 men was sent out aboard the *China*. Aenteckeningen van de timmeragie ongelden montcosten provision ende maentgelden gedaen en betaelt inty equipperen van de joncke als nu genaempt de fortuijne, VOC 1062: 106-121. Coen to *Heeren* 17, 22 January 1620, Colenbrander, *Jan Pietersz. Coen*, 1:519. Pieter de Carpentier and Jacob Dedel to the directors, 8 March 1621, VOC 1072: 376v.
46   'The Dutch East India Company's shipping between the Netherlands and Asia 1595-1795', http://resources.huygens.knaw.nl/das/detailVoyage/91220, accessed December 2014.
47   Parthesius, *Dutch Ships in Tropical Waters*, p. 107. The *last* was a variable Dutch unit to measure cargo capacity. As Parthesius writes, for a 'general comparison with the modern measure of cargo capacity, the "tonnage", the last value can be multiplied by two'.
48   Ibid., p. 107.
49   Aenteckeningen van de timmeragie ongelden montcosten provision ende maentgelden gedaen en betaelt inty equipperen van de joncke als nu genaempt de fortuijne, VOC 1062: 106-121.

not from date of signing but rather from the commencement of service once the recruits reached Southeast Asia. If one added in waiting times and the long sea voyage itself, the result was a longer period of obligation. The contract begins much as a standard agreement that would have been immediately familiar to any one of thousands of Dutch sailors or soldiers. The recruits were required to pledge never to start brawls or engage in fighting, never to gamble, 'drink to intoxication', or 'harass or attack married women and girls'. They were to obey the captain, the helmsman or 'any Dutch authority' at all times both on the ship as well as ashore; never to 'speak back when given orders' and above all 'never oppose with deceit or otherwise the captain or other authorities, or commit treachery against their persons '. Violation of these final provisions would lead to the swift application of capital punishment.

But it was not simply their own bodies that were to be subject to punishment. Diverging from comparable agreements signed with European recruits, the contract pulled in their 'parents, wives, children and guarantors [who] will be punished in the same way as these are also obligated by the contract'. In this way, the Company mandated collective punishment extending to the recruit's family and the guarantor standing security for him who was also listed in the contract. The inclusion of this provision means that the contract represents, at least in theory, a striking expansion of VOC jurisdiction, giving Specx, the head of a minor European trading outpost, the ability to draw the families of his recruits into a VOC juridical web and punish them accordingly. It was by no means clear if the Company had any basis for such an ambitious extension of its authority, but the question of enforcement is less important than the psychological impact of the clause, which was designed to force the recruits into obedience by pegging outsized consequences to their actions.

Despite the harshness of the contract and the clearly hazardous nature of the duty, Specx does not seem to have struggled to find enough men willing to sign on. The handful of recruits that listed their hometowns in the 1615 agreement were overwhelmingly local, drawn either from Hirado itself or from Nagasaki, a bustling port city less than a hundred miles down the coast. Some were surely Christians eager to find a way out of Japan: the list of names includes two Miguels and one Pedro, who were probably either baptised in their youth or born to a Christian family. But the majority showed no obvious Christian connection, and the bulk of the recruits were probably seeking economic opportunity, and hence intended to (and did) return to Japan once their contracts expired. Given conditions in Hirado and Nagasaki, where the trade boom was concentrated in the hands of a relatively small number of local officials and rich merchants, the fact that a regular salary proved enticing is not especially surprising. Hirado, the most important site for recruitment, was, according to descriptions by contemporary European visitors, flooded with unemployed men looking for work. One observer, writing in 1613 when the Company commenced its programme of recruitment, described a town filled with 'base people or Renegados [...] loytering vp and downe the Towne'.[50]

The presence of a large population of what was described as 'divers vagrant people' was closely tied to the progressive closing down of alternative avenues for employment in Kyushu. As the Tokugawa regime consolidated its hold over the archipelago after 1600, it became increasingly difficult to find a place in daimyo armies, which had displayed a seemingly boundless appetite for soldiers during the bloody years of the Warring States period (*Sengoku*, 1467–1568) when Kyushu was convulsed by regular conflict. At the same time, wide-scale piracy, which had drawn in tens of thousands of Kyushu inhabitants at its peak in the sixteenth century, was by 1615 finally suppressed. Although Toyotomi Hideyoshi, the second of Japan's three great unifiers, had officially banned piracy in 1588, these practices had initially mutated into a different form rather than simply disappearing. As late as the first decade of the seventeenth century, ports like Hirado continued to play host to a range of pirate groups, and European vessels sailing through Asian waters regularly encountered their ships on the busy sea lanes of early modern Asia. In 1605, for example, an English vessel, the *Tiger*, cruising off the Malay peninsula, sighted a Japanese pirate junk which 'had been pyrating along the coast of China and Camboia', while in 1607 the commander of a Dutch expedition stumbled upon three junks belonging to Japanese pirates (*Japonesche Zee-roovers*) based in Hirado.[51] By the time Specx began hiring, however, little trace of the pirate industry remained and the Company probably drew at least some of its recruits from the maritime communities that had once participated in Japan's great wave of seaborne predation. That at least some of the 59 would have had a maritime background is confirmed by the expectation that they would crew the *Fortuijn*, which lacked enough sailors of its own, on the long voyage to Southeast Asia, and the contract listed a handful of specialised roles including mast climber and master of the anchor.

Given the closing off of these traditional avenues of employment it is not surprising that Specx's offer of an advance, regular provisions and a reliable

---

50   Satow, *The Voyage of Captain John Saris*, p. 179.

51   Markham, ed., *The Voyages and Works of John Davis*, pp. 178-182; Isaac Commelin, ed., *Begin ende Voortgangh van de Vereenighde Nederlantsche*, p. 77.

monthly wage proved highly attractive, and the head of the rival English factory noted that there was an abundance of 'dasparate, warlike people & ready to adventure for good pay'.[52] While Kyushu was clearly fertile ground, Specx was probably aided by the development of a specialised class of recruiters who had sprung up to cater for the Company's needs. Evidence of this can be found in the contract itself, in which a handful of guarantors stood in for multiple recruits. Sakino Matsy Sejusteroo, for example, offered himself up as security for eight individuals (Ruisero, Anthonio, Michguel, Fikofatsij, Sjosa, Jejusty, Tsjoso, and Paulo), while Amia Eunbigi stood in as security for five recruits (Jonsemon, Kiitsiemon, Kiuffy, Michguel, and Pedro). If these were indeed recruiters, then such practices were a parallel of the system that had sprung up in the United Provinces, where a specialised class of recruitment agent, the so-called *zielverkoopers* or 'soul sellers', emerged to supply the Company's inexhaustible demand for labour. They did so in part by simple entrapment, effectively imprisoning vulnerable recruits in sealed-off boarding houses, but also by selling wondrous dreams of unlimited riches that extended to putting 'a Hammer into [the recruit's] Hands to knock the Diamonds out of the Rocks they shall meet with'.[53]

VOC recruitment hinged in large part on the conviction that the Japanese were, to use the language of a later empire, a peculiarly martial race. In the words of one European observer, the 'Japanese are the most warlike people in this part of the world'.[54] They were thus set apart from the Chinese, for example, who the VOC viewed as compliant settlers capable of being used to populate colonial settlements like Batavia or Tayouan.[55] The problem with this underlying logic was that the Company did its actual recruiting in two cosmopolitan ports, Hirado and Nagasaki, that had a long history of long-distance trade and a diverse population. The result was that even if the Company thought it was hiring Japanese mercenaries it is far from clear if it was always doing so. One clue to this messier reality comes in the last name of one of the soldiers caught up in the Amboina trial in 1623, Thome Corea. If, as the name suggests, he had a Korean connection, this was not unusual in Hirado where the local daimyo had brought back hundreds of Korean captives who had been instrumental in the creation of the famous

52 Farrington, *The English Factory in Japan*, p. 379.
53 Frick and Schweitzer, *A Relation of Two Several Voyages*, p. 227.
54 Blair and Robertson, eds. *The Philippine Islands*, 5:271.
55 For the process of 'co-colonization' in Taiwan, see Andrade, *How Taiwan Became Chinese*. The Chinese were, one writer declared, 'an industrious people [...] on whom completely depends the well-being of Batavia', the VOC headquarters in Asia. Quoted in Blussé, 'Batavia', p. 161.

Mikawachi porcelain industry.[56] We know from the trial records that Thome Corea was 50 in 1623, meaning that he was born in 1573 and was thus likely brought to Japan in the turbulent aftermath of Hideyoshi's invasion.[57] His inclusion in VOC ranks suggests that the Company's recruitment plans allowed space for reinvention as former captives morphed in search of stable wages into Japanese soldiers. And he was not alone. VOC records include multiple references to 'Japanese' soldiers like Corea or Joan Maccau [Macao], whose names suggest origins outside Japan.[58]

Of Specx's 59 new recruits, the most important was their captain, Kusnokij Itsiemon, who was appointed boatswain (*hoochbootsman*) for the duration of the voyage and tasked with managing the Company's new soldiers once they had arrived in Southeast Asia. As a mark of his elevated position, he was given a salary of eight taels, which was more than three times the standard pay for one of his charges , an advance of 25 taels that could be spent immediately, and the right to bring a servant, Rockoso, who was described in the contract as a *jongen* or boy. Unlike most of his new subordinates, Kusnokij was from the distant commercial metropolis of Osaka rather than Kyushu. It is not clear how exactly he came to be in Hirado or why Specx felt that this was the right man to take charge of the contingent but he proved a disastrous choice whose inept leadership produced a string of problems once the *Fortuijn* departed Hirado.

The purpose of these recruits was to act as a spearhead for VOC forces in Southeast Asia. To facilitate this, Specx set about equipping them with a small arsenal consisting of different weapons 'that were needed to arm the Japanese'.[59] These included 40 Japanese firearms (*Jappanse roers*), 11 Japanese bows, and 45 Japanese spears of different lengths.[60] The muskets were not cheap, costing a total of 72 taels, but they packed a powerful punch. Musket technology had advanced in leaps and bounds in Japan through the sixteenth century, driven in large part by the involvement of these weapons in the endemic conflict that characterised the Warring States period. Like other muskets from this period these were slow to reload, but in the hands of

56   For a recent study, see Hwang, To, and Yi, *Imjin Waeran Kwa Hirado Mik'awach'i Sagijang*.
57   This is the conclusion reached by Iwaō Seiichi. Iwao Seiichi, *Zoku nanyō Nihon machi no kenkyū*, p. 257.
58   Resolution, Fort Jacatra, 18 July 1619, Colenbrander, *Jan Pietersz. Coen*, 3:528.
59   Aenteckeningen van de timmeragie ongelden montcosten provision ende maentgelden gedaen en betaelt inty equipperen van de joncke als nu genaempt de fortuijne, VOC 1062:120.
60   Ibid., VOC 1062:120.

well-trained troops they could be lethal, with Japanese commanders perfecting the use of volley fire independently of their European counterparts.[61]

But if the recruits were armed to the teeth, there was a problem; the vessels designated to transport them were in no state to undertake the long voyage to the trading port of Banten on the island of Java. In fact, it would take close to four months from the date of recruitment on 18 November before the two ships were ready for departure in early March 1616. This long delay earned Specx a reprimand from his superiors who accused him of disrupting the wider trading schedule through his incompetent management of the refitting process.[62] For the recruits, however, the delay would have been far more welcome. By 1615, Hirado had earned a reputation as 'a second Sodamye' home to dozens of brothels and taverns clustered along the shoreline. There was, one visitor explained, 'never a house in the towen butt the bassest swabber in the fleete may have wine and a hoore'.[63] The combination of ready alcohol and large numbers of idle sailors created ample opportunities for violence, and observers recorded groups of mariners 'stagring drunk up & downe the st[r]eetes, slashing & cutting ofee each other w'th their knyves, lyke mad men'.[64] To restore some order, local authorities were forced to take drastic measures, including hacking a group of sailors into pieces and throwing these to the town's dogs.[65] The long period of inactivity also gave time for rivalries to fester within the contingent itself. The most dangerous emerged between Kusnokij and a charismatic rival, Ceyemon, who, clearly covetous of his superior's position and privileges, worked to undermine these. The rivalry simmered for months in Hirado before exploding with bloody results when the recruits finally arrived in Southeast Asia.

Finally, after months of preparation, the *Enckhuijsen* and the *Fortuijn* departed Japan on 5 March 1616 with the bulk of the recruits, perhaps forty or fifty men, crammed into the hold of the smaller junk, which was placed under the command of Jacob Joosten van Lodensteijn. Van Lodensteijn was the brother of one of the original *Liefde* mariners who had been shipwrecked in Japan in 1600, but unlike his sibling, who had established himself as a successful merchant, he had little experience of Japan and little facility with the language.[66] The result was that he had to rely absolutely on Kusnokij,

61   Stavros, 'Military Revolution in Early Modern Japan'.
62   Mulder, *Hollanders in Hirado*, p. 130. Colenbrander, *Jan Pietersz. Coen*, 2:105 and 7.1:501.
63   Farrington, *The English Factory in Japan*, p. 813.
64   *Diary of Richard Cocks*, 2:113.
65   Camps to Coen, 15 October 1621, Colenbrander, *Jan Pietersz. Coen*, 7:2:798; *Diary of Richard Cocks*, 2:131.
66   Mulder, *Hollanders in Hirado*, p. 158.

who was posted on the *Fortuijn* to maintain control of the new recruits. Clearly aware of the brewing conflict, Specx elected to place Ceyemon on the *Enckhuijsen* to take charge of the handful of Japanese soldiers there and keep him out of Kusnokij's way.

In total the two ships were to spend 51 days at sea, arriving in the port of Banten on 24 April. For the larger *Enckhuijsen*, the voyage seems to have passed without incident, in part because of Ceyemon's leadership but also because the ship was (in relative terms) far larger and more spacious. Aboard the *Fortuijn*, however, things quickly deteriorated.[67] The life of a VOC mariner, whether European or Asian, was always a harsh one. Likened by one observer to 'subservient slaves', a sailor aboard a Company vessel had to be ready 'on the slightest nod or command of any superior, to do everything he is told without grumbling. At any show of reluctance, he is threatened and beaten with the rope's end.'[68] For the crew of the *Fortuijn*, however, a combination of the poor conditions made worse by the small size of the vessel, unfamiliarity with the ship's routines and inept leadership pushed the recruits close to mutiny. The problem was clearly recognised by Specx who explained to his superiors that shipping out recruits on smaller vessels invariably created more problems. We are, he declared, 'always apprehensive that more discontent and troubles will take place on the junk as the ship'.[69]

On vessels like the *Fortuijn*, the crew would probably have been divided into two four-hour shifts, giving them at most four hours sleep at any one time. The result was that most sailors slept in wet clothes, tumbling into their hammocks as soon as they finished their duties only to have their sleep cut short when the watch changed again.[70] In such conditions, illnesses like dysentery spread quickly and there was little prospect of medical attention.[71] If conditions were already poor in fair weather, they quickly became appalling in stormy conditions. When the weather turned, the hatches were battened down, sometimes for days or even weeks on end. Water seeped into everything, the smell of rotting mixing with the general

67   Coen to Specx, 14 May 1616, Colenbrander, *Jan Pietersz. Coen*, 2:111.
68   Quoted in Boxer, *The Dutch Seaborne Empire*, pp. 78-9; De Graaf, *Oost Indise Spiegel*, p. 30.
69   Specx to Coen, 1 October 1616, Colenbrander, *Jan Pietersz. Coen*, 7.1:199.
70   Iris Bruijn summarises the situation when she writes that the 'combination of poor diet and substandard sleeping and living quarters plus the climate put a severe strain on the physical resilience of the crew'. Bruijn, *Ship's Surgeons*, p. 73.
71   We know from the sources that the 1613 contingent, which was shipped three years earlier, developed a number of tropical illnesses as they moved into warmer conditions. Originele missive door Jacques Specx, geschreven ten ancker liggende voor het veroverde Portugese fort op 't eijlant Tijdoor aen d'Ed. *Heeren* bewinthebberen tot Amsterdam in dato 2 Augustus 1613, VOC 1056.

stench created by crowding large numbers of people into small spaces with inadequate ventilation. With sailors unable to access the primitive toilet facilities, which were usually located in the open on the bow of a ship, the cabin was quickly fouled with excrement and vomit.

To this must be added the inevitable terrors of a long ocean voyage in the age of sail. For those unused to the open ocean, and a significant share of the recruits had probably never been to sea before, the experience was, in the words of one equally unprepared voyager, 'altogether unconceivable'. Conventional bravery counted for nothing: 'tho' I have been oftentimes in great dangers [...] and upon many occasions have, with Courage enough, stood before the Enemy; yet did none of these dangers ever terrifie me comparably to this [experience of a storm]'. In these moments, 'death doth not only seem sure and inevitable, but comes attended with all the Horrour imaginable, and drest in its most hideous and terrifying shapes'.[72] Such fears were of course justified as VOC ships did periodically disappear without a trace. This was the fate of the *China*, which departed Japan in 1620 with a contingent of close to a hundred Japanese mercenaries, but which was lost somewhere along the sea lanes with its crew and passengers drowned.[73]

To make its sailors behave as 'subservient slaves' in the face of such conditions, the Company imposed harsh discipline.[74] The captain of the *Enckhuijsen*, *Fortuijn*'s sister ship, stipulated that anyone found bringing unauthorised alcohol onto the ship would be dropped from the yardarm [*van de rae vallen*] three times and then lashed before the mast.[75] This involved hoisting the culprit up in the rigging, tying his arms and then dropping him, usually around 40 for 50 feet, thereby either dislocating or breaking his arms. The standard punishments used in VOC ships for more serious offences were characterised by a gruesome ingenuity that was calculated to terrify the average sailor into obedience.[76] A mariner involved in a knife fight was forced to place his hand against the mast, so that a knife could be driven into the centre of it. There he remained until he was able to pull the blade through his hand, cutting through flesh and severing tendons in the process.[77] For even graver crimes, the offender might be

---

72   Frick and Schweitzer, *A Relation of Two Several Voyages*, p. 30.

73   De Carpentier and Dedel to the directors, 8 March 1621, VOC 1072. Blair and Robertson, *The Philippine Islands, 1493–1898*, 19:70.

74   De Graaf, *Oost Indise Spiegel*, p. 30.

75   Copie resolutien getrocken in Japan, 18 Augustus 1615 tot 2 Maert 1616; VOC 1061: 247-257.

76   For some of these punishments, see Hoogenberk, *De Rechtsvoorschriften voor de Vaart op Oost-Indië*.

77   Hoogenberk, *De Rechtsvoorschriften voor de Vaart op Oost-Indië*, pp. 285-6.

keelhauled (*kielhalen*), thrown overboard and dragged under the keel of the ship to the other side, almost drowning him while ripping his flesh away on the encrusted hull of the vessel.[78] While such punishments occupied the extreme end of the spectrum, the VOC also enforced a comprehensive system of fines and levies for a range of trivial offenses that seemed calculated to strip sailors of their earnings.[79]

For the recruits, the transition from an extended period in Hirado's welcoming embrace to the life of a VOC sailor must have been jarring. In this, they were broadly similar to tens of thousands of new recruits that departed the United Provinces but crucially, the Japanese contingent shipped aboard the *Fortuijn* lacked the rigid hierarchies that compelled obedience in such circumstances. The task of maintaining order fell to Kusnokij, who was now required to justify his wages and privileges. He proved entirely 'unsuitable for command', an idle and unreliable captain with no capacity to control his increasingly unruly charges.[80] The result was a total breakdown in authority that seems to have brought the recruits to the very edge (if not actually over the brink) of violent mutiny. The recruits were, their Dutch officers declared, nothing more than a 'mutinous rabble', who had 'behaved very maliciously', endangering the safety of the ship and coming precariously close to armed resistance.[81]

When the news of what had happened aboard the *Fortuijn* reached the VOC hierarchy, it prompted a swift response. On 14 May, just a few weeks after the eventual arrival of the junk in Banten, Jan Pieterszoon Coen addressed the problem in a letter to the head of the Japan factory. In future, Specx must 'inspect' (*monsteren*) his recruits more carefully and make sure that any potential troublemakers were weeded out before leaving port.[82] As Coen saw it, the problem could be solved simply by better hiring practices and proper diligence by officials on the ground. Specx should simply line up the recruits on the shore, remove any bad apples and dispatch the rest. Such comments reveal a crucial blind spot that persisted throughout the Company's decade-long experiment with these soldiers. It was, Coen in particular insisted, not a problem with the recruitment plans as a whole but simply a matter of finding the right disciplinary formula. In response, Jacques Specx, who was acutely aware of the difficulties of exerting control,

78   Frick and Schweitzer, *A Relation of Two Several Voyages*, p. 10.
79   Boxer, *The Dutch Seaborne Empire 1600-1800*.
80   Coen to Specx, 23 April 1617, Colenbrander, *Jan Pietersz. Coen*, 2:234-35.
81   Coen to Specx, 14 May 1616, Colenbrander, *Jan Pietersz. Coen*, 2:111.
82   Ibid., 2:111.

pointed out that 'such scum [*geboeften*] can often, as long as they are on land, remain quiet so that they are difficult to recognise and be weeded out'.[83]

Rather than an isolated incident, the voyage provided a taste of things to come. Despite his performance on the *Fortuijn*, Kusnokij had managed to retain his position as head of the Japanese contingent, which had swelled again with the arrival of the *Enkhuijsen* to include his long-time rival, Ceyemon. Their rivalry was swiftly renewed; on 2 March Kusnokij decided to take action by ambushing Ceyemon as he lay in his bunk with his fellow mercenaries, talking and smoking. Stabbed without warning from behind, Ceyemon died immediately. It was a bloody climax to months of simmering tension and the perpetrator was seized immediately for punishment. But if Kusnokij was an incompetent leader, he proved far more ingenious when it came to legal manoeuvring. When he was arrested, he insisted that his actions had been entirely legal and that he was simply fulfilling his role as commander of the Japanese, a charge that had been given to him, he maintained, both by Specx and the daimyo of Hirado. Since Ceyemon had been 'mustered under his command', Kusnokij was entitled to punish him for insubordination and his repeated attempts to 'belittle him and make himself master'.[84] When he stabbed his rival he was, in other words, acting as a properly constituted officer rather than carrying out a private vendetta.

It was a shrewd and essentially plausible defence as the recruits were bound by a contract that stipulated harsh punishments if any of them attempted to subvert or oppose the officials placed in charge of them. It did not, however, satisfy the VOC tribunal, which convened the day after the original incident to issue a verdict. Lamenting the loss of Ceyemon, who had been marked for greater things, the tribunal concluded that such actions were an affront to 'Christian justice and also Japanese custom'. The result was that these offenses could only be punished by death, and ignoring Kusnokij's protests about his authority he was swiftly executed. With the murder of Ceyemon and the execution of Kusnokij, the *Fortuijn* contingent had already lost two potential leaders and Company officials moved quickly to make a new appointment on 10 June, just a week after the incident in the barracks. The new captain Gonssen, who was described as 'an expert at war of their manner and otherwise qualified and trusted,'

---

83   Specx to Coen, 1 October 1616, Colenbrander, *Jan Pietersz. Coen*, 7.1:199.
84   Jaccatra Resolutions, 3 June 1616, Ibid., 4:125-6. The episode is also discussed in Iwao, *Zoku nanyō Nihon machi no kenkyū*, pp. 121-22.

might have wondered what he was taking on but he was at least spared the prospect of another extended sea voyage.[85]

If VOC officials were able to dismiss such incidents as isolated episodes that could be eliminated once the Company located the right disciplinary formula, it was also the case that the recruits performed well when thrust into actual battle. When Coen and others had devised their plans for mass recruitment, they had envisaged Japanese mercenaries acting as a vanguard in attacks against fortified Portuguese and Spanish strongholds. The reality was less impressive as the soldiers transported aboard the *Fortuijn* were thrust into a series of minor marketplace skirmishes that erupted between the English and the Dutch in Banten.[86] The first of these, which took place in July 1617, started as a dispute over the purchase of fish in the marketplace before turning violent.[87] First into the fight, one of the Company's Japanese soldiers was severely injured with a sword cut through his shoulder blade that left him permanently disfigured.[88] In the second incident in November, a large mob of English merchants mixed with local allies and heavily armed with pikes and firearms marched on VOC warehouses intent on violence. The Dutch merchants based in the warehouse wisely opted to flee, seeking shelter in a house belonging to one of the Chinese merchants operating in the port city.[89] This left the Company's Japanese recruits, just seven in number, to defend their employer's goods alone against a force estimated at more than two hundred.[90] They fought ferociously, cutting some of the opponents almost in half, but losing three dead and one severely wounded.

Such engagements established a basic template and VOC records are peppered with praise for the bravery of Japanese mercenaries in combat.[91] One official wrote that 'the Japanese soldiers show themselves as brave as our own. Their banner was first on the walls. Through their great boldness and fearlessness many were injured.'[92] Their willingness to take on the most dangerous tasks meant that these troops participated in most major VOC campaigns in this period.[93] The most significant of these took place in

85   Jaccatra Resolutions, 10 June 1616, Colenbrander, *Jan Pietersz. Coen*, 3:366.

86   First-hand descriptions of both incidents can be found in IJzerman, *Cornelis Buijsero te Bantam.*

87   These incidents are discussed in Iwao, *Zoku nanyō Nihon machi no kenkyū*, pp. 234-35.

88   IJzerman, ed. *Cornelis Buijsero te Bantam*, p. 56-7.

89   Coen to *Heeren* 17, 18 December 1617, Colenbrander, *Jan Pietersz. Coen*, 1:301-2.

90   Citing a different source, Iwao suggests there were just 5 Japanese soldiers involved in this skirmish. Iwao, *Zoku nanyō Nihon machi no kenkyū*, p. 235.

91   Coen to *Heeren* 17, 18 December 1617, Colenbrander, *Jan Pietersz. Coen*, 1:302.

92   Coen to *Heeren* 17, 1 January 1614, Ibid., 1:17.

93   Resolutions, 14 March 1621, Ibid., 3:699.

March 1621 when Coen assembled a large army, including two contingents of Japanese soldiers, to invade and subdue the Banda islands. One of these contingents was rewarded with a personal gift of 30 reals per soldier for their bravery in the fierce fighting that opened the campaign.[94] As military operations morphed into an extended process of violent pacification, the Company's recruits were pressed into a different kind of service as executioners. On 8 May 1621, VOC officials decided to execute 44 elders or *orangkaya* for allegedly plotting to renew hostilities against the Dutch. In a gruesome scene that was widely condemned even within the Company, six Japanese soldiers were ordered 'with their sharp cutting swords' to hack the eight leading *orangkaya* through the middle, then cut off their heads and then quarter their bodies before killing the remaining 36 leaders.[95]

But as was standard, praise for Japanese valour was balanced by ongoing disciplinary issues, which continued to feature regularly in VOC correspondence. One Japanese soldier, Pedro, was found sleeping when he should have been patrolling the walls of the fortress and was promptly executed by firing squad, while another, Saennon, was sentenced to hard labour for a similar offense.[96] The result was a continued search for a reliable method to turn the recruits into 'obliging servants'. Back in Hirado, Specx insisted that VOC commanders needed to use the harshest possible discipline to keep the recruits in line. The 'sabre' was, he argued, the only medicine that the Japanese could understand and it must be used to hold these soldiers in check.[97]

In the months after they arrived in Southeast Asia, the *Fortuijn* contingent was broken up and scattered around the Company's various outposts wherever they were needed. They start to reappear in the records again around 1619 when their initial three-year contracts come to an end. Some, like Tombe, Schoyts, Itsico, Thosoo, Groboo, Johan Fanso, and Joan Maccau, opted to re-enlist at slightly elevated salaries in July 1619.[98] Others, seeing their numbers diminished by sickness or death in battle, decided they had had enough of Dutch service and resolved to return to Japan. Once they reached Hirado in 1620, however, a conflict broke out centred on whether they could claim back wages from 5 March 1616 when their ship had actually departed Japan or from 18 November 1615 when they had first signed their 'letters of article'. It was almost too much to bear for Specx, who wrote

94   Ibid., 3:698-9.
95   Leupe, 'De Verovering Der Banda-Eilanden', p. 427.
96   Iwao, *Zoku nanyō Nihon machi no kenkyū*, pp. 402-3; Resolution, Fort Jacatra, 13 November 1619, Colenbrander, *Jan Pietersz. Coen*, 3:192.
97   Jacques Specx to Coen, 1 October 1616, Ibid., 7.1:200.
98   Resolution, Fort Jacatra, 18 July 1619, Ibid., 3:528.

furiously that the recruits' demands for an extra three and half months of back pay went 'against reason and Japanese custom'.[99]

Viewed as a whole, the experience of the *Fortuijn* contingent encapsulates some of the tensions embedded in the Company's recruitment scheme. And yet despite persistent problems, the VOC officials and especially Jan Pieterszoon Coen continued to issue order after order requiring their subordinates to pick up the pace of recruitment. On 30 March 1618, Coen demanded that Specx dispatch 'the most suitable, brave young men.'[100] In 1620, he wrote that 'for the strengthening of all the garrisons we have sent for good number of Japanese; [...] a good number will also be sent to the Moluccas and up to 3 or 400 shall be sent this year.'[101] The same year he demanded between one and two hundred more Japanese recruits while using every possible opportunity to insist that Specx 'send here as many brave Japanese as time and circumstances permits. They will not be used for labour but for war.'[102]

Remarkably, these instructions endured even as the Tokugawa regime moved to clamp down on the steady flow of soldiers out of the country. In 1621, the *bakufu*, alarmed at the expanding scale of the mercenary trade, barred the Dutch from further recruitment of soldiers in Japan. The edict, dated Genna 7, 5th month, 22nd day, or 11 July 1621, was issued to the daimyo of Hirado. It prohibited the 'taking of purchased men and women to foreign countries' as well as the 'sending out of swords, daggers and other weapons'.[103] Specx provided the best explanation for this shift in policy when he wrote that the edict stemmed from a newly emerged *bakufu* concern that its subjects would 'become involved in foreign wars', thereby drawing the regime, which was increasingly determined to curtail its foreign engagement, into an unwanted conflict.[104] For Coen, however, the ban represented nothing more than a temporary stumbling block and he ordered his subordinates in Japan to spare no effort in overturning the edict: 'It is necessary that you work with discrete diligence to once again gain the previous license to ship Japanese and weapons from the kaiser [shogun].'[105] In another letter, he was even more insistent, instructing his subordinates to 'spare no cost or trouble' in overturning the shogun's ban.[106] Such letters show that VOC

99   Specx to Coen, 24 February 1620, Ibid., 7.1:501.
100 Coen to Jacques Specx, 30 March 1618, Ibid., 2:373.
101 Coen to *Heeren* 17, 22 January 1620, Ibid., 1:519.
102 Coen to Specx, 26 June 1620, Ibid., 2:748.
103 The complete edict can be found in Nagazumi, 'Hirado ni dentatsu sareta Nihonjin', pp. 67-81.
104 Report by Jacques Specx in Hirado, 20 September 1621, VOC 1075:91.
105 Coen to Camps, 2 June 1622, Colenbrander, *Jan Pietersz. Coen*, 3:195.
106 Coen to Camps, 9 April 1622, Ibid., 3:165-66.

ambitions to use Japan as a source of troops remained resilient even after the *bakufu* had acted to suppress the mercenary trade. This only changed in 1623 when the discovery of a terrifying conspiracy on Amboina triggered an emphatic rejection of these troops.

The end of the experiment

On the evening of 22 February 1623, Shichizō, one of the hundreds of Japanese soldiers shipped out from Hirado, asked a Dutch sentry patrolling the walls of the castle in Amboyna how many soldiers manned the fort and how often the guard was changed.[107] This line of questioning quickly aroused suspicions, and he was detained and interrogated. Answering at first that he asked these questions for his own 'amusement and pleasure' (*uyt vermeyen en om plaisier gedaen*), he confessed after torture that he had plotted with the English merchants on the island to seize control of the castle.[108] In his confession, Shichizō incriminated another Japanese mercenary called Sidney Migiell who was then arrested and interrogated, and proceeded to confess. After Migiell all the remaining Japanese in the VOC garrison were questioned and tortured with the same result.

As Shichizō, gasped out the details of the supposed plot, the castle's Japanese contingent morphed from trusted soldiers into shadowy agents of a sprawling conspiracy. Rather than securing territories like Amboyna against outside threat, they became the agent of dispossession, the mechanism by which Amboina could be transferred from the Company's dominion to that of its English rivals. Heavily armed and with free access to every part of the castle, the Japanese were to 'hand over the castle to the English', slaughtering all those who resisted and opening the gates of the fortress for their new paymasters to march in.[109]

Spurred by a series of powerful anti-Dutch pamphlets, much of the writing on Amboina has focused on the English merchants caught up in the conspiracy trial. But, Amboina was also a traumatic episode for the

107 Shichizō's name appears as Hytjeio, Hitieso or a range of alternate spellings in VOC sources. I follow Iwao Seiichi that this is most likely 七蔵 (Shichizō). Iwao, *Zoku nanyō Nihon machi no kenkyū*, p. 256.
108 *Copie autentycq van de Confessien ende Sententien van Mr. Touwerson ende Complicen over de Moordadige Conspiratie op t' Casteel Amboyna voorgenomen, dat door Godes merckelijcke ende genadige beschicking opden xxiii Februario 1623 is aenden dach gecomen als mede de resolutien by den Hr. Gouvernr van Speult & den raet daer over genomen*, VOC 1080, 136v.
109 *Copie autentycq van de confessien ende sententien*, 136v.

Dutch Company, which believed it had uncovered a sprawling plot with soldiers from Japan at the centre. The result was a shift in VOC policy and an abandonment of any further calls to recruit Japanese soldiers. Summoned by the States-General in the Dutch Republic to explain what had happened on Amboina, VOC officials declared that they had lost all faith in these troops. The Japanese have, they explained, 'ever been in good esteeme with us, and have alwaies been much trusted, and not having any occasion of malice, or rancor, or feare of them, or against them'. But in the post-Amboina world this had all changed and 'it behoveth our nation to be alwaies in mistrust of the Japonians, and not so confidently to use or be served of them as before'.[110] In this way, the 1623 conspiracy trial marked a turning point in the Company's experiment although Japanese soldiers already in Southeast Asia continued to feature sporadically in VOC muster rolls.[111]

Given the limited duration and scale of recruitment, how then to assess the Company's experiment with these troops? In the final analysis, there were too few Japanese soldiers in VOC ranks to alter the military balance. The Dutch never recruited more than a few hundred Japanese mercenaries, and although they featured in important campaigns their presence alone was never enough to alter the course of any single conflict. But these soldiers were also more significant than their numbers suggest for they initiated a pattern that was to become increasingly important for the VOC and its English rival, both of which went on to recruit tens of thousands of Asian soldiers over the course of their existence. The Japanese experiment might have ended in failure, but the wider template that they represented proved essential to the success of European empires in Asia.

Works cited

Andrade, Tonio, *How Taiwan Became Chinese: Dutch, Spanish, and Han Colonisation in the Seventeenth Century* (New York: Columbia University Press, 2008).

Baker, Chris; Pombejra, Dhiravat na; van der Kraan, Alfons; Wyatt, David, *Van Vliet's Siam* (Chiang Mai, 2005).

Blair, Emma and Robertson, James, eds. *The Philippine Islands, 1493–1803*, 55 vols. (Cleveland: A.H. Clark, 1902-09).

110   *A remonstrance of the directors of the Netherlands East India Company presented to the Lords States Generall of the united Provinces*, p. 10.
111   A group of Japanese soldiers featured for example in the 1628 siege of Batavia. I am grateful to Mischa Frenks for this reference.

Blussé, Leonard, 'Batavia, 1619-1740: The Rise and Fall of a Chinese Colonial Town', *Journal of Southeast Asian Studies* 12.1 (March 1981).

Boxer, C.R., *The Dutch Seaborne Empire 1600-1800* (London: Penguin Books, 1965).

Bruijn, Iris, *Ship's Surgeons of the Dutch East India Company: Commerce and the Progress of Medicine in the Eighteenth Century* (Leiden: University of Leiden Press, 2009).

Caron, Francois and Schouten, Joost, *A True Description of the Mighty Kingdoms of Japan and Siam* (London: 1663).

Cho, Hung-Guk, 'The Trade between China, Japan, Korea and Southeast Asia in the 14th Century through the 17th Century Period', *International Area Studies Review* 3.2 (2000): 67-107.

Clulow, Adam, "Unjust, Cruel and Barbarous Proceedings: Japanese Mercenaries and the Amboyna Incident of 1623," *Itinerario* 31.1 (2007): 15-34

Cocks, Richard, *Diary Kept by the Head of the English Factory in Japan: Diary of Richard Cocks, 1615–1622,* ed. University of Tokyo Historiographical Institute (Tokyo: University of Tokyo, 1978-1980).

Colenbrander, H.T., ed., *Jan Pietersz. Coen, bescheiden omtrent zijn bedrijf in Indië,* 7 vols. (The Hague: M. Nijhoff, 1919-23).

Commelin, Isaac, ed., *Begin ende Voortgangh van de Vereenighde Nederlantsche Geoctroyeerde Oost-Indische Compagnie* (Amsterdam, 1969).

Cushman, Richard, trans., *The Royal Chronicles of Ayutthaya: A Synoptic Translation* (Bangkok, 2000).

Dam, Pieter van, *Beschrijvinge van de Oostindishe Compagnie*, ed. F.W. Stapel (The Hague: Rijksgeschiedkundige Publicatiën, 1927-1954)

De Bary, Theodore, Gluck, Carol, and Tiedemann, Arthur, ed. *Sources of Japanese Tradition: Volume 2, 1600 to 2000* (New York: Columbia University Press, 2005).

Farrington, Anthony, *The English Factory in Japan, 1613-1623* (London: The British Library, 1991).

Floris, Peter, *His Voyage to the East Indies in the Globe, 1611-1615,* ed. W.H. Moreland (London: Hakluyt Society, 1934).

Frick, Christoph and Schweitzer, Christoph, *A Relation of Two Several Voyages Made Into the East-Indies* (London, 1700).

Fujii, Jōji, 'Junana seiki no Nihon: buke no kokka no keisei', in Asao Naohiro et al. eds., *Iwanami kōza Nihon tsūshi 12* (Tokyo: Iwanami Shoten, 1994).

Goor, Jur van. *Jan Pieterszoon Coen, 1587-1629: Koopman-Koning in Azië* (Amsterdam: Boom Publishers, 2015).

Hoogenberk, H., *De Rechtsvoorschriften voor de Vaart op Oost-Indië 1595-1620* (Utrecht, 1940).

Hwang, Chŏng-dŏk, Chin-sun To, and Yun-sang Yi, *Imjin Waeran Kwa Hirado Mik'awach'i Sagijang: Segyejŏk Pomul ŭl Pijŭn P'irap Chosŏn Sagijang ŭl Ch'ajasŏ*

[The Imjin Wars and Captive Korean Potters At Mikawachi, Hirado] (Ch'op'an. Sŏul-si, Tongbuga Yŏksa Chaedan, 2010).

IJzerman, J.W., ed., *Cornelis Buijsero te Bantam, 1616-1618* (The Hague: M. Nijhoff, 1923).

Ishizawa, Yoshiaki, 'Les quartiers japonais dans l'Asie du Sud-Est au XVIIème siècle', in *Guerre et Paix en Asie du Sud-Est*, ed. Nguyen The Anh and Alain Forest (Paris: Harmettan, 1998)

Iwao, Seiichi, *Shuinsen bōekishi no kenkyū* (Tokyo: Yoshikawa Kōbunkan, 1985).

Iwao, Seiichi, *Zoku nanyō Nihon machi no kenkyū* (Tokyo, 1987).

Katō, Eiichi, 'Rengō Oranda Higashi-Indo Kaisha no senryaku kyoten toshite no Hirado shōkan', in *Nihon zenkindai no kokka to taigai kankei,* ed. Tanaka Takeo (Tokyo: Yoshikawa Kōbunkan 1987).

Kaushik, Roy, *Military manpower, armies and warfare in South Asia* (London: Pickering & Chatto, 2013).

Kondō, Morishige, *Gaiban tsūsho*, in *Kaitei shiseki shūran* (Kyoto: Rinsen Shoten, 1983-1984).

Leupe, P.A., 'De Verovering Der Banda-Eilanden', *Bijdragen tot de Taal-, Land- en Volkenkunde van Nederlandsch-Indië* 2.4 (1854).

Li, Tana, *Nguyễn Cochinchina: Southern Vietnam in the Seventeenth and Eighteenth Centuries* (New York: Cornell Southeast Asia Program Publications, 1998).

Lockard, Craig, '"The Sea Common to All": Maritime Frontiers, Port Cities, and Chinese Traders in the Southeast Asian Age of Commerce, ca. 1400-1750', *Journal of World History* 21.2 (2010): 219-247.

Nagazumi, Yōko, *Shuinsen* (Tokyo: Yoshikawa Kōbunkan, 2001).

Nagazumi, Yōko, 'Ayutthaya and Japan: Embassies and Trade in the Seventeenth century'. In *From Japan to Arabia: Ayutthaya's Maritime Relations with Asia*, ed. Kennon Breazeale (Bangkok: Printing House of Thammasat University, 1999).

Nagazumi, Yōko, 'Hirado ni dentatsu sareta Nihonjin baibai buki yushutsu kinshirei' *Nihon rekishi* 611 (1999).

Parthesius, R., *Dutch Ships in Tropical Waters. The Development of the Dutch East India Company (VOC) Shipping Network in Asia, 1595-1660* (Amsterdam: Amsterdam University Press, 2010).

Polenghi, Cesare, *Samurai of Ayutthaya: Yamada Nagamasa, Japanese Warrior and Merchant in Early 17th Century Siam* (Bangkok: White Lotus Press, 2009).

Markham, Albert, ed., *The Voyages and Works of John Davis* (London: 1880).

Masselman, George, *The Cradle of Colonialism* (New Haven: Yale University Press, 1963)

Milton, Giles, *Nathaniel's Nutmeg,* (London: Hodder & Stoughton, 1999).

Morga, Antonio de. *History of the Philippine Islands from the discovery by Magellan in 1521 to the beginning of the XVII Century; with descriptions of Japan, China and adjacent countries*, translated and edited by E.H. Blair and J.A. Robertson (Cleveland: *A.H. Clark, 1907*).

Mulder, W.Z., *Hollanders in Hirado, 1597–1641* (Haarlem: Fibula-Van Dishoeck, 1984).

Raben, Remco, 'Het Aziatisch legioen: Huurlingen, bondgenoten en reservisten in het geweer voor de Verenigde Oost-Indische Compagnie', in *De Verenigde Oost-Indische Compagnie tussen oorlog en diplomatie*, ed. Gerrit Knaap and Ger Teitler (Leiden: KITLV, 2002).

Ribeiro, Madalena, 'The Japanese Diaspora in the Seventeenth Century. According to Jesuit Sources'. *Bulletin of Portuguese-Japanese Studies* 3 (2001): 53-83.

Satow, Ernest, 'Notes on the Intercourse between Japan and Siam in the Seventeenth Century', *Transactions of the Asiatic Society of Japan,* 13, (1885).

Satow, Ernest, *The Voyage of Captain John Saris to Japan, 1613,* (London: Hakluyt Society, 1900).

Stavros, Matthew, 'Military Revolution in Early Modern Japan', *Japanese Studies*, 33.3 (2013): 243-261.

Turnbull, Stephen, 'The Japanese "Wild Geese": The Recruitment, Roles and Reputation of Japanese Mercenaries in Southeast Asia, 1593-1688', Unpublished paper.

Wray, William 'The 17th-Century Japanese Diaspora: Questions of Boundary and Policy', in

Yamada Nagamasa Kenshōkai, ed., *Yamada Nagamasa shiryō shūsei* (Shizuoka: Yamada Nagamasa Kenshōkai, 1974).

Zheng Ruozeng, *Chouhai tubian*, 9 (China, 1563).

Contact details

School of Philosophical, Historical and International Studies, Faculty of Arts, Monash University, Level 6, 20 Chancellor's Walk, Clayton Campus, Wellington Road, Clayton VIC 3800, Australia
Tel.: +61 3 9905 2193
adam.clulow@monash.edu

8 The East India Company and the foundation of Persian Naval Power in the Gulf under Nader Shah, 1734-47

Peter Good

Abstract

This chapter explores the involvement of the East India Company (EIC) in the creation of a fleet in the Gulf by Nader Shah of Persia between 1734 and 1747. It considers the rationale behind the EIC's assistance to the Persians and what shape it took, considering the pre-eminent position and threat attached by contemporaries to European ships. The chapter draws on the EIC's Persian Gulf Factory Records which shed new light on the ongoing negotiations between the EIC and Persian officials in country. The EIC were active in supporting the construction of a Persian fleet, turning a profit by supplying, not only ships, but also supplies and stores necessary for their maintenance. The provisions provided were a useful means through which the EIC gained favour with the Persian Court in a period of ongoing conflict and uncertainty.

Keywords: Persia, EIC, navy, Nader Shah

Beginning in 1734, Nader Shah, the formidable and brutal ruler of Persia sought to create a navy to match his recently reformed army. In order to do this, he worked to co-opt the English East India Company, which had access to the most powerful naval technology in the region. For decades now, scholars like Carlo Cipolla and others have explored the perceived superiority of European naval technology and the advantages that could be derived from it.[1, 2] The

---

1   Cipolla, *Guns, Sails and Empire* , 1985.
2   Both Chaudhuri and Das Gupta discuss the superiority of European naval technology and the benefit derived from it in the Indian Ocean. Chaudhuri, *Trade and Civilisation in the Indian Ocean*, p. 12; Das Gupta, *India and the Indian Ocean World*, p. 18.

Clulow, Adam and Tristan Mostert (eds.), *The Dutch and English East India Companies: Diplomacy, trade and violence in early modern Asia*. Amsterdam: Amsterdam University Press, 2018
DOI: 10.5117/9789462983298/CH08

focus, however, has always been on how Europeans used this naval power to dominate Asian trading and political bodies. The chaotic political climate in the Gulf region during Nader Shah's reign provided an opportunity to expand his power, and in service of this he engaged the Company who provided ships for loan or sale for a variety of military and diplomatic missions. For its part, the Company was willing to be co-opted in this way, seeing opportunities for both financial and diplomatic gain. To this end, the Company used their forces in the region as a navy for hire, providing the Shah with ships to defeat his enemies in the first instance and then assisting him in acquiring his own, in order to protect their trade and turn a profit. This form of cooperation does not seem to appear in any other relationship between the Company and an Indian Ocean power, although it shares some similarities with VOC submission to the Tokugawa *bakufu* that ruled over Japan and the Dutch Company's subsequent involvement in putting down the Shimabara Revolt.[3]

The strength of European naval power in the Indian Ocean has been widely recognised by scholars. Because of this, it is noteworthy that the Company, which was a significant naval power in this period, used its ships to bolster Persian power rather than to dictate terms to the Persian Empire. Chaudhuri suggests that the experience of the Child's War at the turn of the eighteenth Century, in which the Company had entered into an ill-conceived conflict with the Mughal Empire, had impressed upon the Governors in London and India that they could not hope to militarily defeat the great Asian land empires in open war.[4] The Company's behaviour in Persia is consistent with this idea and indicates the lengths to which it would go to avoid conflict with a major power, even if that meant chipping away at the Company's naval supremacy in the region.

After 1722 and the collapse of the Safavid Empire, Persia and the surrounding region became the nexus of a complex struggle involving the Ottoman Empire, Russia, pro-Safavid restorationists, and the Hotaki Afghan forces that had overcome and occupied the Empire's territories. Eventually, the Safavid dynasty was restored, largely thanks to the efforts of a talented Afshar general, Tahmasp Qoli Khan, better known as Nader Shah. Nader Shah oversaw the empire throughout the largely ineffectual reign of Tahmasp II (1729-1732), who was succeeded by his infant son, Abbas III (1732-1736). Nader Shah eventually disposed of the fiction of Safavid rule in 1736, when he had himself proclaimed Shah in a large public gathering of notables on the Moghan Plain. He then successfully reorganised the army, leading it to

---

3   Clulow, *The Company and the Shogun*, pp. 121-2.
4   Chaudhuri, *Trade and Civilisation in the Indian Ocean* , p. 87.

numerous victories from Iraq to India. Not satisfied with his conquests by land, Nader Shah decided to build fleets on the Caspian Sea and the Persian Gulf. In both endeavours he used Europeans, specifically Englishmen, to help his plans progress. On the Caspian coast, he hired Captain John Elton, a merchant and member of the Muscovy Company to design and oversee construction of a fleet. In the Gulf, Nader Shah sought instead to use the existing expertise of the East India Company, whose ships called regularly at ports on the Persian coast.

This chapter explores Nader Shah's desire to extend his military reach to the Gulf and the East India Company's willingness to serve as a navy for hire. It considers the various ways in which the Company was induced to perform services ranging from the provision of ships for embassies to the pacification of Arab and Afghan rebels on the Gulf coast. Nader Shah's accession meant that the Company lost many of its previous freedoms. Previously the Company had been able to issue passes, tax passing trade and fire upon recalcitrant ships that did not submit to inspection. The status quo after the reassertion of Persian rule over the *garmsirat*, in which the Company had played a central role, was far more delicate, especially after the Company's trade privileges and share of the customs due at Bandar Abbas were voided by the new Shah. In order to regain these, the Company was willing to acquiesce to some of the demands now being made upon them.[5] The focus on the chapter is on the ever more intimate ties which the Company entered into in order to preserve its trading rights in Persia, and the ways in which Nader Shah attempted to use the Company's naval forces against his enemies and rebellious subjects.

First stages

The Safavid Empire at its largest extent covered all of modern Iran along with parts of Eastern Turkey, Iraq, Azerbaijan, Armenia, Turkmenistan, and Afghanistan. The Safavids also claimed suzerainty over the Southern littoral of the Persian Gulf, over what is now the UAE and Oman, as well as the island of Bahrain. After coming to power, Nader Shah resolved to recover

---

5   Three articles deal with the founding of the Persian fleet as a part of Nader Shah's strategy. They are reliant largely on European Company sources, but the two later offerings by Axworthy and Floor borrow heavily from Lockhart, *The Navy of Nadir Shah*. See also; Floor, 'The Iranian Navy in the Gulf during the 18th Century'; Axworthy, 'Nader Shah and Persian Naval Expansion in the Persian Gulf'.

all of these former Safavid possessions. His campaigns in Iraq and India have gone down in history, earning him the title of the 'Napoleon of Asia'. Like Napoleon, he was limited by his inability to rely on naval support for his campaigns. The *Hawala* Arabs, who controlled areas on both shores of the Gulf, and the Imamate of Oman, both represented significant blocks to any campaign in the Gulf. The Omanis had, in fact, become so powerful that EIC vessels would not pursue or harass Omani ships found without Company mandated passes, even though such offenses were usually punishable by heavy fines or the impounding of goods by Company forces.

As the only other naval powers in the Gulf region, European trading companies were seen as a key partner in Nader Shah's campaigns against the independent Arab tribes and the Omanis. In order to secure their cooperation, Nader Shah decided to emulate Shah Abbas, who, desiring naval assistance to capture the island of Hormuz, had offered the Company significant trade privileges should they agree to support him. In order to do the same, Nader Shah first voided the Company's privileges, promising their reinstatement should the Company cooperate with his regime. In this way, the Company's involvement in Nader Shah's campaign was not unusual. What is striking is the way in which the Company appears to have allowed itself to be forced into performing various services for the Shah.

Borrowing and lending: Persian requests for Company ships

The East India Company's trade in Persia goes back to the first decade of the seventeenth century. Reduced to essentials, Persian trade was conducted by the Company as a primary source of bullion for Indian markets where European goods, especially cloth, were not popular. By 1730, the Company was represented by an agent in the port of Bandar Abbas and further representation in the Persian capital, Isfahan, and in the wool-producing region of Kerman. The Company had no more than a dozen Europeans working in Persia at any point, with the possible exception of European soldiers and sailors acting as garrison troops for brief periods.

During the early period of Tahmasp II's reign, it was unclear who was in control of Persia, with both Tahmasp and Nader Shah issuing orders that were sometimes contradictory. Indeed on one occasion the Company applied to Tahmasp to rescind an order issued by Nader Shah.[6] All this was to change, however, when Nader Shah took full control of the government of Persia in

---

6   IOR/G/29/5 ff.106-v Consultation on Thursday 19th March 1730.

1732, having already strongly influenced policy during the reign of Tahmasp II and then his infant successor, Abbas III. The change was marked first by Nader's declaration that all previous agreements with the Europeans were null and void. For the Company, this proclamation resulted in the loss of any claim to customs from Bandar Abbas and 3,000 *toman* owed them by Shah Sultan Hussein, who had been dethroned by the Afghans in 1722.[7] This meant that the renewal of centralised Persian authority suddenly weakened the Company's position with the loss of their privileged position in the Persian trade.

From 1732, when Nader Shah took full control of the Persian state during the minority of Abbas III, his calls for Company ships can be placed into three broad categories; borrowing, chartering, and buying. In the first case, the Shah demanded the use of a Company ship free of charge; the second involved payment for that service; and the third was based on the sale of ships and stores for Persian use. The relationship can further be broken down into actions taken against Persian enemies by the Company at the behest of Persian authorities, the transportation of Persian men and materiel and embassies, and lastly the direct trade in ships and military equipment. The use of the Company's ships and crews was valuable to Nader Shah's regime, especially at this time of instability, due to their greater size, speed and firepower relative to local vessels. This allowed Persian officials to deploy an imposing force able to broadcast the Shah's power diplomatically or militarily. Company ships were used to deflect Arab raids on Persian territory and provide security against land-borne attacks. By providing such vessels, the EIC had the added benefit of being able to denigrate its European competitors, especially the Dutch who, more often than not, refused to carry out such missions. Gaining favour with various officials through cooperation also went some way to alleviate the burden of carrying out these missions. The significant benefit to the Company of ensuring the safety of shipping in Bandar Abbas, where they still claimed the right to exact 1,000 *toman* annually from customs, should also be made clear. This privilege was originally granted to the Company in 1622 and was one of the advantages Nader Shah withdrew when he came to power. It was this, along with other benefits granted historically to the Company that were used to manipulate it into assisting the Persian regime. After stripping away the Company's trade privileges, Nader Shah demanded the use of EIC ships to blockade Arab ports resisting Persian suzerainty in 1734. The Company were told that their cooperation would result in the reinstatement of their

---

7   IOR/G/29/5 f. 185 Consultation on Thursday 7th December 1732.

former rights.[8] The Company acquiesced to this demand, promising to
blockade one port with the *Britannia,* the only ship they had in the Gulf at
that time.[9] The loss of their privileges had weakened the legal standing of
the Company in Persia, which had lost the protections formerly guaranteed
to its employees and property. Nader Shah was therefore clearly using this
erosion of authority and security as a platform to make his demands.

The Shah's demands and requests were not always greeted with immediate
obedience from the Company, which attempted to gain concessions and the
reinstatement of its privileges before deploying its ships. The Company's
servants were no doubt aware of their Persian interlocutors' eagerness to
use their ships and the bargaining power this could give them. The Persian
reliance upon European shipping is revealed through a number of events
which took place during this period, which included the use of Company
ships to capture recalcitrant Persians subjects, blockade ports or suppress
uprisings of Arabs along the Gulf Coast.[10] While the Company predominantly
did this under the promise of a renewal of their privileges, they were equally
capable of bartering for other concessions, using their compliance with
Persian demands as a show both of contrition and strength.

In one case the Company demanded the removal of a merchant who had
attempted to channel all the Company's trade through his person, before
they would take any action against the Arab and Baluchi rebels.[11] In this
way it is possible to discern that the Company was aware of the bargaining
power that they possessed which could be used for more than just regaining
their former privileges. The Company was equally clear on the limitations
on its support for Persian military adventures, refusing to assist Nader Shah
in any campaign that infringed upon the Company's good standing with
the Muscatis, Mughals, and Ottomans, all of whom were important trade
partners to the Company. On one occasion, the Shahbandar of Bandar
Abbas visited the Company's factory on 9 May 1734 and asked its agent for
clarification on what services he could expect the Company to perform.
The Agent, William Cockell, replied that the Company 'could act nothing
against Bussorah [Basra], the Muscat Arabs, The Mogulls Subjects all whom
Wee were in a Strict Friendship and Alliance'.[12] He added that requests to
assist the Persians against their own subjects would be assented to whenever

---

8   IOR/G/29/5 f.225 Consultation on Sunday 3rd February 1734.
9   Ibid.
10   IOR/G/29/5 f.241 Consultation on Wednesday 29th May 1734; IOR/G/29/5 f.225 Consultation
on Sunday 3rd February 1734.
11   Ibid.
12   IOR/G/29/5 f.235v Consultation on Thursday 9th May 1734; Lockhart, p. 7.

possible, as proven by the concurrent action being undertaken against Mohammed Khan Baluchi. Both the EIC and VOC were asked to lend ships to bring the rebellious Mohammed Khan Baluchi (a Baluchi Chief from Eastern Persia) to heel.[13] The Company were clearly engaged in balancing the wishes and expectations of the Persians, while trying to maintain their broader geopolitical concerns.

Assistance to the Persians in their naval experiment was not to be given at any cost, but was a useful means of better securing the Company's trade and political position. The ban on action against the Arabs did not stop the Company from choosing to provide the services of the *Rose Galley* to carry supplies to Mohammed Taqi Khan, the Beglerbegi of Fars, during his campaigns on the Arab Shore, deeming that this did not contravene its orders not to engage in hostilities with the Arabs.[14] The captain, Henry Venfield, was given strict instructions by the agent not to go out of his way to liaise with the Persians or Arabs and that on delivering his charge, consisting of some supplies and reinforcements led by an Arab Sheikh, he should stay no more than three or four days.[15] Another passenger, an Armenian merchant named Khawaja 'Sohawk', was also to be taken with them, though Captain Venfield was instructed to leave him behind if he did not return to the ship within the time allotted in his instructions.[16] Venfield was expressly forbidden from taking any hostile action against the Arabs under any circumstance.[17]

Captain Venfield wrote later that Taqi Khan delayed him numerous times, spuriously claiming that he wished to return with the ship to Bandar Abbas, but never making a certain move to board her.[18] Further requests were delayed by news of an Arab fleet cruising the Gulf and putting a stop to any shipping between Bandar Abbas and the Arab Shore, highlighting the tenuous position of Company shipping in the region at the time.[19] The danger was highlighted when the *Rose Galley* was captured by the Arab fleet and threatened with dire consequences should the ship be caught supplying the Persians again. Captain Venfield was also kept as a prisoner by the

---

13   IOR/G/29/5 ff.235v Consultation on Wednesday 8th May 1734.

14   Taqi Khan Shirazi, close supporter of Nader Shah until his failed rebellion in 1744. He served for a time as Governor of Shiraz. IOR/G/29/6 ff.37v-38 Consultation on Tuesday 13th June 1738.

15   IOR/G/29/6 ff.39v-40 Consultation on Wednesday 21st June 1738.

16   Ibid.

17   Ibid.

18   IOR/G/29/6 f.44 Consultation on Wednesday 19th July 1738.

19   IOR/G/29/6 f.45v Consultation on Friday 21st July 1738.

Arabs for a time.[20] The crew of the *Rose Galley* thereafter refused to carry anything for the Persians to the Arab Shore under any circumstance, causing a minor incident between the Company and the Persians, who requested the use of the *Rose Galley* to carry supplies again.[21] This reveals the complex interplay of factors which governed the regional relations maintained by the Company and their fear of confrontation with an obviously threatening Arab naval force, a concern that overcame the political drive to maintain the Company's privileges in Persia. There were obviously limits to the risks that the Company would take and the clear demonstration of a threat, such as the incident with the *Rose Galley*, was enough to give them pause for reflection.

Transportation of Embassies

In addition to supplying vessels, the Company also engaged in the transportation of embassies for the Safavid and Afsharid state. As before, this was a well-established practice with VOC ships, for example, carrying embassies from Siam to France and Portugal.[22] For the Persians, the presence of the Company as a willing carrier for their embassies opened up new possibilities for contacts with other powers throughout Asia and even Europe, as shown by a voyage to Siam and embassies carried to India.[23] The prestige of being able to use European ships for these embassies, and the reach they afforded the Safavids, made the presence of the Company valuable to successive Persian Shahs.

Philip Stern has suggested that the presence of Europeans allowed for a much greater flow of diplomatic missions, spreading the reach of Persian diplomacy from Thailand to France and Britain.[24] The Persian state continued to use the faster, safer transportation provided by the Company, which, as was the case in the dispatch of the Shirley brothers by Abbas the Great, was useful in broadening their diplomatic horizons. Persian diplomacy, unsurprisingly, had focused more on the Empire's close neighbours and main rivals in India and Turkey. It was common practice, for example, to send embassies on the deaths and coronations of Persian Shahs and Mughal Emperors. The importance of such mission was outlined when an emissary

20   IOR/G/29/6 f.48v Consultation on Friday 28th July 1738.
21   IOR/G/29/6 f.49 Consultation on Monday 31st July 1738.
22   Ruangsilp, *The Dutch East India Company Merchants*, p. 130.
23   See O'Kane, *Ship of Sulaiman*.
24   Stern, *The Company-State*, p. 77.

was not sent to Persia on the death of Shah Tahmasp I, provoking the new Shah, Abbas I, to complain in a letter to the Mughal Emperor, Akbar.[25]

According to Subrahmanyam, prior to the Company's arrival in the Gulf, Persian embassies had to travel to India via Kandahar, a region disputed by the two empires, or gain Portuguese approval to travel via the Gulf.[26] It seems clear, therefore, that the arrival of the Company in the Gulf greatly expanded Persian diplomacy from its immediate neighbours to the wider Indian Ocean world. In addition, the European presence allowed for faster, more secure communication with the Mughals, with whom contact had been halted due to the great distance and risk involved in the overland route. The presence of Europeans on the Gulf littoral also allowed for speedier communication with other European powers, should it be desired, permitting the dispatch of embassies to England, France, and elsewhere.

With his rise to power and prominence, Nader Shah sought to reaffirm these links with the Company, hoping to use them to facilitate his own diplomatic and military ambitions. In 1730, while the last of the Afghans were still holding on in various parts of Persia, including the *Garmsirat*, Nader Shah demanded that the Company provide shipping for an embassy to India. This embassy was led by the *Ishik-Aghasi Bashi* or Chief Mace-Bearer, an honorific title in the Persian Court, Ali Mardan Khan. The request was transmitted by the Company's Armenian broker, who was beaten on the Shah's order and forced to pay 40 *toman* before being permitted to carry his message.[27] The order came after the Company had already been forced to pay various exactions to Nader Shah, for which they were already petitioning the newly crowned Shah Tahmasp II for reimbursement.[28] Despite their ill treatment, the Company was still involved in the pacification of Arab forces resisting the Shah's rule.[29]

It is noteworthy that the Company was willing, despite the aggressive and confrontational nature of its relationship with Nader Shah, to cooperate with him. The Company's commercial interests in Persia were relatively modest, comprising mostly of purchasing Kerman wool and selling European broadcloth. It is true that the Company was compelled to sell British goods abroad, cloth being the major commodity for export, and that Persia provided in return a useful supply of silver and luxury goods, such as Shiraz wine

25   Islam, *Indo-Persian Relations*, p. 55.

26   Subrahmanyam, *An Infernal Triangle*, p. 105.

27   IOR/G/29/5 f.105v Consultation on Saturday 14th March 1730. I believe the beating may have been a warning to the Company about their status within the Empire.

28   IOR/G/29/5 ff.106-v Consultation on Thursday 19th March 1730.

29   IOR/G/29/5 f.106v Consultation on Thursday 19th March 1730.

and rose water, for the Indian markets. This commerce did not, however, represent a large share of the Company's trade in the Indian Ocean. Instead, it seems to have been the Company's legal privileges that were so valuable to them. The share of customs from Bandar Abbas, the freedom from import duties and the Company's ability to charge ships for passes in Persian ports, while not vital to their operations in the Gulf, was highly significant to the Company's hierarchy. It seems that the existence and renewal of the Company's *Farmans* was important not so much for their content, but for the status that written agreements gave the Company and the profit that could be made from them, both financially and diplomatically.

The ambassador had to be stalled initially, being informed that 'the monsoon is as far sett in', with the adverse weather threatening 'Not only the Vessells but every Man on board'.[30] It transpires that the two 'Vessells', the *Severn* and *Edward,* were both privately owned and had little space between decks and so were unsuitable to transport passengers. Moreover, the captain of the *Severn* had refused point blank to carry the Persians.[31] His refusal shows that the Company did not always have the final say on the use of the ships they hired out, a problem that would re-emerge when other requests for shipping were made.

Nader Shah and his subordinates were also more than willing to play the European companies off against each other to meet their ends, alternating between the EIC and the VOC to force one of them into complying with Persian demands. The inability of the English Company to provide shipping in one case led Nader to request the same service of the Dutch, who at first refused, then offered a sloop to carry the ambassador with a few horses and attendants as far as Sind.[32] The Dutch then withdrew their offer the next day, earning an angry response from the ambassador.[33] The following week, after the intercession of various local officials, the VOC repeated the offer to lend the sloop to carry the ambassador, 30 attendants and 15 horses.[34] The Persians, deeming the Dutch sloop much too small, turned again to the English Company, requesting the use of the recently returned *Britannia*.[35] The Company thought it only proper to provide the ship in order to keep up

30   IOR/G/29/5 f.106 Consultation on Thursday 19th March 1730.
31   Ibid.
32   IOR/G/29/5 f.109 Consultation on Friday 17th April 1730.
33   IOR/G/29/5 f.109 Consultation on Saturday 18th April 1730.
34   IOR/G/29/5 f.109v Consultation on Monday 20th April 1730.
35   The disparity in size between the Company's frigate and the Dutch sloop may have been connected with the Persian ambassador's desire to look grand and guarantee that his entourage would be suitably impressive, both in size and in the means of its arrival.

with Dutch pretences to assist the Persian ambassador. They also believed this would help with the ongoing negotiations concerning their privileges that were being carried out at Isfahan. As a result, they agreed that the *Britannia* should be offered for Persian service. Mir Mehr Ali, the Persian governor of Bandar Abbas, welcomed this offer, especially as it was made 'without recourse to frivolous excuses as was practiced by the Dutch'.[36] After a short while, the ambassador decided to use only the Dutch sloop, leaving the *Britannia* at Bandar Abbas to guard against Baluchi or Arab incursions against the town.[37] The action presented multiple advantages to the Company: discrediting the Dutch in the eyes of the Persians, showing the Company's willingness to transport the embassy, and defending the city from the Baluchi and Arab threats. It served the EIC's wider goal of regaining its trade privileges by making the Persian government believe that they were supplying their assistance willingly without threat or coercion.

During this exchange the ambassador said that it had always been customary for the Company to carry embassies on board their ships from Persia, hinting that any refusal might lead to punishment.[38] EIC officials replied that they did not believe they were under any obligation to carry Persian embassies (though they had previously carried an embassy to Siam in 1685), but they would be prepared to lend a ship for this purpose 'out of gratitude and Return were always ready to Shew our attachment to their majestys and out of Friendship and Respect [...]'.[39] It is evident from the Company's account that they were eager to provide the Persians with assistance both for their own advantage but also to discredit the Dutch. The *Britannia* was therefore set aside to carry the embassy, though the Persians were informed that they would need to provide a smaller ship to accompany her, the coast not being safe for a larger vessel to approach. In addition, transportation for the entourage, horses, and baggage of the embassy would need to be paid for by the Persians themselves; the small ship that the Company had intended on lending them in addition to the *Britannia* having been too badly damaged during its capture.[40] Though the account does not report when the embassy left, the *Britannia* returned safely to Bandar Abbas on 14 December 1730, having last called at Bombay.[41]

36   IOR/G/29/5 f. 111v Consultation on Wednesday 29th April 1730.
37   Ibid. and IOR/G/29/5 f.112v Consultation on Saturday 2nd and Monday 4th May 1730.
38   IOR/G/29/5/ f.118v Consultation on Wednesday 22nd July 1730.
39   See O'Kane, *The Ship of Sulaiman*, 1972; IOR/G/29/5/ f.120 Consultation on Wednesday 22nd July 1730.
40   IOR/G//29/5 f.120 Consultation on Sunday 26th July 1730.
41   IOR/G/29/5 f.139v Consultation on Wednesday 14th December 1730.

In 1732, a second ambassador, Mahmud Ali Beg, was appointed to the Mughal Court, and again the Company was expected to provide transportation. This news was delivered in a letter from William Cockell, the Company's Agent, which was accompanied by an order from Shah Tahmasp to carry the embassy. This was an order, rather than a request with the result that the Company complied immediately, promising to provide passage, but only for the ambassador.[42] Although the Company did not consider such orders automatically binding, they attempted to fulfil them where they were able. Other Persian officials were more diplomatic, paying visits to the Agent in order to ingratiate themselves and make a public display of respect while asking for assistance.

These missions were a useful means by which the Company could gain favour from local and court officials, and they were able to use the support from the officials they had assisted to drive home their agenda at the Persian Court. It was through the endorsement of these officials that one can see the major advantage to the Company of acceding to Persian demands for transportation for their embassies. The endorsements and recognition that these acts received at Court were of considerable value to the Company in securing their trade privileges or as a means of escaping financial exactions for the Company's masters or their servants. The EIC was careful to secure these endorsements first and dispatch them with letters of their own, as was the case with those secured from the two agents to India and Latif Khan, which were sent with a Company letter to Nader Shah.[43]

In 1736, Nader Shah ordered that Mirza Mohsen, a new ambassador to the Mughal Emperor, be transported by either the EIC or the VOC to India. As well as this passenger, the sister and family of Sa'dat Khan, a Mughal Vizier, were also taken on board.[44] Despite the Persians having their own ships by this point, as well as having not paid for previous transportation provided to their embassies, the Company agreed to carry the passengers in the hope of securing goodwill from the Shah and the reinstatement of their still defunct *Farmans*. These passengers were charged 1,800 rupees for the use of the *Robert Galley*. As it was not a Company-owned ship, the Agent was not able to simply instruct the captain to accept the passengers.[45] No doubt the Company also hoped that this service done for the family of a Mughal courtier would not harm their activities in India. Previously, such arrangements had been written off as favours to the Persians and thus no

42   IOR/G/29/5 ff.181-v Consultation on Saturday 28th October 1732.
43   IOR/G/29/5 f.315 Consultation on Saturday 3rd January 1736.
44   IOR/G/29/5 f.359v Consultation on Tuesday 30th November 1736.
45   IOR/G/29/5 f.361 Consultation on Thursday 9th December 1736.

payment was expected, whatever may have been promised. The Company instead used such opportunities to garner support. This provides further evidence that the EIC was used as a chartering service for private shipping and the advantage that this usage could secure for it.

The honourable Company as an honourable broker: purchase of shipping for the Persian navy

A major shift in policy came in May 1734 when Nader Shah dispatched Latif Khan, appointed as his admiral, to the Gulf with 'orders to purchase shipping of the Europeans at Gombroon'.[46] The Company and Dutch Agents discussed the matter and concluded that the ships that plied the Gulf belonged not to them, but their superiors in India and Batavia and were therefore not for sale. Along with this polite but firm refusal, the Company offered to organise the construction of shipping in Surat for the Persians, should they so wish. Lockhart mentions in his work that the ships of Surat were famed for their longevity, seaworthiness and resistance to the bad climate of the Gulf.[47] The Persians were slow to warm to this idea; instead repeatedly pressing the Europeans to sell the ships that passed through Bandar Abbas.

The Company sought, along with the Dutch, to woo Latif Khan into putting a stop to entreaties for them to sell passing ships, as the request was beyond the powers of either of the Agents stationed in Persia.[48] The danger was that Nader Shah, always mercurial at best, would decide that the Europeans were of no more use to him and that the creation of a strong navy of his own would allow him not only to expel the Europeans, but stop their trade altogether. This use of a provincial official by the Europeans to influence the centre was not unusual; in this case however, Latif Khan was being used specifically to create a strong advocate for their continued presence. As well as requesting that the Persians stop offering to buy their ships, the Company again mooted the idea of dispatching a Persian official, under Company guidance, to purchase ships for the Shah at Surat.[49] A Persian request that the Company should buy the ships for them, if provided with the money, was deemed impossible without direct orders and permission

46   IOR/G/29/5 f.234v Consultation on Thursday 2nd May 1734; Lockhart, *The Navy of Nadir Shah*, p. 6. Lockhart provides this quotation, but fails to give a reference for it.

47   Lockhart, *The navy of Nadir Shah*, p. 6.

48   IOR/G/29/5 ff.240v and 241 Consultations on the 28th and 29th May 1734.

49   IOR/G/29/5 f.241 Consultation on Wednesday 29th May 1734.

from the Presidency at Bombay.[50] As was typical, the Company attempted to navigate a fine line between Persian demands and their own limitations. They used Latif Khan to assuage the demands of Nader Shah, while pleading the need to follow the orders given to them by their superiors in India.

It was the Company who created the core of a Persian fleet in the Gulf by delivering up Sheikh Rashid, a local Arab chief, along with two ships they had captured during the siege of Kish.[51] Lockhart, in his article on these events suggests that the Persians had purchased the two ships from Sheikh Rashid.[52] In fact, the Company had captured and handed them over to the Persians, with the Sheikh deriving no advantage from the transaction. This ascribes a much more active role to the Company in the formation of the Persian fleet. The Persian desire to build a naval force presented a dilemma for the EIC. The Company's officials were willing to facilitate the creation of a Persian fleet, which would essentially remove the European monopoly on naval strength in the region and thereby damage one of the few bargaining chips they had when it came to their rights and privileges in Persia. It would seem that this concern was not as important to the Company as removing their obligation to provide ships to the Persians when they needed them, suggesting that the Company's attitude to the use of their ships as military tools had shifted. This change may well be due to the fact that most of the shipping travelling in and out of the Gulf was chartered by the Company, thus enjoying its protection, while not being subject to or beholden to fulfil any orders contrary to their contract. The *Britannia* was a Company ship and was therefore under the command of the Agent, leading to its regular use in serving Persian requests.

One of the dangers of having privately owned, Company-chartered ships operating in the region became apparent in 1734 when two ships, the *Ruparell* and the *Patna,* were sold by their captains to the Persians.[53] This made it plain that while the Company might be unwilling to sell its own ships, private traders could fulfil Persian demands, thereby depriving the Company of any benefit. The captain of the *Patna,* Thomas Weddell, died shortly after selling his charge to Latif Khan at Bushehr, having sent his personal effects on from there with a dinghy that brought news of the sales to Bandar Abbas.[54] The Company's response was to censure Richard Cook, the captain and owner of

---

50 Ibid.
51 IOR/G/29/5 f.242 Consultation on Sunday 2nd June 1734.
52 Lockhart, *The Navy of Nadir Shah,* p. 7.
53 Ibid., p. 7. and IOR/G/29/5 f.257v Consultation on Monday 2nd December 1734.
54 Ibid.

the *Ruparell*, for his actions which the Company described as 'Scurrilous'. In order to take advantage of these circumstances, the Agent decided to convince Latif Khan that the ships had been sold to him 'by our connivance' in order to 'make a meritt of it'.[55] This event, reported to the Bombay Presidency by a letter sent on 3 December, was followed up by a positive ban on the sale of ships to the Persians by any party but the Company.[56] The ban, as well as the Agent's attempts to make it appear to the Persians that he had helped arrange the two previous sales, shows the flexibility in the way the Company's servants managed the expectations of the Persian Court, not to mention a good eye for how best to protect their master's interests.

In 1735 the nascent Persian fleet was sent against Basra, where the Company maintained a small residency. Here they met with defeat at the hands of the Turks, who, upon learning of the approach of the Persian fleet, seized the *Royal George* and *Dean Frigate,* two Company ships that had called to trade there. On confronting the Ottoman authorities about the seizure of the Company's ships, Martin French, the EIC Resident, was imprisoned. The Persian ships were subsequently driven off by the superior firepower of these two ships, demonstrating the superiority of European naval gunnery when in trained hands.[57] This act significantly jeopardised the standing of the Company in Persia, leading to a brief withdrawal from their factories in Kerman, Isfahan, and Bandar Abbas.[58] Perhaps more significantly, the seizure of the Company's ships by the Ottomans demonstrated the desire of Asian powers for European naval technology, underpinning the superiority of the trading companies' military strength. Equally, the success of the Ottomans outlined the necessity for adequate training as the possession of European ships was not adequate to ensure victory.

The use of Company ships by the Ottomans to repel the Persian navy at Basra is indicative of the ongoing threat faced by the mercantile companies when dealing with the land-based empires with whom they traded. No doubt it would have been in the power of the captains of the *Royal George* and *Dean Frigate* to resist Ottoman attempts to board their ships, but this would risk provoking a backlash both commercially and politically from the Gulf to the Mediterranean. It was for this reason that the Company decided not to offer the Persians military assistance against Basra, despite the affront of

55   Ibid.
56   Lockhart, *The Navy of Nadir Shah*, p. 7.
57   Axworthy, 'Nader Shah and Persian Naval Expansion in the Persian Gulf', 2011, p. 35; Lockhart, *The Navy of Nadir Shah*, p. 8; Floor, 'The Iranian Navy in the Gulf during the 18th Century', 1987, pp. 39-40. Originally in IOR/G/29/5 f.278v Consultation on Monday 16th June 1735.
58   IOR/G/29/5 ff.299-v Consultation on Wednesday 3rd September 1735.

having their ships commandeered and employees imprisoned.[59] This event underlines the difference in firepower that European ships possessed when compared to what the Persians and their Arab sailors were used to or prepared for. No doubt this disparity was at least partly responsible for the continued pre-eminence of the Europeans in the Gulf along with the desirability of their assistance with military operations and transportation of important officials, supplies and troops. This also shows why Nader Shah desired to purchase or otherwise acquire European ships. A second attack on Basra by the Persians in 1743 led to the Ottomans again attempting to use a Company ship to defend the city, though they were again refused assistance by the Resident. For this refusal Martin French was again imprisoned by the Turks, who forced the ship to manoeuvre to defend the city. Not wishing to repeat the events of 1735, the crew created a leak in the hull of the ship, thereby escaping any need to render assistance to the Turks on pretext of repairing her.[60] The Company's men were evidently capable of learning from their mistakes.

In May 1736, the agent was informed that the ship *Northumberland*, under the command of Robert Mylne, had been sold to the Persians, despite such a sale being banned by the Company.[61] Lockhart and Axworthy erroneously suggest that this ship was seized by the Persians, who then paid off Captain Mylne.[62] It is reported that Captain Mylne received 500 *toman* in silver, which he claimed to be a down payment on another ship he had promised to buy for the Persians, rather than as payment for the *Northumberland*. He also claimed he had a promise for 5,000 *toman* more should he deliver further ships to the Persians, which service he claimed he was forced to offer under threat of punishment by his 'captors'. His story was dismissed by the agent who held him and Eustace Peacock, the *Northumberland*'s supercargo, responsible for the sale of the ship. It seems very unlikely that Mylne, against the orders of the Company and the *Northumberland*'s owners, sailed to Bushehr, the home port of the Persian fleet, in order to sell his cargo, unaware of the likelihood of the Persians' wishing to purchase his charge. This does not seem credible, and was dismissed out of hand by the agent.[63] The Persian purchase of a private ship shows that the Company's plans to limit such sales to their own benefit were slipping. The high prices offered by the Persians, as well as the

59   IOR/G/29/5 f.294 Consultation on Monday 11th August 1735.

60   IOR/G/6/ f.279 Consultation on Wednesday 17th January 1743.

61   IOR/G/29/5 ff.336-v Consultation on Friday 21st May 1736.

62   Axworthy, 'Nader Shah and Persian Naval Expansion in the Persian Gulf', 2011, p. 35.

63   IOR/G/29/5 ff.340v-342 Consultation on Thursday 6th July 1736, consisting of letters between the Agency at Bandar Abbas and Eustace Peacock and Captain Robert Mylne.

desire of private European merchants to make a good profit, were clearly enough to render the Company's deterrents only partly successful.

The sale of shipping by private individuals was of particular concern to the Company as it threatened its position in Persia by making their refusal to sell ships to the Shah seem obstructive at best or antagonistic at worst. A second issue for the Company was that private sales eroded their ability to organise and make a profit from selling their own ships built for the purpose in India. The first instance of a Company-brokered sale was that of the *Cowan* in 1736. The *Cowan* was, in fact, a privately owned frigate bought by the Company at Bombay and dispatched to the Gulf, arriving at Bandar Abbas on 19 November 1736.[64] The arrival of the *Cowan* and its handover to the Persian fleet was accompanied by much fanfare and the firing of salutes from the Persian fleet, the fort at Bandar Abbas, and the Company factory and ships in the road.[65] The Persians then requested that another ship should be delivered to them on similar terms. The sale of the *Cowan* illustrates how Persian officials could achieve their aims by compromising with the Company on the method used to do so. In exchange for a cash payment and the indulgence of the Shah's good favour, the Persians were able to gain a much coveted European ship, while the Company were able to herald the deal as a profitable victory.

Seeing how well received the *Cowan* was, the Company agreed to deliver a second ship, having made somewhere in the region of 200% profit from the 8,000 *toman* sale, as reported by an envious Dutch source.[66] The *Cowan* was later renamed the *Fath-i Shah* at a ceremony in which yet further salutes were fired, including by the Dutch.[67] Despite several mentions in the secondary sources by Lockhart of a second ship being delivered with the *Cowan*, the EIC records contain no such detail. They show that the *Cowan* arrived in company with the *Robert Galley*, though this ship later departed carrying Mirza Mohsen, the Persian ambassador and the sister of the Mughal grandee Sadat Khan. The *Robert Galley* was eventually sold to the Persians in 1742 and not by the Company. Instead the ship was sold by the connivance of the already troublesome Eustace Peacock, who travelled up to Shiraz in order to offer the ship up to Taqi Khan. Peacock sold the *Robert Galley* for 1,000 *toman*, but was forced to give a gift of 150 *toman* to Taqi Khan on his visit to Shiraz.[68]

64   IOR/G/29/5 f.357v Consultation on Friday 19th of November 1736.

65   IOR/G/29/5 f.361v Consultation Saturday 18th December 1736.

66   Floor, 'The Iranian Navy in the Gulf during the 18th Century', p. 41; Lockhart, *The Navy of Nadir Shah*, p. 9.

67   IOR/G/29/5 ff.38v-9 Consultation on Tuesday 3rd March 1737.

68   IOR/G/29/6 f.189v Consultation on Wednesday 27th January 1742 and f.190 Consultation on Sunday 31st January 1742.

Two more ships, the *Mary* and the *Pembroke*, were delivered to the
Persians with naval stores in 1742 at a cost of 186,251 rupees or around 9,312
toman (£23,280).[69] Originally, the Company at Surat had purchased three
ships for the Persians, but the third had been damaged before departure
and therefore had not arrived in Bandar Abbas. The Council at Bombay
requested that these costs be covered by attempting to get the Persians
to pay for the third ship, despite it having not been delivered.[70] The agent
and Council at Bandar Abbas found it impossible to follow this order; the
Persians had bought several European ships already and so it was thought
Taqi Khan was unlikely to be easily duped.[71] Instead, the agent at Bandar
Abbas made sure to get a receipt for the two ships delivered for the full
amount already paid to him, thus putting an end to the issue as speedily
as possible.[72] The actions of the agent, though less than scrupulous, were
somewhat better than the plan suggested by the Council at Bombay. The
agent succeeded in gaining political capital from a potentially awkward and
dangerous situation, balancing the advantage of a quick, risky profit with
accruing the goodwill of Taqi Khan. Though Jean Sutton speaks briefly of
the problems caused by private and Danish trade in arms, the sale of ships
in this way seems to be unique to Company interactions with Persia.[73]

The delivery of the *Mary* and *Pembroke* was accompanied by a fresh issue:
how to crew the expanding Persian fleet adequately. Up to this point, the
fleet had been manned by Arabs from various tribes in the Gulf, whose
loyalty to Nader Shah in his campaigns against their fellow Arabs and
Sunni co-religionists (1738 and 1742) could hardly be counted upon. Indeed,
mutinies severely damaged the fighting ability of the Persian fleet on numerous occasions. This affected the Company as Taqi Khan, the *Beglerbegi*
of Fars and chief administrator over the *Garmsirat*, had decided that the
Indian and European crewmen already serving on the ships would be
more competent, not to mention more loyal, than Arab crews. On getting
wind of this, the Company dispatched their Armenian linguist with the
ships in order to foil any attempt by Taqi Khan to detain the crews and, if
necessary, to bribe the Persians to secure their return.[74] The crews did end
up staying on with the Persians for two months, but insisted on full pay
and served under their own officers. These officers argued fiercely with

69 IOR/G/29/6 ff.188v-9 Consultation on Sunday 24th January 1742.
70 IOR/G/29/6 f.183v Consultation on Wednesday 30th December 1741.
71 IOR/G/29/6 f.187 Consultation on Thursday 21st January 1741.
72 IOR/G/29/6 f.204v Consultation on Monday 19th April 1742.
73 Sutton, *The East India Company's Maritime Service*, 2010, p. 108.
74 IOR/G/29/6 f.201 Consultation on Tuesday 23rd March 1742.

Taqi Khan over whether the Persian or Company colours should be flown over the ships while the Company officers and crews remained aboard.[75] When Taqi Khan insisted on flying the Persian ensign, the crews refused to serve any longer than the two months they had been contracted for, despite an angry response from the Persian grandee.[76] This clearly reveals a tension between the expectations of the Persians and the Company. The lack of a treaty formally cementing the relationship and status of both sides allowed for significant difficulties to arise over questions of sovereignty and authority. This question over manning the ships delivered to the Persians shows weaknesses on both the Company's and the Persian side. On the one hand, the Persians could compel the Company to provide the crews, threatening disfavour at Court and the anger of key local officials, while the Persians had no way of forcing the ships' crews to comply with their orders. This would suggest that the Persians simply had no way to force the crews to comply with their orders, either through reward or duress, underlining the disparities between Company and Persian naval power.

An unexpected advantage lay in the capacity of the Persians to use deserters as military experts. This had originally been prohibited in the agreements made during the Hormuz campaign nearly a century previously, though this, like the Company's privileges, seems to have broken down after the Afghan invasion and rise of Nader Shah. Most notable among these deserters was Captain Richard Cook, who had sold his ship, the *Ruparell,* to the Persians in 1734. Cook afterwards assisted the Persians at Bushehr in 1735, where he intervened with the Persians on the Company's behalf after the defeat at Basra as well as taking part in later negotiations with Arab mutineers on behalf of the Persians.[77] Along with Cook, other European deserters appear to have made their way into Persian service, including those from the *Harwich.*[78] The records do not mention why these men chose to serve the Persians, though the promise of better pay, conditions, or appreciation for their naval expertise may have contributed. They would have been disappointed as the Arab mutinies were sparked, among other things, by a lack of pay and poor provisioning.

Despite these issues, the ships were officially handed over to the Persians on 28 May 1742, ignoring the fact the *Mary* was in need of daily pumping,

75   IOR/G/29/6 f.204 Consultation on Tuesday 13th April 1742.
76   IOR/G/29/6 f.204v Consultation on Monday 19th April 1742.
77   IOR/G/29/5 f.282v Consultation on Monday 23rd June 1735 and Lockhart, p. 11.
78   IOR/G/29/6 f.14 Consultation on Friday 16th December 1737.

owing to leaks in her hull, while the *Pembroke* lacked full rigging.[79] It has
been suggested that taking ownership of the vessels gained Taqi Khan
enough political capital with Nader Shah that he concerned himself relatively
little with the state of the ships themselves, not to mention a further implied
personal financial incentive tied up with the purchase.[80] Despite these
troubles, the agent was informed by Bombay that the Company would supply
two further vessels for the Persians, as long as a bond of 20,000 rupees, or
1,000 *toman*, per ship was provided beforehand.[81] The Persians had previously
requested the use of crews composed of lascars from Bombay, though these
requests had always been denied.[82] The lack of concern shown by Taqi Khan
over the state of his purchases suggests that the Company took some licence
in the quality and cost of the ships they delivered, no doubt with an eye to a
larger margin. This profiteering on the Company's part was ignored by the
equally avaricious Taqi Khan. In this case, the balance struck was highly
beneficial to the Company, who turned a significant profit on the sale of
ships to the Persians, while also earning the gratitude of Taqi Khan, whose
status was augmented in the eyes of the Shah. In this way the Company
maintained its friendship with an important official while also assisting
in the advancement of that official's career.

By 1743 there is significant evidence that the Persians were actively seeking
out ships from other sources. These included other Company ships operating
in Sind, which was now part of Nader Shah's Empire in India, as well as Arab
and Indian ships. These were purchased at Sind or extorted from the Arab
Sheikhs of the Gulf.[83] This diversification in supply shows that the Persian
effort to build up their naval strength was not concentrated solely in the
Gulf, nor limited to a single source. In fact, as Lockhart and Axworthy note,
Nader Shah also worked to build up a fleet in the Caspian.[84] There were also
later reports of the Persians seizing eight ships from Sind and using them
to carry men, horses, and 50,000 *toman* of treasure from there to Bandar
Abbas.[85] In 1743, during the campaign on the Arab shore against Muscat, it
is recorded that a 'large ship from Muscatt of about nine hundred tons and

---

79   IOR/G/29/6 f.215v Consultation on Friday 28th May 1742.

80   Ibid.

81   IOR/G/29/6 f.233v Consultation on Sunday 14th November 1742.

82   IOR/G/29/5 f.367v Consultation on Monday 21st February 1737.

83   IOR/G/29/5 f.242 Consultation on Sunday 2nd May 1734 and IOR/G/29/6 f.274v Consultation
on Wednesday 20th December 1743.

84   See Lockhart, *The Navy of Nadir Shah*; Axworthy, 'Nader Shah and Persian Naval Expansion
in the Persian Gulf'.

85   IOR/G/29/6 f.274v Consultation on Wednesday 20th December 1743.

mounts 50 guns arrived at Bandar Abbas after being handed over by the Muscati Arabs to the Persian forces.[86] The ship was sent on to the Persian arsenal and dock at Bandar-e Laft where she was hauled ashore and her hull cleaned.[87] This highlights a shift in the power relations of the Gulf region, the Persians now being able to flex their own naval muscle in such a way that they could capture and maintain ships from the Muscatis, who had previously exercised almost untrammelled control of the Gulf's shipping, checked only by their fear of the Europeans.

Persian power in the Gulf took a serious downward turn in August 1740, when the Arab crews of the Persian fleet revolted *en masse*, killing the admiral, Mir Ali Khan, along with anyone who resisted them. They then took all the ships they could from the anchorage at Bandar-e Laft. The Company blamed this mutiny on a lack of pay and supplies, adding that the Persian fleet was lost should the Arabs refuse to sail, having no other sources of skilled mariners.[88] In order to put down this revolt, the Persians were forced to request ships from the EIC and VOC. In this way, Persian authorities had to turn to Europeans to defeat a fleet whose primary function was to replace them as the paramount naval power in the Gulf. As the Company were unable to supply any assistance, the Dutch were requested to provide two ships that they had available at Bandar Abbas.[89] The records note that the Dutch felt compelled to assist the Persians, believing that such a dire circumstance necessitated them giving their aid freely, as the backlash should they resist would be severe due to the panic that rippled through Persian officials. The Dutch did, however, need to bribe the ships' crews to proceed past Kishm Island.[90] The Company eventually lent some aid against the rebels by providing a *tranky* (small ship used for coastal voyages) crewed with some of their factory guards and a gunner, who, if the Company report is to be believed, put up a much greater resistance to the Arabs than did either the Dutch or the Persians, both being accused of taking flight at the sight of the enemy.[91] This incident reveals a continued Persian reliance on their European 'navies for hire', especially in a period where the balance of power in the Gulf had not yet settled in Persia's favour, meaning that a mutiny of this sort could set the Persians back to a point where they were again reliant on borrowed European military assets.

86   IOR/G/29/6 f.249 Consultation on Monday 23rd May 1743.
87   Ibid.
88   IOR/G/29/6 f.108v Consultation on Tuesday 26th August 1740.
89   Ibid.
90   Ibid.
91   IOR/G/29/6 f.115v Consultation on Sunday 12th October 1740.

A final way in which the Company was involved in supporting Persian naval expansion in the Gulf was through the provision of naval stores and supplies, as well as, on one occasion, personnel to assist in the construction of ships at Bandar-e Laft.[92] The first major instance of this was recorded in 1735, after the Persian defeat at Basra, when Latif Khan, the Persian admiral, asked the Company to provide him with a supply of tin, iron shot, and gunpowder, all of which he promised to pay for.[93] Despite not having the quantity he requested, the Company gave him a considerable supply of 500 maunds of tin, 2,000 round shot and 10 barrels of powder. Why exactly the Company's factory had such a quantity of shot and powder in the first place is unclear, and it seems unlikely this could have been solely for the factory's use. The store of such a large quantity might have been used either to resupply ships passing the factory, or made available to local merchants or potential buyers. In fact, there is no mention of either of these activities taking place, the only trade in such naval stores being connected with demands from the Persian government, most of which came later than 1735. This seems, therefore, to be evidence either of a clandestine trade in military hardware with the Persians by the Company, which does not appear on their books, or that a private trade was being carried out by someone in such materiel, though if this were the case there would have been some recourse to the owners before it was given as a gift to Latif Khan. Such requests were made to the Company and Dutch sporadically throughout the period of the Persian naval experiment, sometimes with promise of payment, or treated simply as gifts. This evidence, along with the sale of ships to the Persians, solidifies the Company's role as an arms trader in the Gulf.

The Company's purchase of ships and gifts of stores to the Persian fleet provides an interesting case, showing a great level of military involvement in the Gulf region as well as revealing a further level to the political balance struck between the Company and the Persian government. On the one hand, it seems obvious that the Company would benefit from the profits they could turn on brokering the ship sales, while on the other, it would damage any claim to naval supremacy they had in the Gulf. Presumably this would permanently put a stop to any pretence the Company might have to collect money for passes from ships bound to or from India. There were other benefits to the Company in supplying ships; they would be seen to be assisting the Shah in his desire for a fleet, as well as building an effective force to combat piracy and threats by Arab shipping to the sea lanes. This

92   Lockhart, *The Navy of Nadir Shah*, p. 12.
93   IOR/G/29/5 f.282v Consultation on Monday 23rd June 1735.

would alleviate the Company from the need to do so themselves, as they had in the past. The presence of a Persian fleet would also allow the Company to relinquish any responsibility for troublesome requests to transport embassies, troops, and supplies for Nader Shah; after all, this intimate involvement carried risks of gaining the Shah's displeasure should his expectations fail to be met. This required the Company not only to placate him, but also to keep local officials, such as Taqi Khan and Latif Khan, firmly in the Company's camp in order to advocate on their behalf at Court.

Conclusion

This chapter has demonstrated that Nader Shah used the English East India Company's ships as a mechanism to engage in long-distance diplomacy, while taking advantage of European naval technology to achieve his strategic aims in the Gulf region. The desire for European ships and the negotiations that took place to acquire them are a neglected part of the relationship between the European Companies and states in Asia. The military balance between Europeans and Persians is demonstrative of the wider interaction of European naval technology and Asian powers while adding a new dimension to the way the Companies transacted business and diplomacy with non-European states. Unlike in India or Japan, where the Company took on the veneer of vassalage, their attitude towards Persia was based on the historic cooperation between the two powers to drive the Portuguese from Hormuz and the subsequent *Farmans*. The Persians' ability to manipulate the Company with the promise of trade benefits, as well as the threat of expulsion or violence, is a strong indication of the Companies' aversion to open conflict, as well as their respect for written agreements. It also challenges the idea of the Company as having the upper hand in their interactions with Asian rulers. As with the Tokugawa and the VOC, Nader Shah controlled the terms of the relationship with the EIC.

Despite this, relations between the Company and Persia were not entirely stable, requiring a delicate balancing act of differing expectations and interests with influences ranging from the ever-changeable mood of the Shah to the machinations of the VOC. The Persians did not simply dominate a quiescent Company, the employees of which played a constant game of cat and mouse with Persian officials in order to limit their exposure to Persian wrath while operating at a minimal cost to their Honourable Masters. They were able to do this by playing off Persian desire for European ships which allowed them to deal from a position of strength that belied their numbers.

The evidence also reveals a distinct shift from previous periods in the Anglo-Persian relationship, which shows that the Company were given a relatively free hand to act in the Gulf, issuing passes, firing upon non-compliant ships, and taxing passing trade. This *carte blanche* was lost on the accession to power of Nader Shah, whose vision for a renewed Persian hegemony over the entire Gulf region, including the Arab shore and Muscat, drew the Company into a closer relationship with the Persian throne. This new status quo was far more precarious, resting on the Company's desire to regain their privileges, some of which they eventually did, set against the Shah's own wishes and expectations.

In many ways, the Company's presence in the Gulf was central to the naval experiment carried out by Nader Shah until the end of his reign in 1747. Without the Company's willingness to act as a navy for hire, the Persians would have had no basis for their attempt to assert control over the *Garmsirat*. The defeat of the Afghans by Nader Shah precipitated the spread of smaller groups throughout the region. These smaller groups, in league with their Arab Sunni coreligionists represented a significant block to renewed Persian control over the Gulf littoral. The presence of the Company and their willingness to nullify the naval advantage of the Arabs was central to the rebels' defeat. Nader Shah's reliance on the Company for naval assistance was almost certainly a factor in his decision to create a fleet of his own. In this project he again found the Company to be a useful ally, despite initial difficulties in agreeing how ships might be purchased. In this way, the combination of Nader Shah's desire for a navy and the Company's scruples about selling their own ships led to a situation where the Company acted both as hired muscle and a supplier of military equipment. The Company were neither a silent nor an acquiescent partner, carefully balancing acting as a broker for the sale of ships, even feigning this role when private individuals made sales without their knowledge, with that of an independent power. The Persian fleet was therefore the coalescence of two mutually supporting policies. The Persians wished to assert themselves militarily in the Gulf, while the Company, happy to decrease their exposure to Arab piracy, turn a profit in the process, and gain back their extensive trade privileges, supported them in this attempt. Persian demand for the use of Company ships, either for embassies, fighting, or transporting supplies was a nuisance that the Company believed could be circumvented by providing the Shah with his own fleet, rather than a Company navy for hire.

Works cited

Axworthy, Michael, 'Nader Shah and Persian Naval Expansion in the Persian Gulf, 1700-1747', *Journal of the Royal Asiatic Society* (vol. 21, 2011): 31-39.

Cipolla, Carlo M., *Guns, Sails and Empire* (New York: Sunflower University Press, 1985).

Chaudhuri, K.N., *Trade and Civilisation in the Indian Ocean* (Cambridge MA: Cambridge University Press,1985).

Clulow, Adam, *The Company and the Shogun: The Dutch Encounter with Tokugawa Japan* (New York: Columbia University Press, 2014).

Das Gupta, Ashin, *India and the Indian Ocean World: Trade and Politics* (Oxford: Oxford University Press, 2004).

Ebrāhim Moḥammad, trans., John O'Kane, *Ship of Sulaiman* (New York: Routledge, 1972).

Floor, Willem, 'The Iranian Navy in the Gulf during the 18th Century', *Iranian Studies* (vol. 20 no.1, 1987).

Islam, Riazul, *Indo-Persian Relations* (Tehran, 1970).

Lockhart, Laurence, *The Navy of Nadir Shah: The Proceedings of the Iran Society* (London, 1936).

Ruangsilp, B., *The Dutch East India Company Merchants at the Court of Ayutthaya* (Leiden: Brill, 2007).

Stern, Philip J., *The Company-State* (Oxford: Oxford University Press, 2011).

Subrahmanyam, Sanjay, *An Infernal Triangle: The Contest between the Mughals, Safavids and Portuguese 1590-1605* (London: I.B. Tauris, 2012).

Sutton, Jean, *The East India Company's Maritime Service* (Woodbridge: Boydell Press, 2010).

Contact details

Peter Good, Field House, Langley Common Road, Barkham Berkshire, RG40 4TS, UK
Tel.: +447853137235
peter_good@hotmail.com

Epilogue

9 The Dutch East India Company in global history

A historiographical reconnaissance

Tonio Andrade

Abstract
This chapter provides a brief overview of scholarship on the Dutch East India Company, focusing on the work of major figures, including J.C. van Leur, M.A.P. Meilink-Roelofsz, Niels Steensgaard, and Leonard Blussé, among others. It suggests that one can discern a consistent trend in that scholarship: toward a greater appreciation of the power and strength of Asian trading networks. It then reflects on trends in current and future scholarship, including the work of contributors to this volume, suggesting that the network models currently in the zeitgeist are paying dividends in understanding, particularly when one keeps in mind the significance of the Asian networks that underlay and competed with the European networks. The chapter ends by recognising that recent scholarship seems to support a sort of 'global early modernity' whose salient characteristic is a dramatic – and largely reciprocal – increase in intercultural adoption.

Keywords: Capitalism, peddling trade, TANAP, early modernisation, networks

How influential was the Dutch East India Company in Asia? To what extent did it transform or revolutionise Asian trading patterns? And how powerful and resilient were the Asian trade networks that the VOC competed with? For a long time, historians thought they had answers to such questions. In the past, the Company has been portrayed as a catalyst for capitalism and a force that brought modern rational economic practices to world trade, thereby transforming preexisting trading structures throughout

Clulow, Adam and Tristan Mostert (eds.), *The Dutch and English East India Companies: Diplomacy, trade and violence in early modern Asia*. Amsterdam: Amsterdam University Press, 2018
DOI: 10.5117/9789462983298/CH09

the maritime world. Today, however, historians are far more cautious, with new work following a trend toward a greater appreciation of the power and strength of Asian networks. With each passing decade, it seems, historians find the VOC – and other early modern European colonial powers – less influential than previously believed.

But this is not to say that the Company was not important. At the same time as scholars have successfully undercut older views regarding the company's impact, they have also come to a much deeper appreciation of the VOC's own shipping networks, and historians today are particularly interested in the Company's intra-Asian (as opposed to Asia-to-Europe) networks. The Company did indeed create an unprecedented network of routes and trading structures, suggesting that there may well be some truth to the older idea that the VOC had a transformative effect in Asia.[1]

Still, we must keep in mind that the visible networks – that is to say, the official networks most readily apparent in VOC sources – are merely the tip of the iceberg. As historians broaden our use of non-European sources, we are gaining a more precise understanding not just of the Company's networks but also – and more importantly – of how its routes connected with the myriad other routes that crisscrossed the early modern world. We must always strive to remain aware of the complex Asian networks that worked within, against, and alongside the Company's official networks.

The origins of 'Asiatic despotism'

To understand the long arc of VOC historiography, there is no better place to start than Karl Marx. This is not so much because he was a scholar of the VOC – in fact he wrote little about it – but because his writings have been so influential. His perspective on Asia and the rise of European capitalism still affects current-day scholarship in global history in general and the VOC specifically, particularly when it comes to European impact on Asian trading structures.

Marx was far more interested in the English East India Company than in the Dutch East India Company, just as he was far more interested in the nineteenth century than in the seventeenth and eighteenth centuries, and he believed that VOC rule in seventeenth- and eighteenth-century Asia

---

1   This network approach must not blind us to the other phenomena that marked VOC history: war, violence, weather, and, of course the individuals themselves, who sailed the ships, wrote the documents, and loaded the crates.

was a more primitive forerunner of English rule in the 19th century. The British had, he believed, disassembled Indian society and reconstituted it for rational, capitalist plunder. The Dutch, in contrast, were 'parasites', who simply planted European control on top of Asian despotic structures, without restructuring the societies underneath.[2] This argument reflects Marx's famous (or infamous) concept of 'Asian despotism', which was inspired by earlier thinkers including Montesquieu. The concept of Asian despotism has had a huge influence on subsequent thought and continues to affect our understanding of world history today.

So what does Marx mean by Asiatic despotism, and by the related concept of the Asiatic 'mode of production'? In early societies, he believed, humans held property in common. This primal communitarianism was antithetical to capitalism because capitalism called for all goods and services to be translated into monetary exchange. Common property held back the development of capitalism everywhere, but in Europe this communitarian tradition was eventually overthrown, as Europeans – most importantly the British – moved toward a commercial economy. Marx believed that in Asia this early communitarianism persisted because of a despotic imperial system. Asian despotism arose for various reasons – most notably the need for irrigation structures – but the important point is that for Marx the despot did not recognise property rights. The lack of property rights retarded capitalism, and so, Marx argued, Asian economic activity stayed relatively backward, while Europeans stampeded into the future of cold cash and credit.

Marx argued that the VOC, although it emerged in a Europe moving toward capitalism, made its profits not by bringing capitalism to Asia but simply by imposing a European despotism upon the existing Asian despotisms. This piggy-backing despotism was, he wrote, a 'monstrous combination', because Dutch profits were in essence based on 'a system of plunder'.[3, 4] The fundamentals of the Asian economies didn't change

---

2   He quotes with approval Sir Stamford Raffles, who served as English governor of Java during the Napoleonic Wars, from 1811-1815, who says that the Dutch East India Company 'employed all the existing machinery of despotism to squeeze from the people their utmost mite of contribution, the last dregs of their labor, and thus aggravated the evils of a capricious and semi-barbarous Government, by working it with all the practiced ingenuity of politicians, and all the monopolising selfishness of traders.' Raffles, cited in Marx, 'The British Rule in India', 10 June 1853.

3   Marx, 'The British Rule in India', 10 June 1853.

4   Marx, 'The Transformation of Commodity Capital and Money Capital into Commodity-Dealing Capital and Money-Dealing Capital or into Merchant's Capital', p. 437.

– pepper, cloves, nutmeg were still produced in the traditional ways – but the Dutch gained a monopoly over the carrying of these goods. This model brought profits to the Netherlands – and to Europe as a whole – but it was a primitive type of colonialism, suited only for early capitalism. By the nineteenth century, the Dutch East India Company model had become atavistic and was eventually replaced by British capitalistic imperialism.[5] Like his understanding of the VOC, Marx's model of the Asiatic mode of production was simplistic, but it continued to guide discussion, as scholars built upon or challenged Marxian perspectives. The most important of these scholars was the great Max Weber.

From Weber to van Leur

Like Marx, Weber wanted to explain the rise of capitalism, but whereas Marx focused on class struggle and modes of production, Weber's central concept was 'calculability', or predictability. This notion runs through Weber's work, perhaps most obviously in his posthumously-published *General Economic History*.[6] Weber argued that during the pre-modern period, economic activity – indeed life in general – was not susceptible to ready measurement. It was difficult to transport goods because roads were poor and dangerous, and seaways were infested with pirates. It was difficult to guarantee contracts, create reliable credit networks, trust strangers, and build faith in governmental structures. Capitalism, however, required calculability. (For Weber, capitalism is 'the provision of human needs by the method of enterprise, which is to say, by private businesses seeking profit. It is exchange carried out for positive gain, rather than forced contributions or traditionally fixed gifts or trades'.[7]) So long as economic activity was hindered by unpredictability, enterprise would not be able to spread and deepen and become the primary means of providing human needs and wants.

Weber believed that among the most important obstacles to predictability were traditional social and cultural structures and, perhaps most importantly, traditional governmental systems. Asian societies, he argued,

5   Marx, *Capital*, Vol. 3, Part IV, Ch. 18, 'The Turnover of Merchant's Capital. Prices'; and Ibid., Ch. 20, 'Historical Facts about Merchant's Capital'.

6   Weber, *General Economic History*.

7   This is the excellent paraphrase by Randall Collins, in Collins, 'Weber's Last Theory of Capitalism', pp. 21-22.

tended to be characterised by 'patrimonial' systems of government, which vested authority in sovereigns rather than in rational and predictable legal structures. There are here clear echoes of Marxian notions of Asiatic despotism. According to Weber, the West threw off patrimonial systems (or was still in the process of doing so) and built modern legal and political structures, buttressed by new systems of belief that helped strangers conduct business with each other.

What role, then, did the VOC play in Weber's schema? Weber saw the VOC, and also its English rival, as a 'preliminary stage in the development of the modern stock company'.[8] He believed that it helped create some of the conditions of modernity – such as transferable shares and bookkeeping innovations – which helped lead to modern capital accounting, but, like Marx, he also believed that the VOC was a parasitic rent-seeker, which merely imposed a tax monopoly on subject peoples whose economic lives went on much as they had before. He called this system 'colonial capitalism'.[9] Instead of facilitating full-blown capitalism, the VOC's 'colonial capitalism' strengthened feudal conditions, as 'native chieftains' became territorial lords and free peasants became more like serfs.

Yet in contrast to Marx, Weber did conduct significant research into Asian societies. He understood that Asian economic structures could be quite sophisticated. He argued, however, that ultimately they were more backward than those of the West because of, first, the predominance of patrimonial authority and, second, the persistence of structures of belief that led to distrust of strangers and other anti-rational mindsets. He spent a great deal of time looking for the absence of a 'spirit of capitalism' that might have vivified the otherwise sophisticated economic structures that he understood existed in much of Asia.[10]

Weber's research on Asia inspired much work, including that of the most important early historian of the Dutch East India Company, J.C. van Leur. Born in 1908, van Leur became a student in the new field of Indology at the University of Leiden. This was not entirely by choice. He preferred history, but Indology promised a career in the Dutch empire, and van Leur's family was not wealthy. After he graduated, while waiting for his first posting overseas, van Leur had an opportunity to pursue his passion for history: he wrote a PhD thesis using Weberian methods to shed light on Indonesian history. The resulting work had a humble title – 'Some perspectives on the history

8   Weber, *General Economic History*, pp. 281-82.
9   Ibid., p. 61.
10   Gellner, 'The Uses of Max Weber', pp. 48-62.

of Asian trade' (*Eenige beschouwingen betreffende den ouden Asiatischen handel*) – but it ended up being extremely influential. His insights went well beyond the Company itself. In effect, van Leur set in motion a problematic that still underlies much discussion in world history today: he argued that Asian trading networks were far more resilient than previously believed, and hence that the VOC had less of an effect on Asia than had been assumed.

Van Leur criticised the ways in which 'colonial historians', to use his term, tended to overestimate European preponderance, viewing history 'from the deck of the ship, the rampart of the fortress, the high gallery of the trading-house'.[11] Against those who believed that the Dutch influence had been profound and lasting, he argued that up to at least 1650 trade carried by Europeans comprised only a modest share of total Asian trade. Similarly, he suggested that Western commercial structures were not necessarily superior to Asian trading structures. He further argued that even in the eighteenth century, Western influence in Asia remained limited to a number of military outposts that could only be defended with difficulty.

For van Leur, it was the nineteenth century that saw the great disjuncture: only then did the West definitively move ahead. Prior to that point, Asian trade and civilisation remained on a level with that of Europe. This position is strikingly close to the arguments of Kenneth Pomeranz and other so-called 'revisionist' historians, who hold that developed parts of Europe and certain developed parts of Asia followed similar paths until around 1800.[12] To be sure, we must recognise that van Leur's conclusions were not based on significant primary source-based research, and, as we will see, he misunderstood some important aspects of Asian trade. But there can be no doubt of his significance. He set in motion or at least prefigured one of the most important debates in global history, a debate that continues today.

Yet subsequent scholars of the VOC have argued that van Leur was if anything too conservative when it came to the sophistication and strength of Asian trade vis-à-vis that of Europe. This is clear in the brilliant work of historian Marie Antoinette Petronella Meilink-Roelofsz.

---

11   These words come not from his dissertation but from one of his later writings. Van Leur, in a 1939 review of Stapel, *Geschiedenis van Nederlandsch Indië*, cited in Wertheim, 'Early Asian Trade: An Appreciation of J.C. van Leur', p. 168.

12   Wertheim, 'Early Asian Trade', pp. 167-173. Pomeranz, *The Great Divergence*; Wong, *China Transformed*; Rosenthal and Wong, *Before and Beyond Divergence*; Marks, *The Origins of the Modern World*; Andrade, *The Gunpowder Age*.

The 'peddling trade'

Like van Leur, Meilink-Roelofsz was not trained as a professional historian. Although she audited classes at Leiden University taught by figures such as J. Huizinga and J.H. Thiel, she received her degree in secondary school teaching, and unfortunately for her, she graduated during the Great Depression. Unable to find a job, she began volunteering in the Dutch Imperial Archives (Algemeen Rijksarchief), today known as the National Archive (Nationaal Archief). Eventually, her unpaid internship led to a formal job, and she gradually became the world's foremost expert on the archives of the Dutch East India Company, a repository that is one of the world's richest sources of historical material for seventeenth and eighteenth-century global history.

In 1962, she published her landmark work *Asian Trade and European Influence in the Indonesian Archipelago,* a book that has had a deep and abiding influence on VOC historiography.[13] It was largely a response to van Leur. Meilink-Roelofsz greatly appreciated van Leur's contributions and followed him in adopting an Asia-focused perspective. But she believed that van Leur was wrong on a number of counts. First, she showed that van Leur was mistaken in saying that Asian trade was generally limited to luxury goods. Rather, she argued, there was also a significant trade in bulk goods. In addition, she felt that van Leur underplayed the influence of the Portuguese, although she largely agreed that they eked out a position in the Asian trading networks thanks primarily to rivalry between indigenous states, even as she showed how their position in trade was based on interaction with Asians. Similarly, she believed that Dutch influence was far greater than van Leur had believed. As she wrote, 'Economically the company represented a power factor in the Indonesian archipelago with which due reckoning had to be held, and which seriously disturbed or even utterly destroyed various aspects of the native economy'.[14]

Most importantly, however, she argued against van Leur's depiction of Asian trade. Van Leur had argued that Asian trading ports were sophisticated in themselves, but also that they were largely isolated, lacking close connections to each other. The connective tissue was weak, he believed, because it was formed by individual traders, whose routes and organisations were not systematised.

Van Leur referred to these traders as peddlers (*kramers*), and their trade he characterised as peddling trade (*kramershandel*). In English, of course,

---

13   Meilink-Roelofsz, *Asian Trade and European Influence in the Indonesian Archipelago between 1500 and about 1630.*
14   Ibid., p. 10.

the word 'peddler' calls to mind an image like that of Edmund Spenser's poor pedlar, 'bearing a trusse of tryfles at hys backe, as bells, and babes, and glasses, in hys packe'.[15] The Dutch term *kramer* refers to someone who sells items at tents or booths, as at a market or fair. Van Leur did not mean, however, that the Asian traders were just selling things at booths. On the contrary, his peddlers might own or lease large vessels carrying expensive cargos. His point was that this peddler trade was personal: markets were not linked by large or supra-national structures but by individuals making ad hoc economic decisions. He also believed that these peddlers carried primarily luxury goods and that there was little or no mass trade in bulk goods. He believed that these three factors – the lack of transnational credit systems, the individual nature of the trade, and the traders' focus on luxury goods – caused fluctuations of price and supply and decreased calculability, and that these fluctuations, à la Weber, were inimical to the rise of capitalist-type structures. In addition, he believed that this Asian trading system was ancient, having existed for millennia in the same basic form.

Meilink-Roelofsz objected strongly to van Leur's depiction of Asian trade. Asian trade was not, she argued, an ad hoc affair, a matter of individual peddlers sailing about. Rather, it could be highly sophisticated, with formal structures that stretched from the Arabian Sea to the China Seas. She focused on indigenous Malayo-Indonesian structures, detailing the development of trading polities such as Srivijaya and Malacca, and on the long-distance trade of Asian groups such as Arabs, Gujarati, and Chinese who conducted regular voyages between regions.

A decade after the publication of *Asian Trade and European Influence*, another scholar resurrected the 'peddler' argument. Danish economic historian Niels Steensgaard's 1973 work *Carracks, Caravans, and Companies* argued explicitly against Meilink-Roelofsz's depiction of Asian trade, suggesting that van Leur was right: pre-Dutch trade in Asia was indeed a peddler trade.[16] As a result, markets were opaque and prices unstable. Like van Leur, Steensgaard included the Portuguese in this pre-capitalist peddler-type trade, arguing that they were merely tax gatherers focused on a 'redistributive enterprise', who 'might enter the market as peddlers on a grand scale. Their role might be dominating and continuous, but their behavior did not modify the market pattern in which they operated'.[17]

---

15   Spenser, 'The Shepheards Calender', p. 460.
16   Steensgaard, *Carracks, Caravans, and Companies*. This was reissued as *The Asian Trade Revolution of the Seventeenth Century*. I cite from the latter version.
17   Ibid., p. 110.

Here one can discern strong similarities to Marx and, more importantly, Weber, both of whom had argued that until the late 1700s, Europeans were merely placing European political control on top of traditional Asian structures. In this view, Europeans did not restructure Asian trade, rather they just controlled and profited from it. Of course, Marx and Weber felt that the VOC was no different. It, too, merely acted as a European despot planted on an Asian despotism, or, in the words of Weber, as an agent of mere 'colonial capitalism'. Steensgaard argued that this judgment was wrong. The VOC, he believed, had in fact revolutionised Asian trade. His focus was not on Indonesia, but on trade from the Indian Ocean basin to Europe, and he argued that although the Portuguese had pioneered the sea route to Asia, their networks were not robust. They were more medieval than modern, more ad hoc than systematic. Thus, the traditional overland caravan trade had continued much as it had for centuries before. Like van Leur and Weber, Steensgaard's focus was on calculability, and he believed that the unpredictability of the caravan trade and other Asian trading structures caused considerable price fluctuations, which in effect acted as a brake on market forces in Asian areas.

The VOC, however, changed the situation decisively, and to explain how, Steensgaard added a new focus on violence. It of course did not escape van Leur or Meilink-Roelofsz that VOC trade was based on the power of Dutch guns, but Steensgaard argued that violence was *central* to the VOC's trade revolution, a position he illustrated by contrasting the company's use of violence to that of the Portuguese. The Portuguese, he argued, used violence semi-rationally because they were focused as much on religious crusade and glory as on profit. The Dutch, however, used violence 'rationally', with a consistent pursuit of profit. As a result, they achieved a monopoly that brought greater predictability to Asian markets, providing transparency and stability.

Meilink-Roelofsz responded to Steensgaard in a long article, in which she defended the sophistication of Asian trade. Her views on this matter have tended to prevail.[18] Partly this is due to her own spirited arguments. But it's also due to the work of later scholars. The most notable of these was Sanjay Subrahmanyam, who ended up having a deeply significant influence on the debate not just because of his outstanding source-based scholarship but also because he came at the question from a different angle.[19]

18   Meilink-Roelofsz, 'The Structures of Trade in Asia in the Sixteenth and Seventeenth Centuries'.

19   See especially Subrahmanyam, *The Portuguese Empire in Asia*.

The Company in global history: Sanjay Subrahmanyam, Leonard Blussé, and Asia-centered perspectives on the VOC centered perspectives on the VOC

Subrahmanyam argued that Steensgaard was right to discern a major transformation in Asian trade during the seventeenth century but that he was wrong to attribute it primarily to the Dutch East India Company. Many things were changing in Asia, and even more important than the arrival of the Dutch was the expansion of major Asian states, such as the Ottomans, the Safavids, and, most importantly, the Mughals. This consolidation of political control drove the rapid development of indigenous Asian trade. Indeed, according to Subrahmanyam, the expansion of Dutch trade was likely part of a general expansion of Asian maritime trade.

This perspective has become generally accepted, underlying the work not just of VOC scholars, but also of more general works on global history, such as Victor Lieberman's magisterial two-volume work, *Strange Parallels*.[20] Asian trade was not static. It was dynamic, going through booms and busts. During the early modern period, scholars have generally discerned a trend of expansion. Indeed, it may even be the case that the expansion of European trade in Asia rested on indigenous trade expansion. Moreover, European dominance, such as it was, was, in the words of John E. Wills Jr., an 'interactive dominance', which emerged gradually and with the active participation of Asian officials, merchants, and brokers.[21]

Today, the most important figure in VOC history is the polyglot Dutch scholar Leonard Blussé, to whom this volume is dedicated. His work brought this interactivity into close focus, not just in his research and writing but also in his broad connections with scholars around the world. In general, his scholarship supports that of Meilink-Roelofsz and Subrahmanyam, but he has not felt it necessary to argue stridently in favour of their views. He is more interested in drawing out their implications. He, more than anyone else, has set the current focus of VOC studies: to understand the on-the-ground (or on-the-water) interactions that made up Asian trade during the VOC period.

---

20   Lieberman, *Strange Parallels*, Vols. 1 and 2. See also Lieberman, 'Protected Rimlands and Exposed Zones'; and Andrade, 'Victor Lieberman's Strange Parallels'.
21   Wills, 'Maritime Asia, 1500–1800'.

Unlike Marx, Weber, van Leur, Meilink-Roelofsz, and Steensgaard, Blussé has mastered Asian languages.[22] As a student, he lived for years in Taiwan and Japan, and he is at home in both Japanese and Chinese sources, modern and classical. This has enabled him to look at VOC history from all sides, using Asian sources to illuminate VOC history. In this he is much like his fellow pioneer, John E. Wills Jr., who brought an unparalleled range of sources to his studies of interactions between Europeans and East Asians. Blussé has also encouraged his many students and collaborators – including most of the VOC experts represented in this volume – to do the same. To do VOC history today means to learn non-Western languages. That's not to say one cannot make contributions using primarily European sources – there's still much fine work being produced based largely or solely on the rich sources of the VOC. But the most significant scholarship tends to take its inspiration from Blussé and Wills, using non-Western sources to supplement and even critique the Western sources.

The result has been a new understanding of VOC history. Blussé, for example, has used Chinese, Japanese, and European sources to show that despite Dutch military and economic power, it was the Chinese who truly dominated East and Southeast Asian trade through the long seventeenth century.[23] This they did by creating close connections with Japanese, Europeans, Javanese, Filipinos, Native Formosans, etc. His work has directly inspired many other scholars who are interested in intercultural history, such as Adam Clulow, Xing Hang, Cheng Wei-Chung, myself, and many others.

Even more important, however, are the bridges he formed with scholars in Asia, having spent years in Taiwan, Japan, and mainland China. His joint publishing initiatives, such as the *Kong Koan* series, the *Formosan Encounter Series* and others have brought Dutch sources to Asian readers, even as he has been a major force in the publication of Dutch sources in Dutch transcription.[24] But perhaps the longest-term impact of his role as a mediator between Asia and the West is the TANAP Program.

TANAP, which stands for Toward a New Age of Partnership, was an ambitious multinational project designed to lay institutional groundwork for global history. At its centre were two questions: when and how did

---

22 Van Leur did know some Indonesian, but he did not generally use it in his scholarship.

23 See especially Blussé, *Strange Company*.

24 A complete listing of his source publication contributions would take up far too much space, but among the most important are Leonard Blussé and Wu Fengbin 吳鳳斌, *Gong an bu* 公案簿, 13 volumes and counting; Blussé, Everts, Milde, and Ts'ao, eds., *De Dagregisters van het Kasteel Zeelandia, Taiwan, 1629–1662*, Four Vols and Blussé, Everts, et al., *The Formosan Encounter. Notes on Formosa's Aboriginal Society*.

the earth's peoples, cultures, economies, and polities become so closely interconnected? And what role did Asia and Africa play in this process? TANAP addressed these questions by focusing on the VOC, and in a bold new way: by creating international scholarly connections.

The heart of TANAP was student exchange. Between 2000 and 2007, dozens of students came from countries in Africa and Asia to the Netherlands to enrol in an MA programme at Leiden University. Many went on to compose PhD dissertations, which were published by Brill in a series of groundbreaking books.[25] These monographs have managed to connect European and Asian historiographies in unprecedented ways, as the authors, having been trained in seventeenth-century Dutch language, early modern palaeography, and the use of VOC archives, asked new questions and, even more importantly, made connections between Dutch documents and sources in their home countries. As a result, TANAP has not just enriched our understanding of the VOC but also the history of the many lands with which the VOC came into contact: China, Japan, Vietnam, Thailand, Indonesia, etc. In all these places, scholars have turned to VOC sources to understand their own history, because VOC sources contain details lacking in local sources and offer new perspectives.

Conclusions

TANAP graduates are exerting a significant effect on current historiography, which leads to the question: where do we stand now with regard to the great question of the VOC's impact on Asian trade? Today, historians generally agree with the basic thrust of the van Leur thesis. Their work continues to show that Asian trading structures were generally not overturned or destroyed by the VOC. Indigenous networks continued to operate alongside VOC ones. Indeed, in many areas the VOC carried considerably less trade in volume and value than did other groups. In general, the more we learn, the more we appreciate the sophistication of Asian trading structures, institutions, and networks.

Even more intriguing is the fact that historians are increasingly aware of just how much the VOC's own networks were influenced by and constructed upon Asian networks. This was not of course true of the VOC alone. The English East India Company, the other subject of this volume, also depended

---

25   A complete list of these books can be found at Brill's website: www.brill.com/publications/ tanap-monographs-history-asian-european-interaction (accessed 2016-03-04).

closely on Asian trading structures, which often were extremely powerful and resilient. For instance, Ghulam Nadri, in his chapter, investigates the wealthy Gujarati merchants that the British interacted with. The merchant Virji Vohra lent huge sums to the Company. His influence was such that Company officials knew they must tread carefully. As EIC official Edward Knipe wrote to London in 1643, 'Virge Vora, by reason of our continuall mighty ingagements, must not bee displeased in any case. [...] And I conclude that, so long as Virge Vora is so much our credittor, little or no proffitt [is] to bee made uppon any goods wee can bring to Surratt'.[26] It is becoming increasingly clear that the European companies were dependent on Asian and African structures, and that these organisations could be enormously wealthy. For example, it seems clear that the Zheng family of Southern Fujian Province, China, brought in more revenues per year from overseas trade (starting in the late 1640s) than did the VOC from all of its holdings.[27]

These Asian organisations were not just rich. They were also powerful, even in the military sphere where the narrative of European superiority has been most persistent. Indeed, many authors still assume that Europeans had a significant advantage in military power, which they used to impose their will on indigenous powers. But recent studies on the VOC show that, at least through the mid-1700s, Asian polities displayed considerable military dynamism, able to hold the VOC back, even defeat it. To be sure, the VOC did have a formidable military, but even so, it was unable to impose its will upon a range of local political structures or other types of powerful organisations. Scholars such as Leonard Blussé, Adam Clulow, Tristan Mostert, Merle Ricklefs, and many others, including myself, have revealed the military power of many Asian organisations.[28]

But even more interestingly, historians are increasingly painting a picture of global adoption and adaptation, what we might call 'global early modernisation'. For example, in his contribution to this volume, Adam Clulow notes how effectively Japanese soldiers used muskets, arguing – as others before him have done – that they were using the musketry countermarch technique long before Europeans were. But the Japanese were not the only Asians whose musketry innovations were precocious. The Chinese were using the countermarch technique with early firearms, long before the

26   Foster, ed., *The English Factories in India*, 1642–1645, p. 108.

27   Hang, *Conflict and Commerce in Maritime East Asia*. I independently came to the same conclusion. See Andrade, *Lost Colony*, p. 52.

28   Clulow, 'Finding the Balance'; Blussé, 'De Chinese nachtmerrie: Een terugtocht en twee nederlagen'; Andrade, *Lost Colony*; Andrade, *The Gunpowder Age*; Ricklefs, *War, Culture and Economy in Java, 1677–1726*.

Japanese applied it to muskets.[29] Moreover, recent work suggests that the
Chinese were adopting and innovating with musketry technology and
techniques at precisely the same time as the Japanese, and with similar
thoroughness.[30]

This military 'early modernisation' was just one aspect of this process of
adopting and innovating new ideas, technologies, and techniques. And it is
important to note that this habit of inter-adoption did not flow only one way,
that is from Europe to Asia. Everyone copied and adapted from everyone.
For example, as Tristan Mostert has noted, the Makassarese were obtaining
military manuals not just from Europeans, but also from Islamic lands,
and Peter Shapinsky has called attention to the development of a 'hybrid
maritime culture' in East Asia during the seventeenth century, showing,
for example, how Japanese traders sailed Chinese junks with European
rigging, their Chinese and Portuguese navigators deploying dual-language
portolan charts.[31]

Put all of this work together, and we begin to glimpse an early modern
Asia that is far more responsive and adaptive than has long been thought.
But how to theorise this 'early modernization'? What large-scale models
can we use? Here, the work of Victor Lieberman can be very useful.[32] In his
model of *Strange Parallels*, European states are contextualised in deeper
Eurasian context: European states were not unique in their rapid economic
and demographic growth, or political centralisation, or vernacular cultures,
or 'proto-nationalism' (Lieberman prefers the more neutral term 'politicised
ethnicity'). Rather, much of Eurasia was undergoing remarkably similar
trends, and the timing of florescences and crises was eerily similar from
one side of Eurasia to the other. We must see the VOC, the EIC, and other
European overseas organisations in this context. They were part and parcel
of a general expansion across Eurasia and the northern and eastern African
littorals.

Since van Leur we have been compelled to view the Dutch East India
Company as much less influential – at least in Asia – than our metanar-
ratives once implied. But we must not go too far. Asian structures were
certainly more powerful, durable, and sophisticated than once believed,
but the VOC also had unique strength and staying power. It established

29   Laichen, 'Ming-Southeast Asian Overland Interactions, 1368-1644,', p. 500; Andrade, *The Gunpowder Age*, pp. 144–166; Andrade, 'Late Medieval Divergences'.
30   Andrade, *The Gunpowder Age*, pp. 166–187.
31   Shapinsky, 'Polyvocal Portolans'.
32   Lieberman, *Strange Parallels*. See also Lieberman, 'Protected Rimlands and Exposed Zones'; Andrade, 'Victor Lieberman's Strange Parallels'.

an unprecedented structure of international communication. Today, VOC historians are increasingly focusing on the organisation's astoundingly sophisticated networks. The idea of the 'network', the 'web', is of course very much of the zeitgeist. We live in the networked age – our refrigerators talk to our phones. Like all generations, our current preoccupations influence our scholarship, and historians today see VOC trading ports as nodes and hubs, the ships as packets flowing back and forth. This perspective is salutary. The network model yields significant insights. Yet we of course must not lose track of other phenomena in the company's history: war, weather, and, of course, the individual personalities and life trajectories that not only make history rich and interesting but also deeply affect its trends and vicissitudes.

Equally importantly, when we map the VOC's formal networks – which is to say, those routes and connections that are most apparent in Dutch sources – we are viewing only the visible part of deeper networks. Today, internet technology experts distinguish between the surface internet and the deep net.[33] The surface net is that part of the internet that is indexed by search engines and viewable by internet users. The deep net consists of databases, proprietary information, items hidden behind paywalls, and so on that are not indexed by search engines and remain hidden from most users. The deep web is to be distinguished from the dark web, where illegal things happen.[34] But what may be surprising is that the deep web is at least five hundred times larger than the surface web and is growing much more rapidly.

In just such a way, we must keep in mind that the networks we view through the VOC's sources are only the visible tip of deeper structures. There was far more trade and circulation going on that remains invisible to us. Some of this trade involved employees of the VOC, who were constantly dealing under the table, their transactions usually involving Asians. But most of this unseen trade was carried out by Asian organisations that operated alongside or below official VOC structures, and often deliberately hidden from official view. Sometimes, parts of these Asian organisations operated within VOC networks, subverting or co-opting them, often with the active connivance of Company employees.[35]

The Dutch East India Company was probably not the catalyst of capitalism that it was once considered to be, but it helped connect human societies in denser and stronger webs than ever before. These global connections brought

---

33   Wright, 'Exploring a "Deep Web" That Google Can't Grasp', 22 February 2009.
34   See Andy Greenberg, 'Hacker Lexicon: What is the Dark Web?', 19 November 2014.
35   See, for example, Andrade, *How Taiwan Became Chinese*, Ch. 2; and Andrade, 'Pirates, Pelts, and Promises'.

dramatic changes to all sides, as humans found themselves becoming less parochial, less isolated, and far better informed about the increasingly small planet they inhabited.

Works cited

Andrade, Tonio, *The Gunpowder Age: China, Military Innovation, and the Rise of the West in World History* (Princeton: Princeton University Press, 2016).

Andrade, Tonio, 'Late Medieval Divergences: Comparative Perspectives on Early Gunpowder Warfare in Europe and China', *Journal of Medieval Military History* 13 (2015): 247–276.

Andrade, Tonio, 'Victor Lieberman's Strange Parallels', *American Historical Review* 117(4) (2012): 1173–1176.

Andrade, Tonio, *Lost Colony* (Princeton: Princeton University Press, 2011).

Andrade, Tonio, *How Taiwan Became Chinese: Dutch, Spanish, and Han Colonization in the Seventeenth Century* (New York: Columbia University Press, 2007).

Andrade, Tonio, 'Pirates, Pelts, and Promises: The Sino-Dutch Colony of Seventeenth-century Taiwan and the Aboriginal Village of Favorolang', *Journal of Asian Studies* 64(2) (2005): 295–320.

Blussé, Leonard, *Strange Company: Chinese Settlers, Mestizo Women, and the Dutch in VOC Batavia* (Dordrecht: Foris Publications, 1986).

Blussé, Leonard, 'De Chinese nachtmerrie: Een terugtocht en twee nederlagen', In Gerrit Knaap and Ger Teitler, eds., *De Verenigde Oost-Indische Compagnie tussen oorlog en diplomatie* (Leiden: KITLV Press, 2002), pp. 209–238.

Clulow, Adam, 'Finding the Balance: European Military Power in Early Modern Asia', *History Compass* 13(3) (2015): 148–157.

Collins, Randall, *Weberian Sociological Theory* (Cambridge, UK: Cambridge University Press, 1986).

Foster, William, ed., *The English Factories in India, 1642–1645: A Calendar of Documents in the India Office* (Westminster, Oxford: Clarendon Press, 1913).

Gellner, David N., 'The Uses of Max Weber: Legitimation and Amnesia in Buddhology, South Asian History, and Anthropological Practice Theory', in Peter Clarke, ed., *The Oxford Handbook of the Sociology of Religion* (Oxford: Oxford University Press, 2009).

Greenberg, Andy, 'Hacker Lexicon: What is the Dark Web?' *Wired,* 19 November 2014, www.wired.com/2014/11/hacker-lexicon-whats-dark-web/, accessed 2016-03-06.

Hang, Xing, *Conflict and Commerce in Maritime East Asia: The Zheng Family and the Shaping of the Modern World, c. 1620–1720* (Cambridge, UK: Cambridge University Press, 2016).

Laichen, Sun, 'Ming-Southeast Asian Overland Interactions, 1368-1644', PhD dissertation (University of Michigan Department of History, 2000).

Lieberman, Victor, *Strange Parallels: Southeast Asia in Global Context, c. 800-1830*, Vol. 1 (New York: Cambridge University Press, 2007).

Lieberman, Victor, *Strange Parallels: Southeast Asia in Global Context, c. 800-1830* Vol. 2 (New York: Cambridge University Press, 2009).

Lieberman, Victor, 'Protected Rimlands and Exposed Zones: Reconfiguring Premodern Eurasia', *Comparative Studies in Society and History* 50 (2008): 692-723.

Marks, Robert, *The Origins of the Modern World: A Global and Ecological Narrative from the Fifteenth to the Twenty-first Century,* Lanham, Rowman & Littlefield, 2007.

Marx, Karl, 'The Transformation of Commodity Capital and Money Capital into Commodity-Dealing Capital and Money-Dealing Capital or into Merchant's Capital', in Karl Marx, *Marx's Economic Manuscript of 1864–1865* (Leiden: Brill, 2016).

Marx, Karl, *Capital*, Vol. 3, Part IV (1867-1894), www.marxists.org/archive/marx/works/1894-c3/ch18.htm#1a, accessed 2015-11-09.

Marx, Karl, 'The British Rule in India', New-York Herald Tribune, 10 June 1853. At www.marxists.org/archive/marx/works/1853/06/25.htm, accessed 2015-11-09.

Meilink-Roelofsz, M.A.P., 'The Structures of Trade in Asia in the Sixteenth and Seventeenth Centuries: Niels Steengaard's Carracks, Caravans, and Companies: The Asian Trade Revolutions, A Critical Appraisal', *Mare Luso-Indicum* 4 (1980): 1–43.

Meilink-Roelofsz, M.A.P., *Asian Trade and European Influence in the Indonesian Archipelago between 1500 and about 1630* (The Hague: M. Nijhoff, 1962).

Pomeranz, Kenneth, *The Great Divergence: China, Europe, and the Making of the Modern World Economy* (Princeton: Princeton University Press, 2000).

Ricklefs, Merle, *War, Culture and Economy in Java, 1677–1726: Asian and European Imperialism in the Early Kartasura Period* (Sydney: Allen and Unwin, 1993).

Rosenthal, Jean-Laurent and Wong, R. Bin, *Before and Beyond Divergence: The Politics of Economic Change in China and Europe* (Cambridge MA: Harvard University Press, 2011).

Shapinsky, Peter D., 'Polyvocal Portolans: Nautical Charts and Hybrid Maritime Cultures in Early Modern East Asia', *Early Modern Japan* 14 (2006): 4–26.

Spenser, Edmund, 'The Shepheards Calender', in *The Complete Works of Edmund Spenser*, ed. R. Morris (London: Macmillan and Co, 1897), 446–89.

Steensgaard, Niels, *The Asian Trade Revolution of the Seventeenth Century: The East India Companies and the Decline of the Caravan Trade* (Chicago, University of Chicago Press, 1975).

Subrahmanyam, Sanjay, *The Portuguese Empire in Asia, 1500-1700: A Political and Economic History* (London: Longman, 1993).

Weber, Max, *General Economic History*, trans. Frank H. Knight (New York: Greenberg, 1927).

Wertheim, W.F., 'Early Asian Trade: An Appreciation of J.C. van Leur', *The Far Eastern Quarterly* 13(2) (1954): 167-173.

Wills, Jr., John E., 'Maritime Asia, 1500–1800: The Interactive Emergence of European Domination'. *American Historical Review* 98(1) (1993): 83–105.

Wong, R. Bin, *China Transformed: Historical Change and the Limits of European Experience* (Ithaca NY: Cornell University Press, 2000).

Contact details

Tonio Andrade, Department of History, 221 Bowden Hall, 561 S. Kilgo St., Atlanta, GA 30322

Tel.: +1 404.727.4469

tandrad@emory.edu

Index

Printed in the United States
By Bookmasters